PRAISE FOR JA
MURDER HOUSES OF LONDON:

'A gripping tour of London's bloodiest buildings, the particulars of which have been meticulously researched and entertainingly presented.'
Adam Wood, Editor of *Ripperologist*

'I cannot recommend this book highly enough. It is a definite must-have.'
Stewart P. Evans

'Jan Bondeson conducts us on a masterly mystery tour of London's 'black plaque' houses, where murder has left a bloodstained visiting card… Wherever Dr Bondeson shines his torch into dark places, he sheds new light with the application of his powerful logic.
Richard Whittington-Egan

'Jan Bondeson can be guaranteed to tell bizarre and quirky real-life tales and to find stories that were thought to be unfindable.'
Paul Begg

'Jan Bondeson delves into the clandestine corners of city life to reveal stories that would probably have preferred to have been left undiscovered. You'll never look at the closed doors of London the same way again. A catalogue of crime covering more than two centuries, Murder Houses of London combined relentless research with splendid story-telling to produce a book of unrivalled interestingness.'
James Harkin, Head Researcher at *QI*

'Houses of Death: Chilling tales from behind the doors of homes that were the scene of gruesome murders over the last 200 years.'
Daily Mail

'This magnificent volume is a treasure-house of information on the murders and murderers of London.'
Books Monthly

'The chilling details are revealed in a new book identifying London's so-called 'murder houses' – homes which have witnessed terrible crimes and still stand today – and telling their grisly stories. Crime history writer Jan Bondeson – a consultant doctor in his day job – spent 15 years researching and writing his book, *Murder Houses of London*.'
Hampstead and Highgate Gazette

'If you were choosing a city to star as a crime story character, London would be front and centre. Bondeson delves into the many dark corners of the city's history to catalogue the crimes that have occurred everywhere from its narrowest and darkest streets to the stateliest mansions, providing a peek behind its bloodiest closed doors for over two centuries.'
All About History

'Everyone is acquainted with the grisly facts of Jack the Ripper... but there are so many other stories to tell of murder and mystery in London. Jan Bondeson delves into these chilling tales, illustrating that you can never really know what goes on behind closed doors.
Discover Your History

'Every house has a history of some kind but few are as bloodthirsty as these dwellings where behind fresh paint, clean windows and grand entrances lie grisly tales of murder.'
True Detective

'There is more, much more, and although the East End can lay its claim to be a starting point for lurid Victorian murders, Bondeson exhaustively details the grisly history of the rest of London too. So grab the book, grab an A-Z (or actually just tap Googlemaps into your smartphone) and go hunting for London's gruesome past.'
East End Life

'Jan Bondeson is a curious author and I must confess that I approached this book with a mix of apprehension and excitement... there is a fascinating discussion to be had here about murders and 'dark tourism'.'
London Journal

'I once said that Jan Bondeson is incapable of writing a bad book. *Murder Houses of London* once again proves that statement correct... it packs a lot of information into 350 densely printed and liberally illustrated pages. If only walls could talk, what tales they would have to tell. Fortunately we have Jan Bondeson to tell the tales for them. An excellent book, highly readable.'
Ripperologist

'The work contains compelling details not only of famous crimes, but also of homicides ranging from the obscure to the long-forgotten.'
Ripperana

MURDER HOUSES OF SOUTH LONDON

Jan Bondeson

Matador
9 Priory Business Park,
Wistow Road, Kibworth Beauchamp,
Leicestershire LE8 0RX
Tel: (+44) 116 279 2299
Email: books@troubador.co.uk
Web: www.troubador.co.uk/matador

ISBN 978 1784623 340

British Library Cataloguing in Publication Data.
A catalogue record for this book is available from the British Library.

Printed by TJ International Ltd, Padstow, Cornwall, UK
Typeset by Troubador Publishing Ltd, Leicester, UK

Matador is an imprint of Troubador Publishing Ltd

CONTENTS

Introduction ix

1 Southwark, Camberwell and Lambeth 1

2 Wandsworth 46

3 Lewisham, Deptford and Greenwich 129

4 Wimbledon, Richmond and Kingston 178

5 Croydon and South London Suburbs 237

6 Discussion 294

Bibliography 315
Major Newspapers Consulted 316
Notes 317

INTRODUCTION

It might be only on enchanted ground;
It might be merely by a thought's expansion;
But in the spirit, or the flesh, I found
An old deserted Mansion.
A residence for woman, child, and man,
A dwelling-place, – and yet no habitation;
A House, – but under some prodigious ban
Of excommunication.

All epigraphs in this book are from
Thomas Hood, *The Haunted House.*

This book is the second volume of my comprehensive account of London's topography of capital crime: houses inside which celebrated murders have been committed.[1] Since there is no shortage of London murder houses, this volume will deal with Southwark, Lambeth, Wandsworth and all suburbs south of the river. For a crime to qualify as a 'murder', it has to have been classified as such at some stage of its investigation or prosecution, although it does not matter what the ultimate verdict was, or whether the crime was solved or not. For a house to qualify as a 'murder house', the murder must have been committed inside its walls, not out in the street or in the garden. Moreover, the building in question must survive relatively intact. A Victorian or Edwardian murder house keeps its status after being subdivided into flats, but no 'murder flats' in tower blocks and other ungainly modern developments are included in this book.

Deaths after botched illegal abortions were formerly classed as murders, but they have no business to be in this book. Nor will there be any sad tales of desperate families turning on the taps and gassing themselves. Interesting or unsolved murders have been preferred to simple slayings, and I have not felt it worthwhile to include a profusion of cases of insane women murdering their babies [there are many], or similar-sounding instances of drunken husbands murdering their wives [there are very many]. Only a few modern murders have been included, and I have avoided the activities of the present-day gangsters and mindless hoodlums, to concentrate on older murders that are of interest from a social history point of view. Moreover, I have tended to follow what the distinguished crime historian Jonathan Goodman used to call his forty-year rule: after that period of time, a murder lost its horror and squalidity, and instead gained some degree of historical interest.

There does not appear to be any London murder houses that are relics to crimes perpetrated prior to 1800.[2] But the late Georgian and Victorian builders knew their trade: they were able to produce quality houses that would stand for centuries to come. Even the houses intended for the poor were built to last, as evidenced by many of the humble South London terraces surviving to this day, in good order. The historic murder houses of London have faced a trinity of enemies: Decay, the Luftwaffe and the Developer. Clearances of low-quality slum tenements have deprived London of a fair few murder houses. Mr Hitler's concerted effort to rearrange London's architecture meant that his Luftwaffe destroyed many a murder house, not only in the East End, but all over the Metropolis. The Developer has accounted for even more of them, with hideous modern blocks of flats replacing much of the traditional fabric of old London.

Armed with this book and a good London map, you will be

able to do some murder house detection work of your own. Sometimes, quiet suburban terraced houses hide terrible secrets from the past: read about the Brixton Matricide, the Battersea Tragedy, and the Tooting Horror. Unsolved murder mysteries abound in these pages: some of them celebrated crimes like the murder of Charles Bravo at Balham in 1876, others almost completely forgotten, like the Addington Square mystery of 1863, the fascinating and mysterious murder of Jane Soper in the Borough in 1875, and the mysterious slayings of Mrs Tyler in Blackheath in 1898, and Mary Kate Waknell in Brixton in 1900.

CHAPTER 1

SOUTHWARK, CAMBERWELL AND LAMBETH

But Echo never mock'd the human tongue;
Some weighty crime, that Heaven could not pardon,
A secret curse on that old Building hung,
And its deserted Garden.
The beds were all untouch'd by hand or tool;
No footstep mark'd the damp and mossy gravel,
Each walk as green as is the mantled pool,
For want of human travel.

In this book, I have defined the Southwark, Camberwell and Lambeth area to incorporate the Borough, Walworth and Bermondsey, and thus being bordered in the west by Clapham and Battersea and in the east by Deptford. This part of London is notable for its wealth of historic murder houses, many of which are no longer standing. No. 12 Wellington Terrace, just off the Waterloo Road near the Bridge, where the beautiful young prostitute Eliza Grimwood was murdered in 1838, was admired by a large crowd almost around the clock. The Grimwood family admitted paying visitors into the house, to attend an auction where the murdered woman's possessions were sold. The blood-stained carpet in the murder room was purchased by a man who proceeded to cut it up

1.1 Eliza Grimwood and the bricklayer Hubbard, the main suspect for her murder, from the Penny Satirist, June 10 1838.

into little pieces, which he sold to collectors of criminal memorabilia in the street, with good success. The haunted Grimwood house remained one of London's most legendary murder houses for many years, and was admired by the old crime author Guy Logan in his *Famous Crimes* column in 1905: "No. 12, Wellington Terrace, Waterloo Road, is daily passed by thousands who have no idea that it was once the scene of a most mysterious murder. There Eliza Grimwood – fair and frail – was cruelly done to death by a male 'fiend' whom she had permitted to accompany her home from the Strand Theatre – that is, if William Hubbard, who lived with the girl and upon her shame, did not himself commit the deed."[1] The dark and impenetrable Grimwood mystery, with suspects ranging from a royal Duke to an alcoholic bricklayer, remains unsolved to this day.[2] Wellington Terrace was demolished in the 1930s, when Waterloo Bridge was being rebuilt.

1.2 Portraits of the murderous Mannings.

Another notorious address for the London crime historian was No. 3 Miniver Place, Bermondsey, where Frederick George and Maria Manning murdered the wealthy moneylender Patrick O'Connor in 1849. They buried his mangled remains in the back kitchen and escaped with his money and stock certificates. The enterprising Maria Manning ended up in Edinburgh, where she tried to seduce Guy Logan's grandfather, who was then a young army officer, to get his help to sell O'Connor's railway shares! But since Lieutenant Logan did not fancy the flashily dressed Mrs Manning, the cunning plan of the murderess did not work out.[3] After O'Connor's remains had been discovered at No. 3 Miniver Place, the hue and cry was on for the Mannings. After the guilty pair had been tracked down, arrested, tried and hanged for the murder, the local jokers renamed Miniver Place, a short terrace of mean-looking little houses, 'Manning Street' for a while, but other locals objected to the memory of these murderous malefactors being perpetuated. Since the houses would not let, the name was changed once more, and when the houses in Weston Street, in which Miniver Place stood, were renumbered,

1.3 The Manning murder house at No. 3 Miniver Place, Bermondsey.

the murder house became No. 103 Weston Street. Experienced murder house detectives like Guy Logan and George R. Sims were not fooled by this stratagem, and they both reported on the progress of the Weston Street house of horrors more than once, expressing surprise that it was still standing. But remarkably, the murder house outlived both these worthies: increasingly dirty and dilapidated, it stood until 1959, when it was photographed shortly before being demolished, along with the rest of what was once Miniver Place, as part of a slum clearance.[4]

The old crime writer Guy Logan, who had a great liking for

1.4 The murder house at No. 157 Manor Place, and incidents from the murder, from the Illustrated Police News, March 28 1918.

visiting historical murder houses, once spent a day at Walworth's house of horrors, No. 16 Manor Place. Here, back in 1860, William Godfrey Youngman had murdered his mother, two brothers, and sweetheart in a veritable bloodbath.[5] After the murder, the landlady of the house received a guinea from the poor-box, since no person would live in the haunted murder house.[6] No. 16 Manor Place retained some of its notoriety well into the 1920s and 1930s; it was demolished in the 1970s for the construction of the new Walworth Police Station.[7] Some older houses across the road show what it must have looked like: a drab, terraced, three-story building. Murder returned to Manor Place in 1887, when Robert Pickersgill cut the throat of his wife Mary

Jane at No. 125, before committing suicide near the Stoke Newington railway station. In 1918, William Constance murdered his wife at No. 157 Manor Place, and was committed to stand trial for the crime.[8] Manor Place has been extensively developed, and none of its murder houses remain.

No. 39 Upper Prince Street, Lambeth, where Jane Whillett was murdered by an unknown assailant in 1830, no longer stands, nor does No. 3 Milstead Terrace, in the Old Kent Road, where the Frenchman Louis Bourdier murdered his sweetheart in 1867. No. 114 Stamford Street, Camberwell, where the charwoman Fanny Saunders was murdered by an unknown assailant in 1893, no longer frowns upon the passer-by, nor does No. 6 Caspian Street, where William Clarke murdered Emily Dobson in 1895. The prolific poisoner Thomas Neill Cream, who was active in the Southwark and Lambeth area in 1891 and 1892, claimed one of his victims at No. 118 Stamford Street, two doors away from

1.5 The murder house at No. 234 Cator Street, from the Lloyd's Weekly Newspaper, September 28 1897.

where the house where Fanny Saunders had been murdered eight years earlier. No. 11 Boundary Lane, Walworth, where Robert Ward murdered his two daughters in 1899, no longer stands.[9] No. 234 Cator Street, Camberwell, site of the unsolved murder of Mrs Saunders in 1897, has fallen victim to the Developer. Guy Logan made mention of the Cator Street murder house more than once, and George R. Sims added Mrs Saunders' small work basket to his collection of criminal memorabilia.[10] The old lodging-house at No. 156 York Road, where Frederick Jesse murdered and mutilated his aunt Mabel Edmunds in 1923, has long-since been replaced by modern-looking buildings.

The little shop of horrors at No. 22 Wyndham Road, Camberwell, where the entire Darby family was murdered for

1.6 The shop of horrors at No. 22 Wyndham Road, Camberwell, from the Illustrated Police News, January 10 1903.

greed of gain by the bloodthirsty Edgar Edwards [alias Owen] back in 1902 remained one of London's most notorious murder houses for many years. In 1906, George R. Sims wrote that "the shop has changed hands twice since the murders. Country folks have taken it, ignorant of its history, had found out the terrible tragedy that had been enacted on the premises, and had left again".[11] Guy Logan agreed that the murder shop stood vacant for a long time after the Camberwell Horror, since no person wanted to live in a place of such sinister memory, even at a nominal rent. "It had a very desolate look when I passed it some months afterwards, but, on going that way again two or three years later, I found that a saddler and harness maker had set up in business there. I shall hope to write a book one day on the subject of 'Murder Houses of London'."[12] The shop of horrors of Wyndham Road in fact stood for several decades to come, until it perished in the 1940s or 1950s, quite possibly due to wartime damage. There are some remaining old shops in the road today, showing what it must have looked like.

But this is not a book about the 'Lost Murder Houses of London': we must no longer lament the lost historic murder houses of bygone times, but turn to those that are still standing. Ponder the unsolved Addington Square and Borough High Street mysteries, walk in the footsteps of the murderous 'Gentleman Jim', and visit what remains of the Borough Poisoner's old pub. It has long since closed for business, but there are other pubs nearby, if you feel in need of refreshments.

THE ADDINGTON SQUARE MYSTERY, 1863

In 1843, Captain James Wedderburn, of the 4th Royal Irish Dragoons, inherited a considerable sum of money, and an attractive London house, from an aged relative. Captain Wedderburn lost no time before he 'sold out' of the regiment, paid off his debts, and settled down at No. 13 Addington Square, Camberwell. His mistress Mrs Mary Gorman was installed as housekeeper at the premises. To conceal that they were 'living in sin', they called themselves Captain and Mrs Watson. As twenty years went by, both captain and housekeeper were getting well into middle age. He travelled about a good deal, quite possibly to visit other mistresses he was 'running', but she lived contentedly at No. 13 with her teenage daughter Eliza.

In October 1863, Mr and Mrs Grieves at No. 14 Addington Square wanted to attend a funeral. Their neighbour and friend Mary Gorman Watson at No. 13 agreed to look after their house while they were away. The captain was not in residence at the time. In the evening of October 27, when Mary and her daughter walked out into the garden, they saw a light in Mr and Mrs Grieves' bedroom. They found it odd that the Grieves' had returned clandestinely, without thanking them for looking after the house. Mary knocked hard at the back palings dividing the two gardens, and young Eliza threw some large Brazil nuts at the Grieves' window, to attract their attention. Whoever was in No. 14 did not acknowledge them, however, although the enthusiastic girl had thrown one of the nuts hard enough to break a pane of glass.

Worried that burglars might be at large in the house of their neighbours, Mary Gorman Watson pondered what to do. A more prudent woman would have called in the police, but instead she decided to knock at the front door of No. 14 and see who would answer the call. And indeed, some person was heard to come downstairs to answer her call. When the door was opened, Mary Gorman Watson thought it was young Miss Mary Grieves, who had returned early from the funeral She stepped inside and exclaimed 'It's only me, don't mind coming down!', but she walked right into a tremendous punch in the face that catapulted her out of the house, like a rag doll.

A minute or so later, a boy knocked on the door of No. 13 and politely told Eliza that her mother had fainted in the street, but having seen her mother alive and well just minutes earlier, Eliza thought he was joking and told him to get lost. Moments later, Mary Gorman Watson recovered consciousness, however; she reeled up to the front door of No. 13 and was admitted by her daughter. 'Stay with me, or they will murder me!' she exclaimed. Although quite confused, she managed to explain that two men, probably burglars, had been hiding inside No. 14; one of them had knocked her down. He had 'put her lights out' so effectively that she was unable to describe either miscreant. Eliza made sure that the police were called in. They searched No. 14, finding a cricket bat and a 'jemmy' left behind by the burglars. Miss Mary Grieves later testifies that some minor trinkets, and some silver spoons, had been stolen.

The morning after, poor Mary Gorman Watson sported a formidable-looking black eye. Eliza made sure that a jolly young doctor was consulted; he pooh-poohed her concerns and promised that her mother would be up and about again in just a few days. But instead she became bedridden and comatose, and died two weeks later. At the coroner's inquest, two more competent doctors testified that the post-mortem findings indicated that her death was the result of the injury from the blow. A verdict of murder against some person or persons unknown was returned, but not a single clue to the identity of the Addington Square burglars was ever found.[13] The two houses at No 13 and 14 Addington Square still remain, as memorials of one of London's many forgotten mysteries.

THE CAMBERWELL COFFEE HOUSE MURDER, 1874

John Walter Coppen was born in 1843, the son of a Clapham grocer. The 1851 census lists him as a 'scholar' living with his parents and two siblings at Bromels Buildings, Clapham. Ten years later, his father had changed careers, taking over the license of the Britannia Inn, 34 Surrey Street, Croydon. John Walter was working there as a barman. He would be doing so for quite a few years to come, acquiring a taste for drinking beer and gin that would one day become fatal.

In 1873, the now 32-year-old John Walter Coppen married the 18-year-old Emma Scrivington, and they took over the Clarendon Coffee House, at No. 39 Camberwell Church Street. To begin with, their marriage seemed quite a success. John Walter was considered quite handsome by Victorian standards: he had long hair and luxuriant whiskers, and a beard you could lose a badger in. Young Emma was quite pretty, and very popular with the male customers at the Clarendon Coffee House. But one problem remained for the family, namely John Walter's addiction to the bottle. He regularly went on drunken 'benders' in the local pubs, carousing with various undesirable people. When Emma reproached him, he responded by accusing her of being too familiar with the coffee-house customers.

On the evening of August 27 1874, John Walter Coppen went out to have a few drinks. Emma was quite disgusted with him, and she refused to sleep in the same bed as such a sottish fellow. She preferred to spend the night in an extra bed in the room of her sister-in-law Emily Caroline Coppen, who also resided on the premises. In the wee hours, John Walter came lurching home after his 'bender', only to find that he would be alone in the marital bed. But the strategy of Lysistrate, which had worked very well in classical Greece, would misfire badly in this seedy Camberwell coffee house.

The next morning, John Walter woke up with a very severe hangover. It was his normal habit to rise at 5 am, to make the paste for the meat pies they were selling, but this particular morning, he remained incapable of locomotion until well after nine. But instead of belatedly starting work on the pies, he crossed the street and borrowed a large knife from a butcher's shop. In the meantime, Emma Coppen had begun work in the coffee-house kitchen, assisted by her sister-in-law and by the servant girl Charlotte Berry. When Emma walked into the back kitchen to get some provisions, there was the sound of a scuffle, and a cry of 'I'm stabbed!' The carpenter John Peacock, who was waiting for a cup of coffee in the shop, heard the outcry, and saw John Walter walk into the shop, with a large, bloody butcher's knife in his hand, exclaiming 'I have done something for you now, Emma!' When his sister Emily cried out that a doctor must be fetched, the bushy-bearded coffee-house proprietor replied 'A doctor will be of no use!'

And indeed, it turned out that Emma Coppen had been stabbed very hard in the belly. She was carried upstairs to her bedroom, where she expired a few hours later. According to the doctor, she "appeared to be dying in a very pious frame of mind", praying incessantly and exclaiming 'I aggravated Walter to do it, may the Lord have mercy on my soul!' John Walter, who freely admitted that he was the guilty man, was taken into custody by the police. There was much curiosity about the 'Camberwell Wife Murder', as a newspaper expressed it: "Shortly after the dreadful affair became known a crowd assembled outside the Clarendon coffee-house, and there was a crowd outside close upon midnight. Golds Brothers' shop, where the knife was borrowed, was an object of as great attraction."

When John Walter Coppen was on trial at the Old Bailey for the murder of his wife, before Baron Bramwell, things were not looking good for him. Nevertheless, as a newspaper expressed it, "The prisoner, who is a remarkably fine man, with heavy whiskers and beard, pleaded 'Not guilty'". The evidence against him was formidable, however, with a series of witnesses describing how he had stabbed his wife to death. He had himself admitted his guilt, in front of the doctor and another witness. Defending the prisoner, Mr Serjeant Sleight argued that the stabbing might have been an accident, or alternatively that there had been no malice aforethought, thus making the crime one of manslaughter. But in his hostile summing-up, Baron Bramwell nullified this argument by declaring that "if the wound was a wilful one, even if the prisoner had no intention to kill his wife, yet, being guilty of unlawful wounding, and that wounding causing death, the prisoner ought to be found guilty of murder". Accordingly, the jury found Coppen guilty of murder, although they added a strong recommendation to mercy. When Baron Bramwell sentenced him to death, he left out the usual concluding sentence 'May the Lord have mercy on your soul'.

John Walter Coppen was handed over to the Sheriff of Surrey for execution. In spite of the jury's recommendation, an appeal to the Home Secretary failed, and he was hanged at Horsemonger Lane Gaol on October 13 1874.[14] The Clarendon coffee-house ceased trading after the murder, and all its contents were sold by auction. The murder shop is today a branch of the Your Move estate agent business. The shop front may well be original.

THE BOROUGH HIGH STREET MYSTERY, 1875

In 1875, the premises at No. 151 Borough High Street, Southwark, was the Turner Steam Bread and Biscuit Manufactory, a small bakery employing several workmen. Housekeeper at the

1.7 A postcard showing the Borough High Street.

bakery was the 55-year-old Miss Jane Caroline Soper, a middle-aged spinster, who had been working for Mr Turner many years. Early in the morning of Sunday September 12 1875, a man knocked on the side door to the bakery, in King Street. He said that he had been sent from the Terminus Hotel, to get some fresh bread. Although she did not recognize the man, Miss Soper, who was alone on the premises, went to get some bread, since she knew that this hotel was one regularly supplied with bread from Mr Turner's firm. But instead of paying for the bread, the man struck Miss Soper hard on the temple, knocking her out cold.

Without stealing anything, he then calmly left the bakery. When the bakers came to work, they found Miss Soper unconscious in the entrance hall, and she was removed to hospital.

There had been no witnesses to the assault on Miss Soper, and although various people had been observed loitering outside the bakery, there was nothing to connect them with the crime. The police initially made few exertions to investigate the crime, particularly since, on September 22, an optimistic young doctor predicted that Miss Soper would recover completely. The skull was not broken, and she was recovering favourably. She was unable to describe the man who had attacked her, except that he had been wearing dark clothes and that some of her blood must have spurted over his attire. On September 30, the doctor found his patient 'somewhat worse', however, and on October 5 she died unexpectedly, without any of her 'dying depositions' being recorded. More than three weeks after the attack on Jane Soper, the Metropolitan Police belatedly began a murder investigation.

The experienced Scotland Yard detectives Chief Inspector Nathaniel Druscovich and Inspector John Meiklejohn took charge of the murder investigation. Five hundred large and a thousand small posters were pasted up all over London, and in the large provincial cities as well, giving details of the Borough High Street murder, and announcing a £100 reward for the capture of the murderer. It was considered noteworthy that a pair of false whiskers had been found in the murder room. Suspicion soon fell on Christopher Chandler, a former workman at the bakery, since he had been observed near the premises on September 10, and since nine months earlier, he had been wearing a false beard and moustache. But when tracked down in New Brompton, Chandler denied all involvement in the murder, and the evidence against him did not appear strong. Nor did much of value emerge from the coroner's inquest on Jane Soper, except that a certain Mrs Dyer had seen a man in King Street who might have been the murderer. Chief Inspector Druscovich presumed that the murderer had been a thief planning to rob the bakery, but he had lost his nerve after knocking down Miss Soper, and ran off empty-handed.

On November 2 1875, when the murder investigation seemed to be going nowhere, a lad named William Knell contacted the police, with the information that a certain Charles Houghton had told him that his own brother-in-law had murdered Jane Soper. The brother-in-law was identified as Sheridan Fletcher Morley, a baker living at Blackman's Court, Bermondsey. He was known as a rough character, violent and drunken in his ways, but without previous convictions for serious crime. When the police tracked down his wife in Blackman's Court, she told them that Sheridan had deserted her the morning of the murder, and that she had not seen him since!

Chief Inspector Druscovich was convinced that Morley was the guilty man, and also that Houghton was an accomplice who helped to shelter him from the police. To track Morley down, he rented a room over a beer-shop, just opposite Houghton's home, and ordered four police constables to keep it under surveillance around the clock. In the end, this unconventional strategy paid off, and both Morley and Houghton were arrested. Brought before the Southwark Police Court on February 1 1876, they stoutly denied any involvement in the murder of Jane Soper. Houghton said that his chaffing about his brother-in-law had committed the murder had just been a joke. Although Morley was a baker, there was nothing to connect him with Mr Turner's bakery, or with Jane Soper herself. The witness Mrs Dyer could not recognize him as the man she had observed knocking at the door in King Street. Due to the lack of evidence against Morley and Houghton, the magistrate Mr Partridge discharged both prisoners. Chief Inspector Druscovich, who remained convinced that Morley was the guilty man, asked for the witness Knell, who had been so helpful to the police, to receive a reward of £2, and this was granted. Druscovich also asked for the brave constables who had been ordered "to keep observation for upwards of 70 days continuous, they were in a very low neighbourhood in a beer shop, frequently mixing with the customers" to be rewarded for their zeal, but they received nothing.[15]

To assess the strength of the case against Morley and Houghton, it is important also to examine the characters of their main accusers, Chief Inspector Nathaniel Druscovich and Inspector John Meiklejohn. At the time they were investigating the murder of Jane Soper, these two were *bent coppers*, on the payroll of the swindlers William Kurr and Harry Benson. The two detectives, and some of their Scotland Yard colleagues as well, pocketed considerable sums of money, as they repeatedly perverted the course of justice to protect Kurr and Benson. But in the end, the crooked detectives got their well-merited come-uppance. Druscovich and Meiklejohn were both convicted of taking bribes in 1877, sentenced to two years imprisonment, and dismissed from the police force in disgrace.

Now, had Morley in some way got into the way of Kurr or Benson, and had they instructed their bent coppers to frame him for the murder of Jane Soper? This seems unlikely, since Kurr and Benson were relatively sophisticated criminals, and Morley a mere street hoodlum. Or did Druscovich and Meiklejohn deliberately set out to fabricate a 'solution' to the murder, to forward their own careers and cover up the taking of bribes? It is true that the case against Morley was pitifully weak, but what if he had lost his composure when questioned by the police, or if Houghton could have been convinced to give evidence against him, or if Mrs Dyer could have been 'helped' to pick him out as the murder?

The murder house at No. 151 Borough High Street is still standing, a rare survivor in these parts. It is today a small shop, at the corner with King [now Newcomen] Street. The side entrance through which Miss Soper admitted her murderer still remains, although it has been secured with a metal gate, 140 years after the murderer bolted.

THE MURDEROUS 'GENTLEMAN JIM', 1892

James Banbury was born in Camden Town in 1868. At an early age, he was apprenticed to a carpenter, but since he turned out to be a quite vicious and unmanageable young lad, his family sent him off to some relatives in Australia. Here, he robbed and nearly killed an old woman, and was sentenced to eleven months' solitary confinement. James Banbury emerged from the Antipodian prison as angry and mean-spirited as before. His family managed to provide him with a job as a clerk in a tramway company, but he embezzled a large sum of money and took to the bush. He lived rough for many months, hunting kangaroos and other animals, and working as a cowboy when he felt like it. After getting word that his father had died, he made haste back to England in September 1891, to make sure that he was not cheated out of his inheritance.

James Banbury made it all the way back to Camden Town and collected several hundred pounds. In high spirits, he made plans to really enjoy his sojourn in the Metropolis. He discarded his shabby Australian attire and bought some quality suits of clothes instead. Describing himself as 'a gentleman horse-gambler', he was fond of attending race meetings. He gambled hard, initially with good success. His flashy clothes and boastful affluence meant that he 'fitted in' very well with the raffish throng gambling on

1.8 The Grosvenor Park murder house. Like the following two, this image is from the Illustrated Police News, July 9 1892.

the horses. 'Gentleman Jim', as he soon became known, also acquired a mistress, the 18-year-old Emma Oakley, and he moved into her lodgings at No. 81 Grosvenor Park, Walworth. Emma was a pretty young floozie who had tired of working as a domestic servant. Instead she was 'kept' by a string of well-to–do lovers. She led a jolly life with the short, stocky, dapperly dressed 'Gentleman Jim' for several months.

But James Banbury's initial spell of good luck deserted him, and he gradually lost his money. When he was unable to pay the bills, Emma evicted him from No. 81 Grosvenor Park, and he had to find alternative lodgings at No. 6 Brewer Street, Pimlico [the house still exists]. He had been genuinely fond of Emma, and drank hard to forget about his failing fortunes. On July 6 1892,

'Gentleman Jim' came lurching out of a public house at two in the afternoon, drunk as a lord after a lavish luncheon. He hailed a hansom cab, finding that the driver, Henry Richard Briggs, was actually an old acquaintance of his, and a fellow racing enthusiast. Bragging that he had won £30 at Alexandra Park a few days ago, Banbury ordered him to drive to Walworth. They stopped at a pub on the way, to have a couple of glasses of gin each. At another pub in Walworth Road, the thirsty 'Gentleman Jim' emptied another glass of gin before wandering off, telling Briggs to wait for him. After twenty minutes, he returned, puffing at a large cigar. He ordered Briggs to take him to Charing Cross.

When they arrived at Charing Cross, they went off to another public house to have some more gin. Suddenly and unexpectedly,

1.9 The pretty young Emma Oakley.

1.10 The sinister 'Gentleman Jim'.

Banbury said 'Get down and have a drink as I am going to leave you. I have shot a girl'. Laughing, the equally drunk Briggs chaffed 'You have not got the pluck. You could not shoot for nuts!' But the cabbie became apprehensive when 'Gentleman Jim' pulled out a revolver, obviously a relic of his bushranging days in Australia, and said 'It is quite true. I loved her, and made up my mind no one else should have her!' Fearful that the weapon would go off by mistake when handled by the drunken gambler, Briggs snatched it away from him when he looked away. Much worse for wear from drink, Banbury was unable to reclaim his revolver by force; instead he cravenly begged for it to be returned to him, and even offered £50 for it. Again, Briggs thought he was just joking. But as they went back through the station, 'Gentleman Jim' struck him a hard blow on the neck. The sturdy cabbie returned the blow and frog-

1.11 All the major players in the Walworth Shooting Drama, and another sketch of the murder house, from the Penny Illustrated Paper, July 9 1892.

marched his inebriated opponent back to the cab. But when they went past Waterloo Place, Banbury suddenly jumped out of the cab and disappeared into the crowd, without paying his fare.

The cabman Briggs had thought that 'Gentleman Jim' had just been chaffing when he talked about shooting a girl in Walworth. But the next day, having recovered from his hangover, he read in the newspaper about the murder of young Emma Oakley. At the Carter Street police station, he gave a full account of his dealings with the sinister 'Gentleman Jim', handing over the loaded revolver to convince them he was telling the truth. Detective Sergeant Leonard and Police Sergeant Brogden knew all about the murder of young Emma Oatley, gunned down in her lodgings at No. 81 Grosvenor Park by an unknown assailant. They managed to track down Banbury's Brewer Street lodgings. He was not there, but another lodger told them that the evening before, 'Gentleman Jim' had been even more drunk than usual. He had talked about shooting a girl, but again the witness had not believed him. A few hours later, when Banbury returned home, the two policemen kicked open the door to his room and took him into custody.

At the coroner's inquest on young Emma Oatley, the first witness was her father, the coachman Henry Oatley. Although he had known that she had not been in service for several years, he had not made inquiries what kind of life she was leading, since he thought her old enough to look after herself. The cabman Briggs told all about his expedition to Walworth with 'Gentleman Jim', and Detective Sergeant Leonard described the arrest of Banbury at his Brewer Street lodgings. The coroner's jury returned a verdict of wilful murder against James Banbury. They added that it was their opinion that the father of the deceased was deserving of severe censure for his most unmanly conduct towards his child, and that Detective Sergeant Leonard should be commended for his prompt arrest of the prisoner.

At the trial of James Banbury, the same individuals gave evidence. Furthermore, the landlady at No. 81 Grosvenor Park, Mrs Emma Foster, identified Banbury as the man she had seen running away from the premises after shooting Emma Oatley. The drunken 'Gentleman Jim' had confessed the murder to three different people, but none of them had believed him. Since it was clear to all that Banbury had murdered young Emma, the best the defence could do was to try playing the 'insanity card': his grandfather had been a little insane, it was claimed, and his great-aunt had died in a lunatic asylum in Australia. But the Holloway medical officer, who had observed Banbury there, gave the opinion that the prisoner was of sound mind. The jury retired for nearly two hours, before returning to deliver a verdict of Guilty, with a recommendation to mercy on account of the prisoner's age. But before the verdict was entered, there was farce when the Foreman pointed out that two of the jurymen were so deaf that they had been unable to hear the evidence. After the two men had readily admitted that this as the case, the jury was discharged. The case was reheard before another jury, with the same verdict. James Banbury was sentenced to death and executed at Wandsworth Prison on October 11 1892.[16]

While searching for the Grosvenor Park murder house, it soon became clear that the houses had been renumbered at some stage, perhaps after the murder. The present-day No. 81 does not at all match the drawing of the murder house in the *Illustrated Police*

1.12 A postcard depicting 'No. 1 South Villas, Grosvenor Park', today No. 47 Grosvenor Park, situated next door to the murder house at No. 49, and built in a very similar style.

News. Since the readers of this particular newspaper were often fond of gawping at murder houses, its illustrations were very accurate. And indeed, a search of the Post Office directories revealed that they houses had been renumbered a few years after the murder. The old No. 81 became No. 49, and the present-day No. 49 Grosvenor Park exactly matches the sketch of the murder house in the *Illustrated Police News*. It remains virtually unchanged since the days of 'Gentleman Jim' and poor Emma Oatley, and apart from some yellowed newspaper clippings and James Banbury's revolver, which was deposited in the Black Museum, it is the sole reminder of a once notorious crime that has become almost completely forgotten.

THE BOROUGH POISONER, 1903

Severin Klosowski was born in a small Polish village in 1865, the son of a carpenter. After leaving school, he was apprenticed to a barber-surgeon, learning hairdressing and acquiring enough medical knowledge to get a job as an assistant surgeon at a hospital for a while. In 1887, he was still in Warsaw, but in 1888, he moved to London, Whitechapel to be precise, working as a hairdresser's assistant. A restless character, with disdain for conventional morality, he kept 'carrying on' with various floozies. Nor was he a very truthful person, claiming to be a Jew although he was in fact a Christian, and using the names Severino Klosowski and Ludwig Zagowski interchangably. In October 1889, he married the young Polish woman Lucy Baderski, but their marital bliss was severely jolted when another woman arrived from Poland, claiming to be Klosowski's wife from an earlier marriage. For a while, both women cohabited with the immoral barber, until the alleged 'first' wife moved out.

1.13 The murderous-looking George Chapman, from H.L. Adam (Ed.), Trial of George Chapman (Notable British Trials, London 1930).

Klosowski took Lucy with him to New York in April 1891, and then to Jersey City. Here, he assaulted her one day in early 1892, without provocation, and held her down to prevent her from screaming. If a customer had not come into the barber's shop, her life might well have been in danger, since he had a large knife handy. Afterwards, he hinted that if she had 'disappeared', he could just have told people that she had moved back to New York. Rather understandably, Lucy did not want to stay with the sinister Klosowski after this incident, and she made haste to return to London. Her sturdy, moustachioed cad of a husband did not seem to bother much about this, and he kept amusing himself with various floozies. In 1893, he returned to London, where he met a woman named Annie Chapman, with whom he cohabited for a while. Realizing that his foreign-sounding name was hardly an asset in his adopted country, he started calling himself George Chapman.

'Chapman' struck lucky in 1895, when he met Mrs Mary Isabella Spink, who had been deserted by her husband due to her intemperate habits. She had a fortune of £500, which Chapman used for various business ventures, including setting up a barber's shop in Hastings that advertised 'musical shaves': Mrs Spink lathered the customers and then played the piano while Chapman shaved them. Like all George Chapman's schemes, this shop did not last very long: he moved to London, where he used the remainder of the Spink money to take over the lease of the Prince of Wales public house in Bartholomew Square, off the City Road [it no longer stands]. Once he had spent her money, he began to tire of Mrs Spink, who was of no further use to him. He purchased antimony and began dosing her with this compound. Slowly poisoning her to death, he watched her long and painful decline with what seemed like grief and concern.

After the wretched Mrs Spink had died on Christmas Day 1897, Chapman advertised for a barmaid. There were plenty of replies, and he chose Bessie Taylor, a dim-witted young woman who had no objection to doubling as Chapman's wife in a bogus marriage, just like Mrs Spink had done. They moved on to the Monument pub in Union Street, Southwark [it no longer stands], but Chapman soon got fed up with Bessie and poisoned her to death in the same manner. After her death in 1901, he employed another foolish barmaid at the Monument: young Maud Marsh, who soon called herself Mrs Chapman just like her predecessor. They moved to the Crown public house at No. 213 Borough High Street, where the chameleon Chapman posed as an American; the pub was called 'George's American Bar' by some

1.14 Chapman and Maud Marsh, from H.L. Adam (Ed.), Trial of George Chapman (Notable British Trials, London 1930).

of the locals. In 1902, the irrepressible Chapman employed another barmaid named Florence Rayner, at a time when his 'wife' was still alive. She did not have any objections to having an affair with him, but when he offered to take her to America, she told him to think of his wife downstairs. Chapman hinted to her that his 'wife' might soon expire, and indeed, he managed to poison her to death on October 22.

But the doctors attending Maud Marsh were less gullible than those who had looked after her two predecessors. They suspected that she had been poisoned and refused to make out a death certificate without a post-mortem. And indeed, her various organs contained a quantity of metallic antimony. Chapman was promptly arrested and the bodies of his two previous 'wives' exhumed: they were found to contain significant quantities of metallic antimony as well. Chapman was found guilty of murder, sentenced to death, and executed at Wandsworth Prison on April 7 1903.[17]

It did not take long for the Scotland Yard detectives to suspect that Klosowski alias Chapman might have more on his conscience than the murders of his three 'wives'. Here we had a serial killer of superior coolness and cunning, who had callously watched his three 'wives' die painful and protracted deaths. After all, there were few men in London capable of multiple murder. Klosowski had lived in Whitechapel at the time of the Ripper murders, and he had known this part of London well. He possessed some degree of medical knowledge, and he might well have attempted to murder his first wife with a knife. A human chameleon, he was an expert with regard to fitting into his environment, and although he lacked both breeding and education, he was a clever and enterprising man. When there was newspaper speculation that Klosowski was the Ripper, George R. Sims spoke up in his 'Mustard and Cress' column in the *Referee* newspaper, claiming that from private information, he knew that Jack the Ripper had been a doctor found drowned in the Thames in December 1888.

Sims was answered by Chief Inspector Frederick Abberline, who had been one of the leading detectives hunting Jack the Ripper. Abberline found Klosowski a very likely suspect, since he resembled the contemporary descriptions of the Ripper, and since he had been residing right in the middle of Whitechapel at the relevant time. Klosowski's ability to 'fit in' and avoid suspicion was pointed out, and there had been at least one Ripper-like murder in New York at the time Klosowski had been living there. Abberline's proposal of Klosowski as a Ripper suspect has received support from Superintendent Arthur Neil, from Hargrave Adam who edited the *Trial of George Chapman*, from the crime writer Jonathan Goodman, and from leading Ripper author Philip Sugden. Abberline certainly spoke to Lucy Baderski, since he was able to describe Klosowski's assault on her in 1892. Hargrave

Adam's statement that he also questioned her closely about Klosowski's movements back in 1888, finding out that he was often out until the wee hours, is interesting if true. It is by no means certain that Klosowski lived with Lucy as early as 1888, however, and Adam was not the most reliable of writers. Other ripperologists have pointed out the great contrast between the Ripper's frenzied assaults and mutilations of [presumably] randomly selected street prostitutes, and Klosowski's slow poisonings of three women he knew well. Although they have found nothing to definitively disqualify Klosowski as a Ripper suspect, the recent biography of the Borough Poisoner, by Ms Helena Wojtczak, highlights the weakness of the case against him, and the amount of wishful thinking used by Abberline and Hargrave Adam.[18]

The only one of Klosowski's London pubs to remain today is the Crown at No. 215 Borough High Street. This venerable old pub was constructed in 1841, on the site of the old Marshalsea Jail, which, as close students of Dickens' *Little Dorrit* will know, was later used as a debtor's prison. The Crown survived Severin Klosowski and his victims by many decades. When the Crown finally closed in 1976, the ultimate landlord said that he had always found the old murder pub a most spooky place. When he had arrived in 1967, he had opened up four rooms that looked like if they had been boarded up for at least forty years. There were plenty of bumps in the night, and his mother had seen the ghost of a man in one of the upstairs rooms. For a while, the Crown was used as a canteen by a nearby company. Later, it was rebuilt, keeping the original façade, and it is today part of the London Institute of Technology and Research.

MURDER AT THE GREYHOUND PUBLIC HOUSE, 1932

In 1931, the Greyhound public house at No. 336 Kennington Park Road, not far from the Oval, was kept by the 51-year-old Mr Ernest William Mace and his 52-year-old wife Violet. They had been at the pub for more than seven years. Trade was not very good, and Mr Mace feared poverty in old age, blaming the income tax for his difficulties, and also the increasing cost of his license. His executors were pressing him for £250 for the license money, payable at the end of January 1932.

On New Year's Day 1932, the barman Gerald Brown found Ernest and Violet Mace dead in their flat above the Greyhound pub.

1.15 Ernest Mace and his wife are found dead, from the Illustrated Police News, January 7 1932.

Mr Mace had shot his wife in the head, and then committed suicide. A letter to their son Jack was found on the dressing table. At the inquest on the Maces, the coroner Mr Douglas Cowburn said that stress had caused Ernest Mace to worry unduly. The income tax had not been at fault, and there was no evidence that the Inland Revenue authorities had been pressing Mr Mace for money due, although trade had definitely fallen off as a result of the increase in beer duty. The jury returned a verdict that Mr Mace had murdered his wife and then committed suicide while of unsound mind.[19] As for the murder pub, it remained the Greyhound for many years, but is today part of the Brown Derby chain.

ANOTHER MURDER IN CAMBERWELL CHURCH STREET, 1935

James Robert Vent was a young Scot who left school at 14 and got a job in a mine, but his mental balance was found wanting, and he soon became an inmate of Bells Hill Mental Home in Glasgow, where he remained for some considerable period of time. He then joined the army and served in India for a while, but his mental problems continued, and he was sent to Columba Asylum in Bombay. Leaving the army, he married and had a daughter, but his wife soon left him. In 1925, he was sentenced to nine months in prison for having sex with a girl aged fifteen. Since he was feeble both physically and mentally, he could not find a job even as a kitchen porter, and had to enter the Westmoreland Road Institution, Walworth, as a long term unemployed. His married sister, Mrs Florence Clowther, tried to help him as well as she could, but the dismal Vent showed her little gratitude.

In the institution for the unemployed, James Robert Vent met a long-term resident named William James Balchin, a dodgy-looking cove who had been there for not less than seven years. He had a wife named Clementina who lodged at No. 70 Camberwell Church Street, and although he had left her ten years earlier, he thought Vent might benefit from making her acquaintance. And indeed, after Mrs Clowther had managed to get Vent out of the institution, he went to see Mrs Balchin. She was a friendly, middle-aged matron, who felt pity for the miserable Vent. Although she and her two sons lived in two small rooms at No. 70, she allowed Vent to move in with them in 1934. The sons, shop porter James and glass worker William, thought Vent an odd fish, who did no work and seemed far from sane, but their mother, who was the person making the decisions in the household, allowed him to remain in the house.

In spite of the age difference (she was 56 years old, and he just 32), Mrs Balchin and James Vent became good friends. The weirdo Vent began to have fantasies of marrying her, or at least sharing her bed. But although her motives in allowing a young man to share her lodgings may be questioned, it does not appear as if Mrs Balchin had any plans of making the dismal Vent her 'toyboy'; she felt pity for the gloomy, feeble-minded Scot, rather than sexual desire. In fact, she had no shortage of 'gentleman friends' of her own age, and they regularly came to take her to the pub, later returning to No. 70 for some late-night 'fun'. Vent thought this most improper, but Mrs Balchin just ridiculed him. On January 12 1935, the drunken Vent went into Mrs Balchin's bedroom early in the morning. He was jealous when she spoke of her affairs with other men, he told her, and now he would cut his throat. Annoyed to be woken up in the middle of the night, Mrs Balchin just told him not to be silly. The infuriated Vent pulled out a razor, seized hold of her, and cut her throat. He then ran out of the house, all the way to Camberwell Police Station. Bursting into the station, he raised his blood-stained hands and screamed 'I'm mad! I'm mad! I've done a woman in!'

James Robert Vent provided a full account of the murder to the police, giving the motive as jealousy. On trial for murder at the Central Criminal Court, he pleaded guilty, and it took only five minutes for him to be found guilty and sentenced to death. He is recorded to have shrugged his shoulders and smiled in the dock. An appeal was dismissed, and the 'smiling murderer', as Vent was called in the newspapers, was due to be executed at Wandsworth Prison on March 20. But although the senior medical officer at Brixton Prison had found Vent sane and fit to plead, the Wandsworth prison doctors disagreed. In the end, there was a medical inquiry under the Criminal Lunatics Act, resulting in Vent receiving a late reprieve, and being removed to Broadmoor.[20] The murder house at No. 70 Camberwell Church Street still stands, not far from the house at No. 39 where the bushy-bearded John Coppen had murdered his wife back in 1874.

THE MURDER OF 'COCK-EYED MAISIE', 1945

In the 1920s and 1930s, Gertrude Marjorie 'Maisie' Rose was quite a well-known London prostitute. She claimed that her father was Edward Rackshaw, an old railway worker, who lived in Redfield Lane, Earl's Court, but present-day genealogical tools provide nothing to suggest that this humble labouring man ever had a daughter named Gertrude or Marjorie. Instead, there is a Gertrude Rose born in Sunderland in 1897, who married a man named Cunningham in 1915. Maisie used to say that she married a Canadian soldier during the Great War, and gone with him to his native land, returning to London a few years later after she had become fed up with him.

Maisie Rose enjoyed good success as a prostitute for many years. She does not appear to have had a steady pimp. Maisie was friendly and likeable when sober, but could become violent and argumentative when drunk. In the early 1930s, she fell in love with a black man named Charlie Bascombe, a sailor and prostitutes' bully. Maisie 'pinched' Charlie from another streetwalker called 'German Paula', and they had a short and tempestuous affair, before 'Big Gracie' pinched Charlie for herself. Maisie retaliated by breaking the windows of Gracie's flat. She then settled down to a calmer and more promising long-term relationship with a barman named Tom Jones, who pulled pints at the Russell public house.

In the mid-1930s, Maisie moved into No. 19 Southey Road, South Lambeth, a three-story purpose-built block of flats situated at the crossing with Cranworth Gardens. It was a four-room flat with its own bathroom, and she possessed her own furniture. Although she was losing her looks, with a nasty squint and false teeth in her upper jaw, she remained quite a successful prostitute. Maisie led a comfortable life at No. 19: a cleaner came once a week, the paper boy delivered the morning and evening newspapers, and the milkman made sure she had a regular supply of milk. Cock-Eyed Maisie, as she was called, had a number of regular customers who used to come visiting in the evening, but she also had a 'beat' outside the Crown and Anchor public house in St Martin's Lane, where she could pick up various late-night 'gentleman friends' and bring them home to No. 19 Southey Road.

The Second World War initially hampered Maisie's business, but when London filled up with American soldiers on leave in 1943 and 1944, her prospects were looking brighter than ever. Although she was now 47 years old, she was still perfectly capable of securing a steady supply of sex-starved transatlantic servicemen. The neighbours in Southey Road, who knew Maisie's profession, were amazed at the number of uniformed Yanks who kept visiting her; one of them, a young man in an officer's uniform, seemed to be quite fond of her.

On March 16 1945, Maisie did not open the door to the milkman or the paper boy. Her cleaner Mrs Frances Archer, who had her own key to the flat, was aghast to find Maisie dead on her double bed, with extensive head trauma from a series of blows with a heavy shillelagh. The injuries to her hands and forearms indicated that she had put up a violent struggle against her assailant. Dr Keith Simpson, who performed the post-mortem, found evidence of recent sexual intercourse, and secured some hair samples from the killer. Signs of latent syphilis, and recent gonorrhoea, were too obvious to be overlooked. Some chemical stains in the murder room indicated that the killer had used a 'prophylactic kit' issued to the US military to prevent venereal disease. The Irish shillelagh used as the murder weapon turned out to be one that Maisie had kept on the premises for her own protection.

The police made inquiries in the London underworld to find out more about Cock-Eyed Maisie and her habits, but with little success. This mystery woman had volunteered very little about her past, and seems to have delighted in telling lies about her family and connections. A certain Mrs Armswood identified herself as Maisie's sister, but both her parents were presumed to be dead. Charlie Bascombe had been working as a grease-monkey on board a merchant ship at the time of the murder, and the barman Tom Jones also had a solid alibi. Instead, the detectives tried to find out more about Maisie's transatlantic customers, but the witness descriptions of their faces and uniforms were wildly divergent. One of them was aged 35 or 40, with a pugilist's nose and dressed in what looked like a corporal's uniform. Several letters to Maisie from Lt. Grover O. Powers, of the 44th Bomber

Group, were found inside the murder flat. He was clearly the 'regular' who had been quite fond of her. Since Powers had been on leave at the time of the murder, he was questioned by the police. The transatlantic aviator freely admitted knowing Maisie Rose, and consorting with her at No. 19 Southey Road, but he had a solid alibi for the day of the murder.

In April 1945, Corporal Maurice J. Gaston was interviewed by the police, since he resembled the suspect with the broken nose, but no witness could identify him or tie him to the murder scene. There were newspaper murmurations that the murder of Maisie Rose might be related to some other unsolved wartime murders of women [Audrey Irene Stewart, Evelyn Hatton]. In November 1946, following press speculation that Neville Heath, who had just been executed for the murder of Margery Gardner, might well have claimed earlier victims, the police established that Heath had been in South Africa at the time Maisie Rose had been murdered.[21]

So, who killed Cock-Eyed Maisie? One key finding from the crime scene was that she had hidden two folded pound notes, presumably the money she had been given by her 'customer', underneath a pillow. This indicates that she was not with one of her 'regulars' the night she was murdered, but with some individual she did not quite trust: a random pick-up with suspected violent tendencies. Had be become disgusted when he saw the diseased state of the prostitute he had 'bought for the night'? Or had some insulting remark about his recent 'performance' in bed triggered a furious attack?

As for the murder house in Southey Road, it is clearly stated in the police file on the murder to be situated near Cranworth Gardens, with another similar block of flats at No. 21 opposite. There is only one house that matches this description, namely the present No. 1A Cranworth Gardens. It was not renamed as a result of the murder, but remained No. 19 Southey Road as recently as the 1980s.

A STRANGE STORY FROM CLAPHAM ROAD, 1963

Frederick William Randall had enjoyed an adventurous life as a trapeze artist and circus performer. In his old age, he opened a small lodging-house in the large terraced house at No. 114 Clapham Road, together with his much younger wife. In January 1963, he died aged 82. Three months later, his old dog Snoozy also expired.

In late 1965, the 55-year-old hospital porter James William Barber was arrested by the police and charged with raping a girl aged nine. While in police custody, he made a remarkable admission. Back in 1963, he had stayed at the lodging-house at No. 114 Clapham Road, and there he had murdered old Mr Randall by poisoning him with barbiturates. He had poisoned the dog too, just for the fun of it. At first, the police detectives were incredulous, but since Barber was clearly a person capable of serious crime, they questioned Mrs Randall about her husband's death. She could well remember that Barber had been in the house, and that when she had found her husband dead in bed, he had put his arms around her and said 'Don't upset yourself!' She had never suspected murder at the time, but it was true that the dog Snoozy had also died mysteriously. The police found out that soon after Mr Randall's death, Barber had remained in the lodging-house until April 1963, when he had gone to Bristol.

The only way forward, the detectives reasoned, was to exhume Mr Randall and Snoozy; both bodies turned out to be contain a barbiturate drug. They found out that Barber had shared his landlady's bedroom after her elderly husband had died, and thought they had found the motive for the murder. With what must have been a very narrow margin, it was decided that Barber should face trial at the Old Bailey for murdering Mr Randall. The evidence against him was ably summarized, and Barber admitted to sharing Mrs Randall's bed, although he denied asking her to go away with him. He was currently serving a ten-year prison sentence for the rape he had committed. Probably at the advice of his legal team, Barber said that he had confessed to the murder and canicide in a state of 'muddled thinking'. Since he knew that he would be charged with rape, why not confess to something even more serious, and confound the police, he had reasoned. He had given Mr Randall, who had been very ill and frail, a barbiturate tablet or two to soothe his pain, but his story of slipping 20 or 30 such tablets into the old man's cocoa was a complete invention. Mr Randall had been quite unwell for some time before he had expired, and the dog Snoozy had also been elderly and infirm.

Although he was undoubtedly a nasty piece of work, Barber seemed sincere when he denied murdering Mr Randall. The alleged motive, that he had been lusting for the elderly trapeze artist's wife, hardly seemed credible. The jury returned a verdict of Not Guilty both on the charge of murder and on the charge of maliciously administering a poison.[22] Barber was returned to his prison cell, where he must have been feeling rather apprehensive, since the newspapers had exposed him as a 'nonce' who had raped a young girl. Such nonces were hated by the other inmates, and had all kinds of unpleasant accidents happening to them in prison.

Although it is clear that the evidence against Barber was insufficient to convict him of murder, his confession was taken seriously by some experienced detectives, and there is still the question why the dog's remains contained barbiturates. If Mr

Randall had really been murdered, along with his elderly canine companion, it was an entirely pointless and mysterious crime. The house of mystery at No. 114 Clapham Road still keeps its dark secret: is it haunted by the shuffling gait of an old man, and by a spectral dog, or have Mr Randall and Snoozy found peace?

MURDER OF A PENSIONER, 1967

In 1967, the 78-year-old Mrs Agnes Jones lived at No. 20 St Stephens Terrace, Lambeth, with her husband and her 14-year-old granddaughter Susan Lees. In November, the ailing Mr Jones had to go into hospital. Agnes Jones had been visiting him there on November 8, but after she had returned to the tidy little terraced house at No. 20 St Stephens Terrace, she would never be seen alive again.

Later the same day, Mrs Ina Weekes, who lived opposite Agnes Jones in St Stephens Terrace, was walking her son home from school, when she saw Susan Lees run out from No. 20, screaming hysterically. Since Susan had left the front door open, Mrs Weekes could see the recumbent body of Agnes Jones, murdered by some intruder. She called the police straight away. They presumed that Agnes Jones had disturbed a thief, who had callously beaten the old lady to death. Susan Lees had probably missed the killer by minutes. Mrs Weekes told a journalist that Agnes Jones had always been a very sprightly old lady. There was no reason at all for a thief to target her house, since she did not have much money.

Detectives led by Superintendent J. Wilson launched a massive manhunt for the killer. They received help from Susan Lees, who claimed to have seen the killers, a gang of three teenagers. First there was a girl with long blonde hair, aged between 15 and 17. Then there was a long-haired hippie teenager.

The third villain was an ugly, foreign-looking cove, also aged around 17. Intriguingly, Susan claimed to have seen these three before, in the Brixton and Stockwell areas. The hippie might well be a guitarist who used to 'busk' in the streets, using the name Ian Roe or Rowe. The ugly bloke was called 'Plonk' and the girl 'Jen'. Susan Lees was guarded by the police, since they were fearing that the gang would come looking for her next. She helped to make an identi-kit image of Jen, and an artist's impression of Plonk was also issued, and both were distributed in thousands by the police. But in spite of the local people being very cooperative to solve the brutal murder of a harmless old lady, and in spite of the detailed descriptions of Jen's long hair and baby-faced looks, and Plonk's ugly mug and untidy hair, the trio of killers were never traced.

After a few weeks, the detectives began to doubt whether the three teenagers existed at all. They knew most of the local vagabonds and street musicians, and when these characters were interviewed, they had never heard of Ian Roe, Plonk and Jen. So was Susan Lees deliberately planting false leads to confound the police, to hide that she (and an accomplice?) had murdered Agnes Jones? The compiled a dossier of evidence against her, and presented it to the public prosecutors. In February 16 1968, she appeared before the Lambeth juvenile court magistrates, accused of having murdered her grandmother, and was remanded for six days. On March 11, she was sent in custody for trial at the Central Criminal Court, accused of murdering Agnes Jones. Mr A.C.L. Levisohn, for the defence, said that she pleaded not guilty, and reserved her defence.

Due to the painful nature of the crime and trial, and the young age of the person accused of murder, nothing was reported in the newspapers about the trial of Susan Lees, but the ultimate verdict was one of not guilty to murder. She pleaded guilty to the charge of impeding the apprehension of another person for murder, and was sent to an approved school.[23] The main point seems to have been that although there were many suspicious circumstances attending the case, it would hardly have been possible for a 14-year-old girl to bludgeon a sprightly old lady to death in such a brutal manner. The police suspected that Susan Lees had let an accomplice into the house, and she had lied to make sure this individual would not be caught, but although the police investigation went on until late 1969, no other person was charged with the murder. The murder house at No. 20 St Stephens Terrace still stands, the sole reminder of one of London's many mysterious unsolved murders. It is as neat and tidy as when Agnes Jones lived there. The police files on the case are closed until 2045.

THE TALE OF A MURDER SHOP AND TWO MURDER PUBS, 1991-1993

Ahmet Abdullah was a Turkish immigrant who had made a name for himself in the South London gangster world. He associated himself with the Arif family, who were involved in a gang war with another notorious gangster clan, the Brindles. In September 1990, 'Turkish Abbi', as he was known, quarrelled with Stephen Dalligan, an associate of the Brindles, while drinking at a club. Abdullah pulled a gun and shot his adversary seven times. Dalligan was not badly injured, but it was thought that Anthony Brindle, leader of the gangster family, would not take it kindly to have one of his loyal followers gunned down.

Ahmet Abdullah was well known as a drug dealer, operating in the Walworth area. On March 11 1991, he went into the William Hill betting shop at No. 25-27 Bagshot Street, presumably to have a flutter on the dogs or the horses. But suddenly, two men came bursting into the shop, brandishing revolvers. Abdullah was shot and badly wounded. Trying to use another customer as a shield, he pleaded with his attackers to spare him. Finally, he reeled out into the street, where he was shot once more, and killed. Later, the brothers Anthony and Patrick Brindle were tried for the murder, but they were acquitted due to lack of evidence. To testify against gangsters of this calibre could be decidedly dangerous for your health.

The murder of their follower Ahmet Abdullah was just one of a series of disasters for the Arif family in 1991. The convictions of Dennis and Mehmet Arif led to the Brindles gaining the upper hand in the gangster war. But another family, the Dalys, instead declared war on the Brindles. In August 1990, several gunmen, believed to be associates of the Brindles, had burst into the Queen Elizabeth pub, trying to extort money from the landlord, at gunpoint. This landlord was John Daly, brother of the gangster Peter Daly. In August 1991, the 23-year-old gangster David Brindle entered the Queen Elizabeth pub, which was well known as a regular hangout for the Dalys and their friends. He tried to intimidate some of his adversaries, but was confronted by the notorious hard man Jimmy Moody, who beat him up with a glass ashtray and a baseball bat. The Dalys were fearful that the injured David Brindle would put out a contract on them after being the recipient of such a brutal beating. They decided to strike a pre-emptive blow.

The gangster Ahmet Abdullah had not been a particularly attractive individual, but at least two people kept his memory alive, or so at least it was thought. Shortly before closing time on August 3 1991, two masked gunmen burst into the Bell pub, situated at No. 51 East Street, Walworth. Screaming 'This is for Abbi!' they opened fire at David Brindle. He was killed as he tried to dive over the bar to retrieve his own firearm. The barman John Plows threw a bar stool at one of gunmen, but the killer retaliated by shooting him four times in the stomach and legs. The murderers also killed an innocent bystander, the 47-year-old Stanley Silk.

The police suspected that the murder of David Brindle had been contracted by the Dalys. The reason the gunmen had shouted out 'This is for Abbi!' may well have been to put suspicion on the near-defunct Arifs. They also suspected that one of the gunmen had been Jimmy Moody, a very dangerous gangster who had started his career already in the 1960s, as an enforcer for the Richardson family, although he did some 'freelance' work for the Krays as well. In 1967, Moody had been imprisoned for manslaughter, serving five years behind bars. Later, he became a member of the Chainsaw Gang, who robbed security vans, cutting away the side of the vehicles to gain access to the money and valuables. In 1979, Moody was again imprisoned, to await trial for armed robbery. His cellmate was the notorious IRA man Gerard Tuite, who was known for his cunning and cleverness. In 1980, these two villains escaped from Brixton Prison, digging through cell walls using tools smuggled into the prison. There was widespread outrage that two of the most dangerous criminals in Britain could abscond from prison with such ease.

Jimmy Moody and Gerard Tuite made it all the way to Ireland, where the IRA employed Moody as a hitman, making good use of his murderous skills. Moody did not care about Irish politics, and was never a proper IRA member, but he was very good at killing people. By the late 1980s, Moody became fearful that he was overstaying his welcome among the volatile, trigger-happy IRA men. He decided to return to his old stomping-grounds in London, but was dismayed to find that in his absence, drug dealing had become the main source of income for the gangster fraternity. As an old-fashioned 'hard man', he disapproved of involvement in the drug-dealing business, but still, the Dalys found him a very useful associate.

Moody hoped that his fearsome reputation would save him from his long list of enemies. In June 1993, he was drinking at his favourite pub, the Royal Hotel [now the Royal Inn on the Park], Hackney, when a tall man with greying hair came up and shot him dead from close range, before calmly exiting the premises to make his escape in a stolen white Ford Fiesta. The Brindles were of course the main suspects for the murder, since they were known for their long memories, and good access to hitmen. But Moody's enemies also included various other London gangsters, some very dangerous 'old acquaintances' from Ireland, and the British Secret Service.[24] To simulate a 'gangland killing' would not have been particularly difficult for either of these organisations.

The William Hill betting shop at No. 25-27 Bagshot Street is still kept by the same company. Both murder pubs are also open for business. When I visited them, there were no gangsters or gunmen lurking about, and the Royal Inn on the Park had quite an upmarket atmosphere.

CHAPTER 2

WANDSWORTH

The startled bats flew out – bird after bird -
The screech-owl overhead began to flutter,
And seem'd to mock the cry that she had heard
Some dying victim utter!
A shriek that echo'd from the joisted roof,
And up the stair, and further still and further,
Till in some ringing chamber far aloof
It ceased its tale of murther!

This chapter will cover another large chunk of London south of the river, including Brixton, Clapham, Peckham, Battersea, and Balham, and extending north as far as the border with Lambeth, south as far as the border with Tooting and west as far as Putney. Again, this part of London contains a wealth of historical murder houses, many of which are no longer standing. The stables of Granard Lodge, off Putney Park Lane, where Daniel Good murdered and dismembered his common-law wife Jane in 1842, stood long enough to be admired by Guy Logan in 1905, but today only the original gates and gatehouse remains of Granard Lodge.[1] No. 4 Springfield Cottages, a terrace of 12 houses once standing on the north side of Acre Lane, Brixton, was the site of a mysterious murder in 1853. The 84-year-old Mr William Jones had been brutally done to death, and his tall, muscular servant

2.1 John Selby Watson murders his wife, from the Illustrated Police News, October 28 1872.

2.2 The Watson murder house at No. 28 St Martin's Road, Stockwell, from the Illustrated Police News, October 21 1872.

Elizabeth Vickers stood trial at the Old Bailey for having murdered and robbed the old man, but with what must have been a very narrow margin. 'Cruel Lizzie' Vickers was acquitted. Of No. 4 Frederick Terrace, Gordon Grove, off Loughborough Road in Brixton, once home to the baby-farmers Margaret Waters and Sarah Ellis, not a brick remains. No. 28 St Martin's Road, Stockwell, where the author and scholar John Selby Watson murdered his wife Anne in 1871, no longer exists, although there are some older houses in the road to show what it must have looked like.[2] Rushcroft House in Rushcroft Road, Brixton, where the prostitute Elizabeth Clark, who called herself Lily Templeton, was murdered in 1909, longer frowns upon the passer-by.

2.3 Lily Templeton is found murdered in her flat at Rushcroft House, Rushcroft Road, Brixton, from the Illustrated Police News, December 4 1909.

Although this book does not tend to deal with modern 'murder flats', I will mention two Wandsworth flats briefly, since particularly gruesome murders have taken place within their walls. In 1959, the impecunious clerk Ronald Herbert Benson came to ask his elderly relative Miss Elizabeth Ivatt for money, visiting her flat at Chesham Court, a modern block off Trinity Road. She was not disposed to give him any, so he brutally beat the 88-year-old former headmistress to death, and murdered her 60-year-old companion Phyllis May Squire as well. Benson was convicted of murder, and sent to Broadmoor.[3] In 1982, a gang of three young drunks were at large in a flat at Coleby Path, an unprepossessing modern block in Brunswick Park. The hoodlums John Bowden,

2.4 A portrait of Lily Templeton, and a sketch of the murder flat in Rushcroft Road, from the Illustrated Police News, December 4 1909.

David Begley and Michael Ward lured the alcoholic former park worker Donald Ryan up to the flat, where they attacked him with a machete just for the fun of it. They threw him into a bath full of scalding hot water, and proceeded to dismember him while he was still alive, making use of a handsaw and an electric carving knife to sever his arms, legs and head. The three killers then went out for a few drinks, discarding various body parts on the way, but they were soon arrested, tried and convicted. The jury was once adjourned, after the horrid crime scene photographs had reduced some of them to tears. John Bowden was sentenced to 25 years in prison, but after he had taken a prison governor hostage in 1984, ten more years were added to his sentence. He escaped from prison in 1992, and again in 2008, but was recaptured each time. John Bowden was in the news as recently as 2012, after having allegedly sent love letters from prison to a Glaswegian poetry teacher.[4]

THE GREAT BRAVO MYSTERY, 1876

In a search for London's greatest murder mystery, the case of the young barrister Charles Bravo, who was poisoned in 1876, has much speaking in its favour. It concerns wealthy and socially prominent people living in a grand Balham country house, there is a multitude of potential suspects, and the moral standards of the people involved leave much to be desired. Such a spicy tale of love, sex and murder in Victorian London has attracted the attention of many authors, whose analysis of the mystery has been wildly divergent.

As a young girl, Florence Campbell seemed to have everything going for her. Good-looking and vivacious, she was born into a rich Scottish landowning family. In 1864, she married a handsome young officer, Captain Alexander Ricardo, whose family was also very wealthy. The problem was that Ricardo was an alcoholic, who drank like the proverbial fish, particularly after he had left the army. Florence left him after he had beaten her up in a drunken rage, and returned to her parents. Although she said that she would not return to her cad of a husband under any circumstances, they persuaded her to become an inpatient at the

Malvern hydrotherapeutic establishment of that upstanding practitioner, Dr James Manby Gully.

James Gully was a fashionable society doctor, known for his excellent bedside manner rather than his diagnostic skill or prominence as a medical scientist. He was a proponent of the 'water cure' for various diseases. In the Malvern hydro, the patients could look forward to lengthy baths, and plenty of water to drink. Present-day medical science would suggest that the benefit of the 'water cure' was largely that the florid, hard-drinking patients were fed a light and easily digestible diet, and not allowed any alcohol. Dr Gully gave the impression of being a solid, reliable family man, and a good father to his brood of children. There was a Mrs Gully, but she was much older than him, and he had put her in a home in Brighton.

When Dr Gully met Florence Ricardo, he was in his mid-sixties, and thus old enough to be her grandfather. A short, sturdy, bald-headed man, he was nothing much to look at. But nevertheless, it did not take long for this extraordinary practitioner to seduce his beautiful young patient. He arranged to become her legal guardian, and she lived openly as his mistress. When Alexander Ricardo dropped dead from vomiting blood, Florence inherited forty thousand pounds, an enormous fortune in those days. She made use of this money to purchase the lease of a fine mansion in Balham, known as the Priory. The besotted Dr Gully bought another property nearby, so that he could continue to keep an eye on his favourite patient. Florence employed a full staff of servants at the Priory, and also got herself a lady companion, a rather sinister-looking widow named Jane Cox, who served her with commendable loyalty. When Florence got pregnant after some anti-contraceptive mishap, Dr Gully performed an abortion in her bedroom at the Priory, with Mrs Cox acting as nurse.

But in the meantime, Florence's respectable parents were

2.5 All the major players in the Bravo drama, from the Penny Illustrated Paper, August 5 1876.

becoming seriously worried about their daughter's immoral conduct. Her affair with Gully was widely known, and her reputation in society suffered as a result. And indeed, the fickle Florence was beginning to tire of her elderly lover, particularly as she had met a more promising swain, the young barrister Charles Bravo. An intelligent, cultured gentleman who was the same age as Florence, he was a vast improvement, with regard to looks and general vigour, compared with the aging doctor. It did not take Florence long to marry Charlie Bravo, and leave her favourite practitioner high and dry. Gully was very much displeased about losing his dear Florence, but there was nothing he could do. Since their affair was quite well-known in society, Florence confessed to Charlie, who took the news quite well. Indeed, he promised to give up his own long-time mistress if Florence never saw Gully again.

But Charlie Bravo gradually showed a more sinister side of his personality. A male chauvinist even by the standards of the time, he wanted to be master in his own house, the Priory, although Florence had actually purchased the property. He had a strong sexual appetite, and insisted on Florence being 'available' at all times, even after she had suffered a miscarriage. Charlie was remarkably mean and avaricious, and Florence must have suspected that he had married her for the money. He made himself obnoxious by insisting on domestic economy, and dismissing some of the servants. One of them, the coachman George Griffiths, who very much disliked being sacked from his comfortable job, was overheard cursing Mr Bravo, and predicting that he would not live for very long. Florence was becoming fearful that Charlie's threat to dismiss also her loyal friend Mrs Cox was not an empty one.

On April 18 1876, Charlie Bravo wanted to take a ride round the grounds of the Priory, but the horse bolted with him, and he returned home very shaken and exhausted. He ordered the maid Mary Ann Keeber to prepare a hot bath for him to recover from his ride, and it is an illustration of both his parsimony and his defective sense of hygiene that he told her to leave the dirty water in the tub, for use the following morning. By dinnertime, Charlie had recovered enough to eat a three-course meal, and drink four glasses of burgundy from the decanter. He was still in a truculent mood, after having received an obnoxious letter from his stepfather, about his unsuccessful gambling on the Stock Exchange. Conversation was minimal, and Florence and Mrs Cox sat gloomily watching Charlie as he was puffing hard on his pipe.

2.6 Two contemporary sketches of Charles and Florence Bravo.

Although she had drunk champagne with her luncheon, and although she and Mrs Cox had polished off two bottles of sherry between them at dinner, Florence ordered a glass of sweet white wine. When going to bed, she wanted another tumbler of white wine and water, and Charlie complained about her incessant tippling. All grew quiet at the Priory, until Charlie Bravo came lurching out from his bedroom, screaming 'Florence! Hot water!' in a terrible voice.

The maid Mary Ann Keeber clearly heard Charlie Bravo's outcry. Too timid to dare to enter her master's bedroom, she knocked at Florence's bedroom instead. Surprised that no person answered the knock, she opened the door herself, to find Florence asleep in bed, and Mrs Cox sitting knitting by the fire. When Mary Ann explained that Mr Bravo had been taken ill, Mrs Cox accompanied her into his bedroom. They found him standing by the open window, vomiting spasmodically. He then turned and fell, but Mrs Cox managed to break his fall. Seeing that he was clearly very ill, she ordered Mary Ann to fetch mustard and hot water, and to make sure that the coachman was sent to fetch a doctor. Mary Ann herself took the initiative to wake up Mrs Bravo, whom she had seen in bed, seemingly comatose. As soon as the drunken Florence had understood that Charlie was ill, she leapt out of bed and insisted that another doctor, who lived closer to Balham, should also be fetched. The medical team was later reinforced by Mr Royes Bell, a surgeon who was a friend of Charlie Bravo, and the distinguished physician Dr George Johnson, who took charge of the case. The volatile Florence made various far-fetched diagnostic suggestions: the ride on the bolting horse might have upset Charlie's constitution, he might have suffered a fainting fit, or he might have eaten something that disagreed with him. But it was clear to the experienced doctors that this was a case of poisoning. Either Charlie Bravo had taken poison himself, or some person had made a determined attempt to murder him.

The question was which poison had been used, and here the doctors were in a quandary. Mrs Cox told one of them that she thought Charlie might have drunk chloroform, but the doctors did not believe her, since there were signs that a strong irritant poison had been made use of. Mrs Cox did not tell the doctors that a sample of the patient's vomit was available outside the window, and she made sure that his blood-stained nightshirt was thrown away and exchanged for a new one. When poor Charlie passed some blood-stained stools, she ascribed the effect to him drinking red wine with his dinner!

When Charlie Bravo regained consciousness, helped by the various ministrations from the doctors, he denied taking any poison. He had rubbed his gums with some laudanum for the toothache, but had not swallowed any. Even when harshly spoken to, and reminded that if he denied attempting suicide, suspicion might fall on some person accused of murdering him, the dying man still denied having swallowed any poison. That amazing Mrs

Cox then told Royes Bell that before the doctors had arrived, Charlie had confided in her that he had taken poison! The angry surgeon shouted at her for not telling any person about this vital fact earlier, but when confronted with her statement, Charlie again stoutly denied having attempted to destroy himself. In spite of the celebrated physician Sir William Gull being called in, as a last resort, Charlie Bravo died after two and a half days of agony.

The autopsy and forensic analysis showed that Charlie Bravo had been poisoned by tartrate of antimony. This corrosive substance had literally eaten his intestines away, and it is a testimony to his strong constitution that he had been able to linger for more than two days. At first, it was suspected that the poison had been administered through the burgundy Charlie had drunk with his dinner, but since antimony makes wine go cloudy, and since its effect sets in within fifteen minutes, this could not be the case. Although Charlie had drunk four glasses of wine, his health had appeared fine until he reached his bedroom. Since it was his habit to drink thirstily from a large carafe of water before going to bed, and since no other suitable receptacle for the poison was detected, the doctors suspected that the antimony had been mixed with the water in this carafe. The only drawback to this theory was that one of the doctors had himself swigged from this very decanter, without any ill effect! Clearly some person, probably the poisoner, must have emptied, rinsed, and then re-filled it?

The police investigation of the mysterious murder of Charlie Bravo, led by Detective Chief Inspector Clarke, made disappointingly little headway. Mrs Cox gave nothing away, and the police did not think that Florence Bravo appeared like a guilty woman. There was a coroner's inquest on Charles Bravo, held privately in the dining room at the Priory, which returned an open verdict. This suited many of the people involved in the case, but the problem was that the active and scandal-mongering newspaper

2.7 The Bravo jury sees the body, from the Illustrated Police News, July 22 1876.

press had found out about some of the most sensational issues, like Florence's affair with Dr Gully, and the role played by Mrs Cox. As a result, a second inquest was held, in public this time, at the Bedford Hotel, Balham [it still stands]. In this 'Trial by Crowner's Quest', Florence and Mrs Cox had their back against the wall. While undergoing a hostile examination, the slimy Mrs Cox changed her story once more, claiming that Charlie had told her that he "had taken poison for Gully. Don't tell Florence." This statement let the cat out of the bag, and offered Florence up for some searching questioning, as Mrs Cox had probably intended. Florence wept bitterly and pleaded for mercy, as she was forced to tell all about her relations with Gully. The good doctor himself faced an equally hostile questioning, and both he and Florence were professionally and socially ruined, for good. Gully was hounded out of his clubs, and the newspapers were full of the

2.8 Mrs Cox gives evidence before the coroner's jury.

merry goings-on at the Priory. At the inquest, both Florence and Mrs Cox made much of Charlie Bravo's cruelty and mean-spiritedness, and they tried their best to allege that he was near-suicidal from his jealousy of Dr Gully. But Charlie's letters made no mention of suicide, or any serious pangs of jealousy for that matter, and his loyal friends stoutly denied that this money-loving young barrister had ever entertained any suicidal notions. The jury eventually returned a verdict of murder against some person or persons unknown.

The verdict from the coroner's jury came as a disappointment to the Bravo family, and was another hard blow for Florence and Mrs Cox. The newspapers did their best to emphasize the infamy of Dr Gully, the immorality of Florence Bravo, and the sneaky

2.9 Florence Bravo, from the Illustrated Police News, September 28 1878.

behaviour of Mrs Cox, although the laws of libel prevented them from making any open accusations. There was also an illustrated magazine about the case, in seven penny issues, entitled *The Balham Mystery*, with some ribald images from the coroner's inquest. It is sad but true that Florence Bravo drank herself to death in September 1879, expiring at the house where she had sought refuge, at No. 19 Eastern Parade, Southend [it still stands]. Dr Gully died in obscurity in 1883, giving instructions that his remains should be disposed of in an unmarked grave. In contrast, that extraordinary Mrs Cox lived happily ever after. Having cashed in a considerable inheritance, she could live in comfort and have her sons educated in some style; this wicked woman did not expire until 1917, at the age of 90.

Over the years, there has been much speculation about who really murdered Charlie Bravo.[5] Agatha Christie, who liked speculating about true crime mysteries, opted for Dr Gully as the guilty man, although she did not explain how the obese, unfit doctor could have acquired Spiderman-like superpowers, enabling him to enter the Priory, put the poison into Charlie's water-jug, and then leave the premises undetected. As for the coachman Griffiths, he had a solid alibi, being at work in Kent at the evening of the murder. The remaining domestics at the Priory lacked a motive to murder Mr Bravo, although I would have been interested to know more about the maid Mary Ann Keeber, and her relations with her master. Amazingly, Sir William Gull, who was known for his stubbornness, stood up at the coroner's inquest to testify that in his opinion, Charlie Bravo had most likely committed suicide. But why would an educated man, who had some knowledge of toxicology due to his legal training, use such a painful and protracted way to kill himself, instead of making use of a handgun or a bottle of morphine? The old crime writer Yseult Bridges, who liked to think up 'solutions' for celebrated murder mysteries, proposed the unlikely version that Charlie wanted to poison Florence, but drank the poison himself by mistake! Professor Mary Hartmann, an American academic who took an interest in feminist aspects of crime, suggested that Florence had wanted to put some antimony tartrate in Charlie's water jug to make him feel nauseous, in order to prevent him pestering her for sex, but that in her drunken condition, she made a mistake with the dose. But there is no independent corroboration that Victorian wives made use of this dangerous poison to control the sexual appetites of their husbands, and anyway, the dose poor Charlie had swallowed had been enough to kill him several times over.

The more cerebral commentators on the Bravo Mystery have concentrated on the two main suspects: Florence and Mrs Cox. The novelist Elizabeth Jenkins and the crime writer John Williams both thought Florence guilty. A story has been going around that when Captain Ricardo's body was exhumed, antimony was detected in his remains, but this story was invented by the mischievous alienist Dr Forbes Winslow, who sometimes tried to falsify 'solutions' for historical crimes. That great Edinburgh chronicler of crime, William Roughead, thought that Mrs Cox had poisoned the obnoxious Charlie Bravo, in order to keep her comfortable job at the Priory, and the crime writers Bernard Taylor and Kate Clarke agreed. Mrs Cox must surely have heard Charlie's outcry, but she did nothing until she had been summoned by the maid. She told a number of untruths at the inquest, and gave the impression of being quite a conniving, wicked woman. But in the most recent book on the Great Bravo Mystery, journalist James Ruddick effectively disposed of the theory that Mrs Cox was keen to keep her job for financial reasons: she had a quite considerable inheritance coming her way, something she was well aware of. Ruddick thought Florence the guilty woman, with Mrs Cox as an accessory after the fact.

James Ruddick's hypothesis is a good one, and it deftly explains some of the mysterious matters about the murder: the volatile Florence was able to keep her cool since her loyal friend was supporting her, and the two women had had good time to coordinate their stories and accuse Charlie of being suicidal at the inquest. Sensing the hostility against herself, and aware of the various untruths she had already told, Mrs Cox then cleverly made use of 'Plan B', telling another pack of lies about Charlie taking poison for Gully, to make sure attention was shifted away from herself onto Florence and her immoral shenanigans. The exuberant 'blurb' for Ruddick's book, and the exhortations of a number of silly and over-enthusiastic London journalists, pronounced the Great Bravo Mystery 'solved', but this is far from being the case. Although Ruddick has shed much new light on the case, the mystery remains.

If one thing is clear about the Bravo mystery, it is that Mrs Cox knew the identity of his murderer, and that she tried her utmost to protect this person from being detected. I would also suggest that the murderess was either Mrs Cox herself or Florence Bravo, or most likely the pair of them acting together. Mrs Cox is likely to have been the dominant partner in such a murder conspiracy, being clever and possessing admirable coolness of mind, whereas Florence was impulsive and volatile. There is also the matter of a pension which, according to a confidential letter to William Roughead, was paid to Mrs Cox by one of Florence's brothers: was this for 'services rendered'? As for the source of the poison, and the toxicological expertise affecting its choice, we must contemplate that witnesses saw Mrs Cox and Dr Gully together several times in the months leading up to the murder. Hell hath no fury like a doctor scorned, and Gully's defective grasp of medical ethics may well have extended to providing some friendly advice to Mrs Cox about how to get rid of his impudent younger rival, for good.

As for the murder house, it is reported to have been haunted by Charles Bravo's restless spirit for many years. The father of Mr James Clark, a chronicler of London ghosts, knew the Priory as a haunted house in the 1940s.The Bedford Hotel, where the inquest had taken place, was also haunted.[6] The Priory has today been subdivided into flats, but the haunting has continued. According to the abovementioned James Ruddick, Charles Bravo haunted his former bedroom with such frequency that one of the residents called in a priest to perform a ceremony of exorcism. This ceremony is said to have had the desired effect.[7]

THE BRIXTON MATRICIDE, 1884

In the 1860s, Mr Frederick Relton, a travelling accountant in the employ of the Great Western Railway Company, was living at

Victoria Place in Newport, Monmouthshire. This impressive terrace of twelve grade two listed houses dates back to the 1830s, and still stands today, one of the few streets in central Newport with any claim to architectural merit. But when there was an outbreak of typhoid fever in Mr Relton's house, he blamed the local authority for the unsatisfactory drainage in Victoria Place. Two of Mr Relton's children died, and the third, young Seymour Boyer Relton, became an invalid. After being rebuffed by the Newport sanitary authorities, Mr Relton moved to Chepstow with his wife and remaining son. Poor Seymour was very feeble-minded, and "scarcely considered accountable for his actions," as a newspaper expressed it.

Later, Mr Relton moved to London with his family. After his death, he left his widow Mary and young Seymour well provided for. The latter, who had his lucid intervals, took an interest in the classics and obtained a 3rd class degree in Latin at London University in 1878, by private study. He then went on to become a stockbroker, but his delicate mental and bodily health meant that he was unable to fully devote himself to this profession.

In 1884, the 62-year-old Mary Relton and the 27-year-old Seymour were living at No. 35 Spenser Road, Brixton. Seymour had for some time been very strange in his manner, and incapable of attending to business. He spent much time in bed, and complained that both he and his mother were being systematically poisoned. He contacted his aunt telling her that there was a plot to murder them, and gave her some salad to be analysed for poison. On March 18 1884, Seymour was very fussy about his food, complaining that there was too much pepper, and that the meat was very tough. His mother spoke to their servant Harriett Reffin, who had prepared the meat, but she had noticed nothing abnormal about it.

Later the same day, Harriett Reffin heard a heavy fall, and Mrs Relton's little poodle dog started barking furiously. When Harriett

2.10 Seymour Boyer Relton is discovered after having murdered his mother, from Famous Crimes Past & Present.

went into Mrs Relton's room, she saw the limp body of her mistress lying on the floor. It looked like if her throat had been cut with considerable force. Seymour, who was standing over her, had blood on his left hand. He called out "Harriett, your mistress has got a razor; she has cut her throat, and I want help!" When Harriett returned after fetching a neighbour, Mrs Relton's face and eyes were much bruised, like if some person had beaten or kicked her. Dr Barraclough, the local practitioner, did not waste words; as soon as he saw the recumbent Mrs Relton, he said "She is dead; she could not have done it herself!"

Seymour Boyer Relton was pulled out of his bed and arrested by the police, and the inquest on his mother returned a verdict of wilful murder against him. No motive for the murder could be discerned, except that Seymour was stark raving mad. When Seymour was on trial at the Old Bailey, Dr Orange, the medical superintendent of Broadmoor, testified that in his opinion, the prisoner was of unsound mind, and unable to plead.[8] The Brixton Matricide was sent to Broadmoor, where he remained incarcerated until his death in 1940, aged 82.

PAINFUL CASE OF MATRICIDE, 1892

Mrs Elizabeth Hudson, an elderly widow, lived at No. 39 Fullerton Road, Wandsworth, with her invalid daughter Edith. Poor Edith's mind had always been very feeble. She had once been engaged to marry, but her sweetheart had died shortly before the wedding was to take place. This tragedy had made her quite deranged, and she had attempted suicide, through cutting

2.11 Sarah Hudson murders her mother, from the Illustrated Police News, January 20 1894.

her throat or drinking fusel oil. On January 11 1894, Edith Hudson went to Wandsworth Police Station and confessed that she had just murdered her mother, through suffocating her with a pillow. A police constable and a doctor were dispatched to No. 39 Fullerton Road, where they found the 76-year-old Elizabeth Hudson unconscious but alive. But although artificial respiration was resorted to, she died not long after. At the coroner's inquest, no clear motive for the murder emerged. Edith claimed that her mother had been an invalid, who needed to be put out of her misery, but other witnesses testified that Elizabeth Hudson had been looking after her daughter, not the other way around. Edith had cashed in £4's worth of insurance money when her sweetheart had died unexpectedly just before they were to be married, but her mother's life had not been insured. Since Edith Hudson was obviously insane and unable to plead, she was incarcerated in an asylum.[9]

HUSBAND MURDER IN BATTERSEA, 1896

In 1888, the year of Jack the Ripper, the house decorator Mr Thomas Preston held the lease of the terraced house at No. 10 Stanmer Street, Battersea. Since it was larger than the other houses in the street, with double doors opening to the yard behind the house, Mr Preston and his wife thought it prudent to let two first floor rooms to a lodger. In 1888, that lodger was a certain Mr John 'Taffy' Dennison, aged 65 and a native of Wales, of no occupation, The Prestons were concerned that Dennison invited a number of young boys, some of them little better than guttersnipes, up to his rooms. At these strange concertos, a barrel-organ was badly played, and the boys sang hymns as well as they could. There was no such thing as a paedophile in 1888, but nevertheless the

Prestons thought their lodger a most sinister cove. But Taffy assured them that he was just practicing with his band of juvenile musicians, who were splendid little athletes, and showed evidence of great talent.

But Taffy Dennison's passion for recruiting singing boys went to extremes. He put an advertisement into several newspapers, saying "Boys (respectable) wanted, to sing a little. Not over 14. Wages 10s to 12s. a week. Write or call... " He received many replies from various foolish or impecunious people who had young boys to spare, and after some tuition at No. 10 Stanmer Street, Taffy took his troupe of musicians on tour to Margate, Ramsgate, Canterbury and Dover. The boys sang and grinded a barrel-organ, holding a sign saying "We are orphans, and get our living by our music." The Welsh Fagin stood a safe distance away, wringing his hands with glee as the kind people of Canterbury filled the begging-bowl of his little accomplices. At Dover Castle, the band made another bravura performance, singing to the soldiers of the garrison. The tour went on to Portsmouth, Hyde and Tunbridge Wells: the bandmaster regularly send backward or recalcitrant boys back home, and received new recruits to replace them. Although the boys could make 30 shillings in an afternoon, the each received only threepence in pocket-money per week. But after Taffy had returned to London with his band, a number of angry mothers confronted him, claiming that he had abducted their sons for his despicable begging charades. As cool as a cucumber, the veteran child exploiter refused to give them a penny, since the boys had joined him from their free will, but this turned out to be a bad business decision on his part, since the mothers went to the police and the newspapers.

'Charge of Kidnapping Boys!' exclaimed the *Morning Post* of May 7 1888, and many other newspapers followed suit.[10] The mothers and stepmothers of the exploited 'singing boys' had joined forces to make sure that the Welsh Fagin was put behind bars, and taken out a summons against him at the Westminster Police Court. Some of them provided evidence, real or spurious, that their sons had been forcibly abducted from home. Taffy had a reasonably strong case that the boys had joined him with the goodwill of their families, but unwisely he had failed to destroy a diary that exposed the full extent of his dishonesty. For several months, he had travelled the south coast with his stable of singing boys, who were paid a very low salary, whereas their master filled his boots with the money donated for the benefit of these alleged 'orphans'. The last we hear from John 'Taffy' Dennison is that he was carted off to prison, to face further prosecution for imposture and child abduction.

★★★

'Cor Blimey!' I can hear the readers exclaim. 'We were expecting murder houses, with plenty of blood and gore, and all we get is a 'child abduction house'!' But before you stomp off to return this book to the booksellers, read on about the *next* lodgers at No. 10 Stanmer Street. The respectable Prestons were of course much put out by the Dennison scandal, and particularly that their

2.12 Mr and Mrs St John, from the Penny Illustrated Paper April 18 1896.

own name and address had been published in the newspapers as the headquarters of the Welsh Fagin. They must have feared that it would be an uphill struggle to get another lodger for the two empty first-floor rooms vacated by the alleged child abductor, but as soon as they were advertised, the 33-year-old Mr Frederick St John moved in right away, with his wife Alice. Another native of Wales, Haverfordwest to be exact, he had just moved to London, and did not know about the recent notoriety of No. 10 Stanmer Street. The recipient of a generous allowance, as the result of a legacy, he did no work at all. An odd-looking little cove with a large bowler hat and a bushy moustache, he drank much more than was good for him. Mrs Alice St John, a tall and sturdy woman, shared this predicament.

The respectable Prestons once more worried about their lodgers, since Frederick St John was seldom seen sober. He often quarrelled angrily with his wife, and these arguments sometimes ended in blows. But the drunken and rowdy behaviour of the lodgers did not result in their eviction from No. 10 Stanmer Street, since they were both perfectly lucid when sober, and paid their rent with commendable regularity. The 1891 Census lists the occupants of No. 10 Stanmer Street as Thomas and Catherine Preston, their four children, the permanent lodgers Frederick and Alice St John, aged 36 and 40 respectively, and two young labouring men.

In March and April 1896, Frederick St John drank harder than ever. He could empty ten bottles of whisky in a week, and spent much of his time lying in bed. In the evening of April 9, the Prestons heard their lodgers quarrel angrily. Mrs St John had the habit of clapping her hands when she was trying to get some point across to her sottish husband. The following morning, Alice St John came knocking at the Prestons' bedroom, exclaiming 'Teddy is dead!' This was the name she used to call her husband.

2.13 The Stanmer Street murder house, from Lloyd's Weekly Newspaper, April 12 1896.

Believing that Mr St John had developed the DTs, Mr Preston went to investigate, but he found the lodger lying dead in his bed, with his face and head much bruised and swollen. Mrs St John seemed much upset, exclaiming "Oh, my poor Teddy! I wish he was alive!" She was herself very drunk and dishevelled. Dr W.H. Kempster was called, and his verdict was that since the head of the deceased had been battered almost to a pulp, and since his body was bruised all over, this clearly had to be a case of murder. The unfortunate Welsh dipsomaniac's head had taken such punishment that it was almost twice its normal size.

Alice St John was duly arrested and charged with the murder of her husband. The coroner's inquest, led by Mr W. Schroeder at Battersea, returned a verdict of wilful murder against her. This

2.14 Mrs St John is arrested, and the murder house at No. 10 Stanmer Street, from the Illustrated Police Budget.

was largely due to the post-mortem evidence, which showed that Frederick St John had been strangled to death with considerable force, since the hyoid bone was fractured. It was rightly concluded that such an injury could not be the result of a fall, or of suicide. Alice St John did not make a good impression at the inquest. A newspaper reporter described her as a tall, strong, unwholesome-looking woman, with a yellowish, pallid complexion. A newspaper sketch of her fully corroborated this unflattering impression.

On trial for murdering her husband at the Old Bailey on June 10 1896, before Mr Justice Hawkins, Alice St John was in a difficult position. There had been no other person in their rooms at No. 10

Stanmer Street when her husband was killed, and the medical evidence favoured wilful murder, and tending to rule out suicide or accident. But in court, the Prestons gave evidence that was very much in favour of the accused woman: Frederick St John had always been a very mean-spirited, violent-tempered man, who had treated his wife cruelly when he was drunk. He could consume three bottles of whisky in a day, and had several times been in hospital with delirium tremens. In contrast, Alice St John had always been very kind to her worthless husband, they said. She came from a refined background, and could speak several languages. The night Frederick St John had died, the Prestons had heard him cry out "Alice! Whisky! Whisky, Alice!" and then a sound resembling a loud clapping of hands. Mr E.W. John, a solicitor practicing at Tenby, identified himself as the brother of the deceased, who had adopted the prefix 'St' to his name sixteen years earlier. Frederick St. John had lacked both occupation and profession, and led a very intemperate life. Importantly, Mr John testified that Alice St John would not in any way benefit from her husband's death, since his income would cease upon his death, and since his life was not insured. Although the stalwart Dr Kempster repeated his damning evidence without hesitation or contradiction, the prosecution was in considerable difficulties. In cross-examination, the helpful Thomas Preston had added considerably to his evidence at the coroner's inquest: Frederick St John had been "a perfect brute" and "a madman when in drink", and he had often spoken of committing suicide. Even the normally severe Mr Justice Hawkins was clearly affected by this description of the deceased, since in his summing up, he recommended the jury not to overlook Frederick St John's violence and brutality towards his wife, over a period of many years. If they were satisfied that the prisoner had accidentally caused her husband's injuries while protecting herself from his assault on her, then she was entitled to an acquittal.

Without hesitation, the jury acquitted Alice St John, and she walked free from the Old Bailey.[11] Whether the outcome of the trial had been different if the original charge had been one of manslaughter is difficult to tell, but it is certain that Mrs St John was a very lucky woman, in that even the prosecutors themselves obviously did not appreciate how very damning the medical evidence against her really was. The conspiracy theorist might speculate that some relation of Frederick St John had designs on his private income: disappointed by the sottish Welshman's reluctance to die, he had arranged for Mrs St John to murder him, and to disguise his death at an attack of the DTs. When this scam did not work, he bribed the Prestons to perjure themselves at the Old Bailey, with complete success, and the conspirators lived happily ever after. Such a scenario is less than likely, however, and most probably it was just a domestic dispute gone wrong, with the tall, strong Alice St John strangling her little Teddy to death with her large, powerful hands, as his feet were drumming spasmodically against the bedpost.

But we must spare a thought for the Prestons, who had been so very unlucky with their lodgers at No. 10 Stanmer Street. If they once more advertised their rooms to let, surely they must have added 'Welsh People need not Apply', since the respectability of their neat terraced house had been so badly let down at the hands of natives of that Principality. Or perhaps the Prestons allowed the two first-floor rooms at No. 10 to remain empty, like some weird Battersea bluebeard's chamber, sometimes haunted by the sound of a ghostly barrel-organ, and the squalling of unschooled voices, at other times by the outcry "Alice! Whisky, Alice!" followed by a horrible gurgling sound. As George R. Sims rightly put it, London's hidden mysteries are sometimes its most gruesome ones, and these horrors are still all around us, if we bother to unearth them.

THE BATTERSEA TRAGEDY, 1896

William Sutton was a sergeant-major in the 89th Foot, who had served in India for many years. After retiring from the military, he became a prison warder, first at Millbank and then at Wormwood Scrubs. He married, but his wife, who suffered from chronic mental depression, left him in 1887 after more than 20 years of marriage, due to his cruelty and fondness for drink. They had a son named William Albert and a daughter named Mary Anne; she had married the platelayer John Donoghue, who lodged at No. 8 Colestown Street, Battersea. After she had left her husband, Mrs Sutton faced hard times, since he was unwilling to pay her any maintenance. In the end, she moved in with the Donoghues at No. 8 Colestown Street, just around the corner from where 'Little Teddy' St John had been done to death just a few weeks earlier.

William Sutton was an angry, morose man, who very much resented his wife for leaving him. He used to make all sorts of allegations about her habits of life, but never tried to seek her out at No. 8 Colestown Street. He himself lodged at No 13 Walmer Road, Notting Hill, where he could lead a comfortable and idle life on his not ungenerous pensions from the army and the police. But on June 1 1896, an unknown man came calling at No. 8, asking for Mrs Sutton. The landlady Mrs Cosby said that she did not live on the premises any more, since she was in St John's Hill Infirmary for her melancholia. She asked him if he was Mr Sutton, something he denied. He said that he had been sent with an important message for either Mrs Sutton or her daughter, and the landlady called Mary Ann Donoghue. She came downstairs with her hat and cloak on, since she was about to go out. Facing the caller, she exclaimed 'Hello, father, how are you?' William Sutton's response was to pull a large army revolver and shoot her

2.15 William Sutton, Annie Donoghue, and the murder house at No. 8 Colestown Street, from Lloyd's Weekly Newspaper, June 7 1896.

three times in the belly. He then shot himself in the chest and dropped dead, on the spot.

Poor Mary Ann Donoghue, who was very severely wounded, groaned aloud with pain. When she saw her husband, she exclaimed 'Oh, John, I am dying!', and she did expire at St Thomas's Hospital soon after. At the coroner's inquest, William Albert Sutton identified the body of his 60-year-old father. He testified that the former sergeant-major had become odd in the head after suffering from sunstroke in India, and that he was in the habit of drinking much more than was good for him. The motive for this angry, long-minded man to come calling at No. 8 Colestown Road was obvious: that his wife had taken out a summons against him to get her hands on part of his pension. This did not explain, however, why he had shot his own daughter dead when it turned out that his wife was in the asylum. She was still in St John's Hill Infirmary at the time of the inquest, and the doctors were said to be pondering how to break the dreadful news of her husband shooting her daughter dead and then committing suicide, without doing further damage to her already fragile mental health. The inquest returned the verdict that Mary Ann Donoghue was wilfully murdered by her father William Sutton, who then committed suicide whilst temporarily insane.[12] The murder house at No. 8 Colestown Street still stands.

MURDER AT LINOM ROAD, 1897

Mrs Elizabeth Locke had married into a wealthy and respectable Derbyshire family. For many years, she lived comfortably in Derby with her husband, a well-to-do draper, and their several children. After Mrs Locke was widowed in 1880, her daughter Fanny suggested that they should move to London, where she wanted to set up a dressmaking business. Although Mrs Locke was now 70 years old, she agreed to move to the Metropolis with her daughter. Fanny Locke's dressmaking firm had considerable success, and she employed several needlewomen in her large workshop.

Both Mrs Locke and Fanny were prudent, parsimonious people, fond of various penny-pinching schemes. Although they were very well off, they had several lodgers in the house. One of them was a young man named Henry Brown, who described himself as a painter and decorator. He paid court to Fanny, and although she was 38 years old and he just 28, they got married in 1892. Mrs Locke did not care very much for her new son-in-law, since he seemed idle in his habits and elusive with regard to his plans for the future. Just a few months after the wedding, a constable knocked at the door, telling Mrs Fanny Brown that her

2.16 The murderer Henry Brown, from Lloyd's Weekly Newspaper, December 20 1896.

husband was wanted by the police for stealing a pony and trap. Henry was arrested soon after and sentenced to three years in prison. The following day, a troop of bailiffs came to the Brown family home and removed all the furniture, which the miscreant had procured "through the hire system".

Chastened by these dismal experiences, Mrs Locke and Fanny Brown moved to another house, No. 14 Linom Road, Clapham. Fanny concentrated on her dressmaking and stayed away from wicked men. Three years went by, as the two ladies lived contentedly at No. 14, and Henry Brown rattled the bars of his prison cell. But in early November 1896, a surly-looking cove came knocking at Mrs Locke's front door, asking 'Don't you know me?' 'Oh yes, it's Henry!' the dim-witted old lady replied. She let Henry into the house, where Fanny was 'rather upset' at seeing her jailbird husband again. Henry moved into one of the first floor bedrooms at No. 14 Linom Road. He was gloomy and morose, and showed no inclination to look for paid employment. He lamented that the furniture had been removed, and blamed his wife for this calamity. He suggested to Mrs Locke that he should instead sell the front room chairs to raise some capital for unspecified 'investments', but she firmly said 'Henry, I can't see how you can sell them; I have been the landlady eighteen months and I think you are in my debt!' Henry looked very angry, but did not press the point. Some days later, he asked Mrs Locke whether chemists sold poison without a label, a question the old lady was unable to answer. A few days later, her tea tasted very bitter, and she vomited profusely.

The two timid ladies became increasingly apprehensive about what the sinister Henry was up to. On November 9, Fanny Brown went up with her mother's breakfast, saying 'Mother, I have had something in my tea, the same as you had last week!' Fanny looked very ill, and she soon ran downstairs to vomit. Old Mrs Locke, whose instincts of self-preservation were seriously defective, then drank thirstily from her own cup of tea! It did not take long for her to experience the same symptoms. As she sat retching into the chamber-pot, Mrs Locke heard her daughter scream for help, but the dose of poison in her tea had made her very ill, and she was unable to run downstairs. The milkman Samuel Matthews was just then coming up to the house, however. He heard Fanny Brown's outcry, and the sound of repeated heavy blows. Through the stained-glass panels of the front door, he could see Henry Brown beating a recumbent figure with a large coal hammer. The milkman knocked at the door and shouted 'Stop it, I shall know you again!' but the only effect was that Henry came up to the door and bolted it. He then went upstairs, where he met Mrs Locke in the landing. He seized hold of the defenceless old lady and hammered away with a hearty goodwill, beating her until she was well-nigh dead. Henry then went to his own room, barricaded the door with furniture, and stabbed himself in the chest seven times.

The milkman Matthews went to fetch the police, and two sturdy constables broke down the front door of No. 14 Linom

Road. Its three senseless inhabitants were all removed to hospital. Fanny Brown soon died from her extensive head injuries. Mrs Locke's life was more than once despaired of, but the old lady eventually recovered from the brutal beating she had received. One of her fingers, which had been flattened by the heavy hammer, had to be amputated. The murderer Henry Brown also recovered completely, since none of his stab rounds had penetrated the chest wall. He was fit to stand trial for the murder of his wife on December 14 1896. The 86-year-old Mrs Locke gave evidence against him. It also transpired that Henry Brown had been an inveterate thief all his adult life. From January 1885, when he had been twenty years old, until December 1896, he had spent 89 out of 144 months in prison, for repeatedly stealing horses and carriages. The motive for the murder remained unclear: perhaps Henry suspected that his wife and mother-in-law had acted dishonestly about the furniture, or even denounced him to the police back in 1892. More likely, the callous thief had planned to murder the two harmless women, steal their money, and sell the contents of the house. Henry Brown was found guilty of murder, sentenced to death, and hanged at Wandsworth Prison on January 5, 1897.[13] The murder house at No. 14 Linom Road still stands, although its front door, through whose stained-glass panels the milkman Matthews saw the murderer at work, has been replaced with one of more modern design.

THE MYSTERY OF WATER LANE, 1900

In 1881, the Lambeth labouring man Charles Henry Burgess married the young local lass Mary Kate Bowers. Soon, they had a daughter named Harriett and a son named Robert. But Charles Henry Burgess died in 1885 and Mary Kate was alone with two children to support. She worked as a needlewoman and mantle maker, and earned just enough money to keep poverty from the door. In 1892, she married a seedy bloke named Arthur Waknell, who worked as an assistant in Messrs Parking & Gotto's shop. They did not get on particularly well after the wedding, and Mary Kate began to suspect that Arthur had married her because she was expecting an inheritance.

This suspicion turned out to be well-founded: as soon as Mary Kate's elderly aunt had died, and the inheritance had been banked, Arthur left his job and spent the money. He beat Mary Kate up if she refused him money for drink, and behaved most obnoxiously. For several years, Arthur ruled the household with an iron fist, but when the money was nearly all spent, he left his wife and went back to his job at the shop. Once more, Mary Kate Waknell was alone with her two children. But by now, Harriett was able to find a situation as a servant, and the lad Robert obtained work as a shirt-cutter at a factory. Since Mary Kate was fearful that the cad Arthur would track her down, and subject her to further ill-treatment, she frequently changed lodgings.

In early 1900, the now 42-year-old Mary Kate Waknell was living in two basement rooms at No. 44 Water Lane, Brixton. The kitchen doubled as the bedroom of her son Robert, and her own bedroom as her mantle making workshop. But Robert noticed that in recent months, his mother had in fact done little work. Instead, she often went out in the evenings, quite flashily dressed, and returning home late at night with a 'gentleman friend'.

On the evening of Friday May 11 1900, everything seemed normal at Mary Kate Waknell's humble abode at No. 44 Water Lane. Robert came home after a long day at work, and 'banked' his weekly earnings of eight shillings with his mother, who allowed him fivepence a day for his train fare and luncheon. Mary Kate was once more fearful that Arthur would track them down,

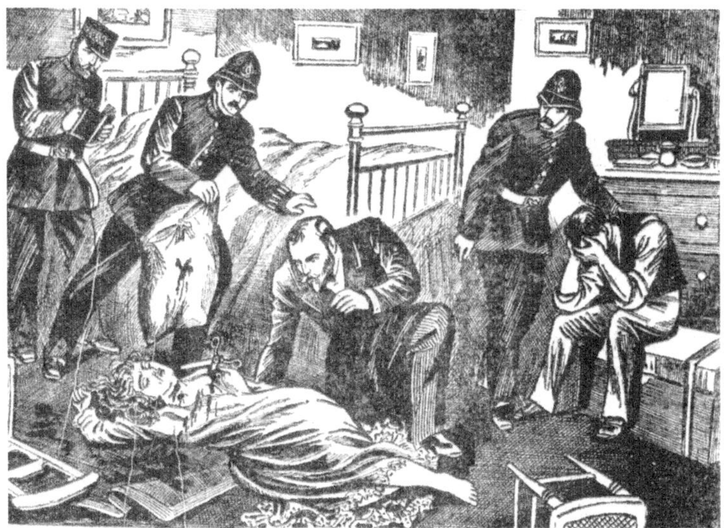

2.17 The murder of Mary Kate Waknell, from the Illustrated Police News, May 19 1900.

and she had arranged for them to move to new lodgings in Lime Street in the following week. She went out late in the evening, and the exhausted Robert went to bed and slept soundly all night. On Saturday morning, he went into his mother's bedroom. To his horror, he found the room liberally spattered with blood, and his mother lying dead on the floor, with multiple deep stab wounds, and a large pair of scissors protruding from her chest.

The police were promptly called in. On being informed by Robert that he thought that his mother was prostituting herself, they suspected that she had 'picked up' some gentleman friend in a pub and brought him back home for some 'fun'. But this particular 'gentleman's' ideas of fun had been more in the line of those of Jack the Ripper: he had seized the large scissors Mary Kate had been using in her mantle making business, and stabbed her again and again. It was rightly considered remarkable that neither the lad Robert, who had been sleeping next door, nor the other three families living in the house, had been woken up by a scream or the sound of a scuffle. There was a newspaper story of a man being arrested on Monday May 14, due to the finding of bloodstains on his shirt-cuffs, but nothing more seems to have come of this, except that the suspect's night-shirt and bed-sheets had also been liberally stained with blood.

After Robert and Harriett Burgess had told the police about the cad Arthur Waknell's ill treatment of their mother, and her great fear of him, he briefly became a suspect. But Arthur gave himself up to the police and provided a solid alibi for the evening and night of the murder. His account of his movements was so satisfactory that he was not even detained by the police. At the coroner's inquest on Mary Kate Waknell, the police had to admit defeat: the man Waknell was clearly innocent, and all their exertions to track down the real murderer had been in vain. Mary Kate's killer had clearly been let into the basement rooms at No. 44 Water Lane without a struggle, making it likely that she had let her 'customer' in herself. Since the corpse had sported a black eye, he might well have felled her with a blow and then stabbed her with the scissors in a frenzied attack. He had then stolen her paltry savings of a few shillings, and let himself out through the front door. As the police themselves expressed it: "the assailant left not a single vestige of evidence which could be followed up, and the officers engaged in the case freely confess that they are without a clue."[14]

It is of course possible that the murder of Mary Kate Waknell was the handiwork of some disciple of Jack the Ripper, intent on murdering a prostitute just for the fun of it. But surely, such an individual should have brought with him his own murder weapon, instead of making use of the large scissors left in the room. If profit had been the motive, the culprit had been singularly inept, choosing a middle-aged part-time prostitute who was herself as poor as the proverbial church mouse. There are also some suspects closer to home. What if the cad Arthur Waknell had really hated his estranged wife, and paid some rough of his acquaintance to murder her, making sure beforehand that he himself had a rock solid alibi. And what about the boy Robert? Had he perhaps been deeply ashamed of his mother's immoral life, and decided to murder her? It would have been easy for him to sneak into her bedroom after the 'customer' had left, and stab her to death with the scissors, the location of which he knew well. It is true that he convinced the police detectives with his candour, and his obvious horror on discovering that his mother had been murdered, but some adolescents are clever actors and liars. The sole reminder of this intriguing, and strangely little-known, Brixton murder mystery is the house at No. 44 Water Lane.

MURDER AT FARLOW VILLA, 1906

John Franklin, a young Putney lad, became an amateur pugilist, boxing under the name John Saracca. In 1898, he went to Malta, where he married and became a canteen steward. But his marriage with the five years older Mrs May Franklin was childless, and John started to suspect that she was 'carrying on' with two other Englishmen, and possibly with a Maltese cook as well. There were frequent angry scenes, and May became fearful that John would make use of his pugilistic skills to beat up his suspected rivals. She persuaded him to return to London, where they lodged in a house called 'Farlow Villa', situated at the corner of Farlow Road and Felsham Road, Putney.

The Franklins had brought with them a young Maltese lad,

2.18 The murder house, Farlow Villa in Felsham Road, from the Illustrated Police Budget, July 14 1906.

who wanted to have a look at the Metropolis. John Franklin had tried to submit a patent of some description, but was rebuffed. He made no attempt to find paid employment, but sat at Farlow Villa all day, looking very morose and disgruntled. On July 9 1906, he locked himself into the first floor bedroom, and three revolver shots rang out. The neighbours found that he had murdered his wife and then committed suicide. In an envelope were eight pages of foreign writing-paper, on which Franklin gave a detailed account of why he had harboured suspicions against his wife.

There was also a will, in which he left all he possessed to his young Maltese friend.[15] The murder house, which was featured in the *Illustrated Police Budget*, still stands today, as No. 164 Felsham Road.

MURDER IN THE 'DUKE OF CAMBRIDGE', 1906

On August 25 1906, the crane driver Thomas Larkman, his brother Walter and their colleague George John Warren went out for a pub crawl in South London. They went from the Wheatcheaf at No. 126 South Lambeth Road [it still stands] to the Builder's Arms [no longer active under that name], and then on to the Duke of Cambridge, at the corner of Thorne Road and Lansdowne Gardens. Here, they were joined by Thomas Larkman's wife Kate, and Warren's mother. These two had also had quite a lot to drink, and soon became quarrelsome. When Kate asked Warren for sixpence that he owed her, the young crane driver angrily thrust it to her, exclaiming "Yes, take your sixpence, you are very sharp about it!" Later, in the urinals, the drunken Warren seized up a knife and showed it to Walter Larkman, exclaiming "This is for Kate!" Larkman thought he was joking, but when they were back in the saloon bar, there was a scuffle between Warren and Kate. Thomas Larkman thought that Warren had struck his wife, and he returned the blow with interest. Then there was an outcry of "She's stabbed!" and indeed the coward Warren had stabbed Kate hard in the chest, severely wounding her.

When a police constable came up to them, Thomas Larkman pointed out Warren, with the words 'There is the man that stabbed my wife!' As soon as Constable Sayer had seized hold of the miscreant, Larkman continued 'Dirty cur, what did you do that for, to a woman?' 'Beer was the cause of it!' Warren laconically replied. Dr Michael Enum, who lived next door at No. 44 Thorn Road, made sure that Kate Larkman was swiftly taken to St Thomas's Hospital, where the surgeons operated to try to stop the internal bleeding, but the patient died from her injuries soon after. An autopsy showed that the cause of death was a stab wound severing a major pulmonary vein.

When George John Warren was on trial for murder at the Old Bailey, there was no question that he had stabbed his colleague's wife to death. His mother Frances Warren, who had been a witness to the murderous assault, testified that Kate had slapped Warren's face just before he stabbed her. Apart from her evidence, which was no backed up by any other witness, only Warren's youth (he was just 19), his drunkenness and the rather dubious character of his victim spoke in his favour. The jury found him guilty of murder but added a strong recommendation to mercy. This recommendation was acted upon, and Warren's death sentence was commuted to life imprisonment.[16] The Duke of Cambridge murder pub at No. 45 Thorne Road still stands today, although it has been converted into flats.

THE CLIFTON GARDENS MYSTERY, 1910

Thomas Weldon Anderson was born in Much Woolton, a small village outside Liverpool, in late 1861. He decided to become an actor, and changed his name to the more sonorous and characteristic Weldon Atherstone [as he shall forthwith be called]. In that redoubtable record of the British thespian world, the old *Era* newspaper, there is regular mention of Atherstone's activities from 1884 onwards. He spent much of his time touring the countryside with various theatrical companies, usually playing supporting roles. A tall, handsome man with an excellent voice, he specialized in Shakespearian productions, and in traditional melodramas.

In 1886, while living in theatrical lodgings in Liverpool, Weldon Atherstone met the young actress Monica Kelly. After marrying in 1888, they lived at No. 20 Barlows Road, Salford, and described themselves as 'comedians'. They soon had a son named Thomas Frederick Anderson, but the marriage was not a happy one. The old crime writer Isobel Mary Thorn, who used the pen-name Elizabeth Villiers, claimed to have met Atherstone and his wife: she noted that the actor was an angry, jealous man, and the baby "a forlorn mite, with bickering parents". This marital discord did not prevent Atherstone and his wife from having another son named William Gordon Anderson, and two daughters as well. The *Era* newspaper files suggest that Weldon Atherstone kept touring and acting throughout the 1890s. Small-time provincial actors were notoriously badly paid, and Atherstone lacked the verve and talent to progress to more important roles on the London stage. In the late 1890s, he left his wife, for good.

In July 1899, when Weldon Atherstone was acting in the play 'The Power of Gold' at the Theatre Royal in Sheffield, he met the young actress Elizabeth Earle. Born in America in 1875, she had been on the stage since 1892, with Mr Hermann Vezin's company. In an early photograph, she is quite pretty, with soulful eyes, regular features and a mass of curly hair looking rather like a wig. Weldon Atherstone and Elizabeth Earle fell in love, and wanted to live together. She left the stage in 1902 and moved in with her mother in a ground floor flat at No. 17 Clifton Gardens, in Prince of Wales Road, Battersea. Atherstone lived with her when he was not on tour in the provinces. No. 17 Clifton Gardens was a large three-story building with a purpose-built flat on each floor. In spite of the name of the terrace, there were hardly any gardens at all, just a tiny front enclosure and an equally minuscule yard at

2.19 Newspaper portraits of Weldon Atherstone and Elizabeth Earle in younger years.

the rear. Nor had security been a great concern when Clifton Gardens had been constructed: there was a small alleyway between No. 17 and the larger house at No. 19, which was a school at the time. Only a low wall separated this alley from the rear garden of No. 17, with its unguarded door to the ground floor flat, and inviting cast-iron outside stairs to the other two flats.

Initially, Weldon Atherstone and Elizabeth Earle lived quite happily together at No. 17 Clifton Gardens. When old Mrs Earle died in 1905, Elizabeth inherited the flat. She made her living by teaching students at the Academy of Dramatic Arts, and instructing private pupils in her flat. She took an interest in the two Anderson boys, who worked as humble East London labouring men, and gave them some acting lessons for free. The boys, who had perhaps not experienced much in the way of parental affection in their lives, became very fond of her. But still, all was not well in the household at No. 17 Clifton Gardens. Weldon Atherstone was no longer young, and there were worrying signs that his acting career was slowly but steadily going downhill. Albeit still able to 'ham it out' in some conventional play or melodrama, his old-fashioned mannerisms precluded him from participating in modern theatrical productions. He was good at reciting the ballads of George R. Sims at various music halls and backstreet theatres, but although the dreadful pathos of ''Twas Christmas Eve in the Workhouse' could still enthral the plebeian audience, rowdy yobs sometimes found it quite hilarious to mimic the actor's sonorous voice, making use of naughty phrases of their own composition.

In 1906, Miss Earle's flat was burgled, and the gas meter broken open. The timid former actress began to worry about the flat's exposed situation, but when she gave the landlord notice that she was leaving, he offered her the use of the first-floor flat instead, and she accepted it. In January 1907, there was a strike among London's music hall performers, for better pay and conditions. It is characteristic of his professional downfall that Weldon Atherstone was one of the 'blackleg' performers at the Euston Palace of Varieties during this strike. He shared the stage with the American singer Belle Elmore, also known as Mrs Cora Crippen. Neither of these two second-rate performers appears to have had a particularly happy time with the rowdy music hall audience; in just a few years' time, they would again be sharing the limelight, in very different circumstances.

As the years went by, Weldon Atherstone became increasingly bitter and paranoid. His acting career was not going anywhere, and he was incapable of saving money for his old age. He was quite jealous of Elizabeth Earle, and forbade her to take any male drama students, since he was fearful that they might have impure designs on their teacher. Thomas Frederick Anderson was seeing a lot of Elizabeth Earle at No. 17 Clifton Gardens, but the jealous actor does not appear to have resented this. When Atherstone went to see Elizabeth Earle in May 1910, he openly challenged her with having been entertaining another lover behind his back. When she denied, the cowardly actor struck her across the face and walked out of the flat. A troubled man, Atherstone took lodgings in Great Percy Street. According to Hargrave Adam, an old crime writer with good police contacts, Atherstone's eccentricities were well known, and some regarded him as a 'mad actor' like Richard Prince who had murdered William Terriss; he was a familiar figure in certain downmarket pubs and bars in the neighbourhood of the Strand.

In the evening of July 16 1910, the now 35-year-old Elizabeth Earle was entertaining the 21-year-old Thomas Frederick Anderson in her flat. They would later claim that all of a sudden, there had been two loud shots from the rear yard. Elizabeth thought some person had been shooting cats, but young Anderson speculated that a householder might have fired off a couple of shots

2.20 Elizabeth Earle and the odd-looking Thomas Frederick Anderson at the time of the inquest.

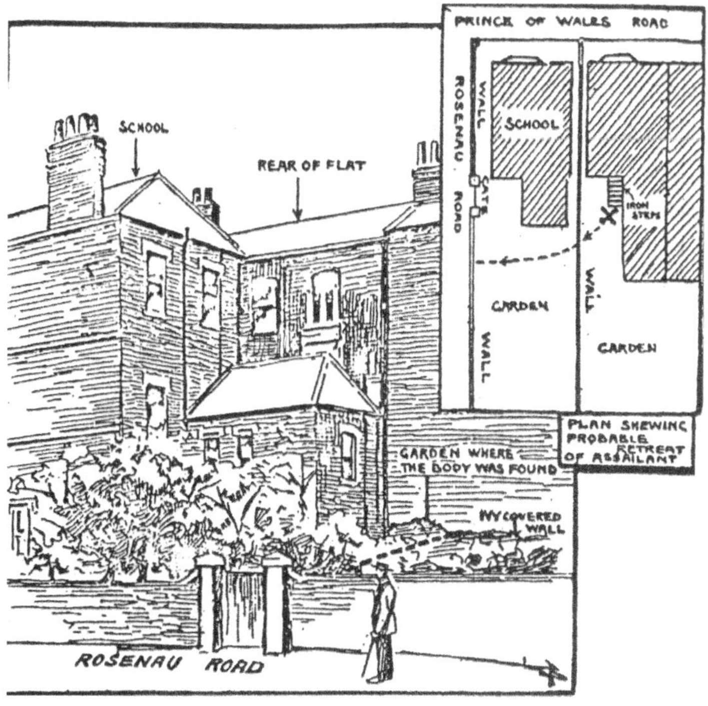

2.21 A drawing of the murder house at No. 17 Clifton Gardens.

to frighten off a burglar. Neither of them went downstairs to investigate, but it did not take long for a police sergeant to come calling at No. 17. It turned out that the chauffeur Edward Noice had come to Battersea Bridge Road police station to report that he had heard two shots, and seen a man leap down from the wall of No. 19 Clifton Gardens and run down Rosenau Road towards the river. Both the ground floor and top flats at No. 17 were empty when Sergeant Buckley came to call, but Elizabeth Earle admitted him and told him that she had also heard the shots. Sergeant Buckley found both Miss Earle and her young visitor very calm and unperturbed. Anderson accompanied the policeman down the cast-iron stairs into the rear yard, where they found an unconscious man lying in the downstairs scullery. Since the victim had been shot twice in the head, he was not a pleasant sight, with one eye hanging down his cheek, and Sergeant Buckley told Elizabeth Earle to remain inside her flat. Two doctors soon arrived at the scene, but the victim died soon after, without regaining consciousness. Thomas Frederick Anderson had clearly seen him, but showed no sign of recognizing him. When the police searched the victim's pockets, they found that he was carrying a large, home-made cosh. The man had taken off his boots, and was wearing carpet slippers. Detective Inspector Geake, who took charge of the case, also found a business card. When he asked young Anderson if he knew a Weldon Atherton, there was a hesitant response that he in fact knew a Weldon Atherstone, an actor who was his father. He could not believe that his father was the victim, however, unless he was wearing a false moustache. Later, when confronted with the dead body at the mortuary, he immediately identified the Clifton Gardens murder victim as his father, however.

The police of course suspected that the young man seen leaving the crime scene after the shots rang out was the murderer. The chauffeur Noice, and four other witnesses who had seen the fugitive running down Rosenau Road towards Petworth Street, described him as young (23-30 years old), between 5'3" and 5'6" tall and wearing a dark-jacketed suit. Noice was certain that the man he had seen was not the tall, lanky Thomas Frederick Anderson. At the coroner's inquest, it was commented that for some reason or other, Weldon Atherstone had gone to No. 17 Clifton Gardens to spy on Elizabeth Earle, armed with a cosh and wearing carpet slippers. His pocketbook contained a number of cryptic notes indicating that he was obsessed with Miss Earle, and convinced that she was seeing a rival. He had once found some flowers in the dustbin at No. 17, and suspected that these had been a gift from his unknown rival. The identity of this individual

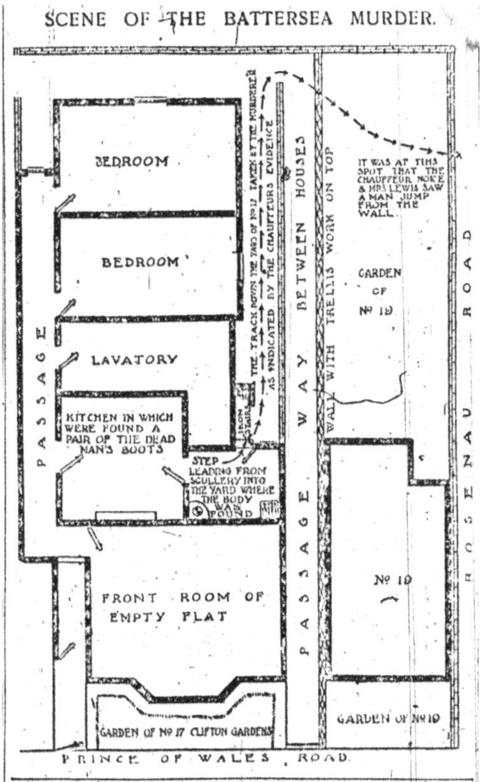

2.22 A plan of the murder house, from a press cutting in the archives of Mr Stewart P. Evans, reproduced by permission.

was never hinted at, and the four men named in the pocketbook diary were all cleared by the police.

Although the newspaper headlines were dominated by the sensational Crippen case, in which Atherstone's erstwhile acting colleague had been found murdered at No. 39 Hilldrop Crescent, there was a fair bit of interest also in the Clifton Gardens Mystery. There was much speculation about Atherstone's strange activities, and whether he might have arranged a meeting with a rival or

SCENE OF THE MURDER.

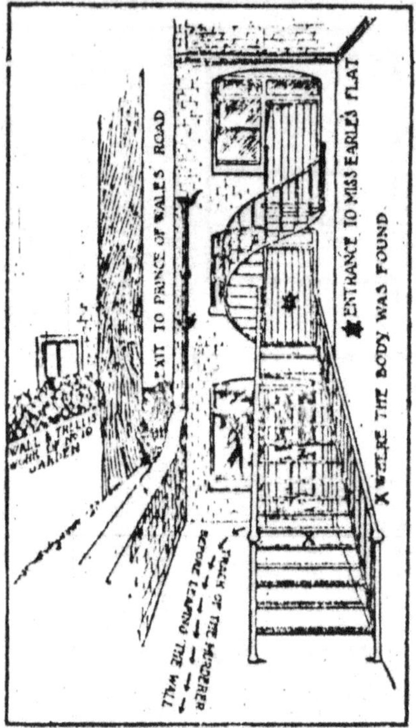

The sketch shows the back of 17, Clifton Gardens, with the door at which the body was found, and the iron staircase leading to Miss Earle's flat.

2.23 The rear entrance to the murder house, from a press cutting in the archives of Mr Stewart P. Evans, reproduced by permission.

enemy on the fatal evening. Elizabeth Earle gave the impression of being almost prostrate with grief, but she did not attend Atherstone's funeral; nor did the actor's widow. All four children were in attendance, however, and many old theatrical colleagues had sent wreaths. The evening newspapers published some quite odd illustrations of the dramatis personae of the Clifton Gardens Mystery. Weldon Atherstone is depicted as handsome and very youthful-looking; the drawing is probably based on a photograph of him in his acting heyday. In contrast, Thomas Frederick Anderson comes across as an awkward-looking fellow, with a long nose and a pinched face, looking much older than his 21 years. As for the newspaper drawing of Elizabeth Earle, it clearly depicts the same person as the youthful-looking photograph of her; the change in the shape of her face can be blamed on edentulousness and ill-fitting dentures.

When the coroner's inquest resumed, there were painful scenes when Elizabeth Earle gave evidence about her long association with the murdered man and his sons. It was rightly considered peculiar that she and Thomas Frederick Anderson had not made any effort to investigate the gunfire in their small rear yard. Young Anderson faced some searching questions about his inability to recognize his father, but he blamed the darkness of the evening and the victim's facial injuries, and gave the impression of telling the truth. As for his younger brother William Gordon Anderson, he had an alibi, having attended a cricket match at Willesden and then returned to his lodgings. The inquest returned a verdict of murder against some person or persons unknown, and there matters have rested ever since.[17]

The majority of later commentators on the Clifton Gardens Mystery have favoured the theory that the morbidly jealous Atherstone had gone to spy on Miss Earle, suspecting that his [probably non-existent] rival might appear at the scene. But instead, a burglar comes bursting into the rear yard, and when the furious actor attacks him, he is gunned down by the armed intruder. According to Sir Melville Macnaghten, a gang of armed German burglars were at large in South London at the time. Hargrave Adam, who had seen a police photograph from the no longer extant file on the case, added a theory of his own, perhaps influenced by contacts at Scotland Yard: it had been Atherstone who had brought the gun along, but it had been turned against him in the struggle with the burglar. This is not as silly as it might sound, and fully consistent with the descriptions of Atherstone's wounds.

The distinguished crime historian Jonathan Goodman brought forward a theory of his own, namely that Elizabeth Earle had conspired with the two Anderson brothers to murder Atherstone, an unsatisfactory lover and father, and a lousy actor who was sponging on them. After Thomas Frederick Anderson had murdered his father, his brother dashed off with the revolver. But William Gordon Anderson had an alibi according to the police, and the man seen escape was much older than sixteen years old. If we presume that Thomas Frederick Anderson had hired a contract killer to murder his father, that problem would disappear, but would a penniless young warehouse worker be able to afford a reliable gunman? Or had the killer's intention merely been to give Atherstone a fright, or beat him up, only for things to go badly wrong then the furious actor pulled his revolver? Nor is there an obvious motive for the murder: the two Andersons appear to have been closer to their father than to their mother, and the lachrymose Elizabeth Earle does not seem like a suitable person to swear into a murderous conspiracy. She told the newspapers that she wanted to go to Australia to look after her consumptive brother, but there is nothing to suggest that she made it to the Antipodes. We know, however, that Thomas Frederick Anderson left London soon after the murder, to become a seaman in New Zealand. He settled down in Auckland, married [not Miss Earle, but a woman his own age] and had four children. After decades of trade union activism, not without success, he admitted the wholesale theft of union funds before his death in 1964.[18]

The burglar hypothesis is in my mind fully credible, but there are also some arguments against it. Why would an armed burglar want to break into a house in a lower-class part of London, wearing an elegant suit? The dangerous German gang previously alluded to do not seem to have made their presence felt elsewhere, and the home-grown burglars seldom carried loaded firearms. At one stage, I had suspicions against Miss Earle: had she also changed her name upon commencing her acting career, and had she married some other bloke in secret, under her real name? The research of Richard Whittington-Egan has demonstrated that Elizabeth Earle was born in America in 1875, however; she had not even made use of the female thespian perogative of lying about her age! Thomas Frederick Anderson's subsequent antipodian defalcations are not devoid of interest, since they provide evidence of a cunning and dishonest intellect; still, many greedy politicians and crooked trade unionists have been merrily pilfering away from the public purse, and from union funds, without ever entertaining parricidal ambitions.

As for the murder house at No. 17 Clifton Gardens, it has long been presumed to be lost. There is no Clifton Gardens today, nor is any street by that name visible on early editions of Bartholomew's *Reference Atlas of Greater London*. But Richard Whittington-Egan, who knows that part of London well, pointed out that Clifton Gardens was not situated *off* Prince of Wales Road, but actually *in* that thoroughfare: it was once the name for the terrace of houses between Battersea Bridge Road and Rosenau Road. Upon closer inspection, this turned out to be perfectly true: one of the houses still has a plaster plaque saying 'Clifton Gardens' and the layout of the murder house at No. 17 has not changed much since 1910. The deletion of Clifton Gardens from the street names of London seems to have erased also the notoriety of the murder house: no blood-stained spectre wearing carpet slippers has haunted the rear staircase, waving its cosh about in impotent rage. In his collection, Richard Whittington-Egan has the carved stone figure of the head of a man, acquired from above the portico of an old house in Rosenau Road; the sole surviving witness to the flight of the Clifton Gardens murderer.[19] Sometimes London's most fascinating mysteries are its forgotten ones.

TAUNTS END IN TRAGEDY, 1913

Albert and Ada Williams were a recently married couple living in Battersea, and they had two children alive. He was a labouring man and she a barmaid. Ada's reputation was far from the best, and she had often stolen from the publicans who employed her. She had a bastard son named John Patrick Dunn, born before she had met her husband, and the cruel Albert was often taunting her about her shameful secret. When drunk, he beat her up more than once, and in the end, she left him and went to live at No. 21 Comyn Road, not far from Clapham Junction.

But Ada Williams was not happy without her beloved Albert. She got the idea that if she 'got rid of' her little son, Albert might

2.24 The Comyn Road murder victim, from the Illustrated Police News, November 13 1913.

take her back and they would live happily ever after. On November 8 1913, she strangled the helpless boy to death and then proceeded to dismember the body. She cut both legs and one arm off and proceeded to burn them in the grate. But the sheer horror of what she was doing became overwhelming, and she gave herself up to the police and confessed her crime, showing them the mangled remains of her little son with the words 'I have murdered him! Tell Mr Williams that he is now free to walk the streets as he pleases!'[20]

At the coroner's inquest on John Patrick Dunn, Albert Williams was censured for his cruelty to his wife. There was a considerable amount of sympathy for the young and attractive Ada Annie Williams, as she was called in the newspapers: was this not one of the cases where 'woman pays' for her loyalty and devotion to a worthless man? The sordid and brutal end of little John Patrick's short and blameless life, his severed limbs left to roast in the grate, was conveniently forgotten, and Ada Annie Williams became something of a newspaper heroine. Described as a tall, slim woman of refined appearance, she was supported not only by the proto-feminist brigade, but also by a number of 'celebrity' busybodies who had been moved by her pathetic story, including the Dean of Manchester, numerous other clergymen, two London magistrates, and the author George R. Sims. The *John Bull* newspaper started a petition on her behalf, and the *Daily Mirror* published her photograph on the front page.

But nevertheless, the ordeal of Ada Annie Williams continued: she was committed to stand trial at the Old Bailey in December 1913. She had already confessed to murdering her son, but her barrister Mr R.D. Roome urged that her despair, poverty and misery would justify the charge being reduced to one of manslaughter. There was not a person in court, he claimed, whose heart was not wrung with pity for her. But Mr Justice Riley coolly stated that he could not see any ground on which it was possible to reduce the offence below the crime of murder. The jury returned a verdict of guilty, and Mr Justice Riley sentenced her to death.[21]

But Ada Annie Williams had one more trump card to play: there was sensation in court when she claimed to be pregnant, and demanded a stay of execution. For the first time since the Richmond murderess Kate Webster had (vainly) 'pleaded the belly' back in 1879, a 'Jury of Matrons' was convened to examine her, and their verdict was that Ada Annie Williams was really pregnant. The execution was postponed, and the Home Secretary later commuted the death penalty to penal servitude for life. This was the last time a Jury of Matrons was employed in a British court.

2.25 Ada Annie Williams in court, from the Illustrated Police News, November 13 1913.

Ada Annie Williams' newspaper supporters exulted that their heroine had been saved from the gallows. For a few months, they published regular updates about her life in prison, but soon she joined the ranks of yesterday's celebrities, and was forgotten about. According to the police files on her case, she gave birth to a healthy boy at Holloway prison in March 1914; he was taken away to the Wandsworth Union. Ada Annie Williams was a truculent, difficult prisoner, who was in constant trouble with the authorities. After being removed to Liverpool Prison in late 1918, she behaved herself better, and was actually discharged on license in July 1921. She was taken care of by her respectable civil servant father, Mr Charles Dunn, of No. 31 Bonar Road, Peckham [it no longer stands], and by her invalid mother. Ada Annie Williams took up nursing for a while, but failed to pass her exams. This did not prevent her from working as a mental nurse for a while, but not with much success: one of her patients attempted suicide, and she was blamed for this and urged to take up another career. In 1928, she was herself incarcerated in Epsom Mental Hospital, but she was out of there the following year, and still under the care of the Aylesbury After-Care Association as late as December 1935.[22] This is the last that is known about her.

MURDER BY A BLIND MAN, 1922

Arthur Alfred Meader, a young London labouring man, enlisted in the Devonshire Regiment and fought in the trenches in 1914 and 1915. His eyesight was becoming affected, however, and he was invalided home. There were differing accounts how Meader had been blinded: he had been gassed (unlikely), had mud sprayed into his face by a ricochet (possible), or suffered from some kind of degenerative eye disease (favoured by the doctors at the time). It is unlikely (albeit still possible) that he was a malingerer, since the army doctors were alert to such tricks, and since competent ophtalmologists back in London agreed that he was no longer fit for army service. In fact, he was admitted to St Dunstan's Hostel for the Blind, where he was taught mat making.

At first, Arthur Alfred Meader seemed reasonably content to be back in London, where he belonged, away from the horrors of the western front. But he was out of the frying-pan and into the fire when he decided to marry, after a dangerously short acquaintance, a young London floozie named Mabel Merry. In late 1916, she persuaded him to apply to the St Dunstans authorities to set up a mat making business in Highbury, and this was granted him. The Meaders then quickly sold the business and went to Brighton, where the volatile Mabel went off with a cabbie. But in 1920, when Arthur Alfred had been able to secure a comfortable little house at No. 21 Boundaries Road, Balham, the wicked Mabel moved back in with him. They seemed reasonably happy for a while, and had a daughter named Irene, presumed to have been fathered by Meader.

The house at No. 21 Boundaries Road had been let to Meader, on favourable terms, by St Dunstan's Houses for the Blind, after this magnanimous organization had forgiven the caper when he sold the mat shop and made off with the money. It is sad but true, however, that Meader's habitual dishonesty continued. He and Mabel lived in the ground floor and basement of the house, and illicitly sub-let the top floor to a needy tenant. Hoping that the kind people at St Dunstans would make sure he was not evicted, he was badly in arrears with the rent. As for the incorrigible Mabel, her conduct plumbed novel lows. She stole money from her husband, spent lavishly on clothes and jewelry, and set up a secret identity for herself as a party girl in the West End. As 'Maisie Carter', she posed as a single woman, and led a very immoral and vicious life, with many dodgy boyfriends. A habitué at various sleazy Soho night clubs, she caught venereal disease from one of her 'gentleman friends' and passed it on to poor Meader. Not long after, 'Maisie' swallowed her false teeth during a drinking binge, and nearly choked to death. For the remainder of her days, a callous doctor informed her, she would have to carry her 'snappers' with her in her stomach. But this wicked woman's days were in fact numbered; her sins were catching up with her fast.

From time to time, the dismal Alfred Meader tried his best to win his wife back, but she just laughed at him. He tried to spy on

2.26 Incidents from the Meader case, from the Illustrated Police News, July 20 1922.

her to catch her 'in the act' with some bloke, but this was difficult due to his partial blindness. Instead he ransacked her belongings, finding a thick bundle of letters addressed to 'Maisie Carter' from various male admirers. The very next day, July 12 1922, Mabel came to No. 21 Boundaries Road, hoping to extract some money from her hapless husband. There was a furious quarrel about the letters, and Mabel struck her husband a glancing blow on the head. Meader seized hold of her with a hearty goodwill, and strangled her to death. After pondering his options for a while, he went to the Balham Hotel, where he had a few drinks, before pulling out the razor and cutting his throat. But Meader did not die, far from it. When the police arrived at the hotel, they found that his injury was quite superficial. Referring to his wife, he said 'I hope she is dead! I shan't hang for it!' Handing the bundle of letters to another policeman, he said 'there is enough in there to justify me doing her in!' And indeed, the letters were of a very graphic description, detailing Mabel Meader's descent into depravity.

When Arthur Alfred Meader was on trial at the Old Bailey for murdering his wife, he had found support from unexpected sources. Several big London newspapers, including the *News of the World*, openly supported him, the blind war hero, whose wife had behaved so abominably. Was Mabel Meader not 'the modern woman' and thus every good old-fashioned family man's worst nightmare? Meader was ably defended in court, by a legal team instructed by the solicitors of St Dunstan's: several witnesses attested to his intolerable situation in life, and 'Maisie's' letters were read from at length. Medical experts attested that Mabel had had a particularly large thymus gland, making it easy to strangle her. Meader suffered from neuritis, he said, and the blow on the head had exacerbated this condition. The only 'inconvenient' testimony came from Mabel's mother, who said that Meader had often tried to spy on Mabel, and that he had been able to see well enough when it suited him! Still, the verdict was one of 'not guilty' of murder. Meader admitted the second charge of attempting to commit suicide, for which he was bound over.[23] He disappeared into obscurity, successfully dodging the genealogists through his habit to use the names 'Alfred', 'Arthur' and 'Robert' interchangeably. It is recorded that an 'Alfred A. Meader' married a woman named Chapman in Islington in late 1923, but otherwise there are no clues as to the later activities of this Boundaries Road mystery man.

Arthur Alfred Meader was a very lucky man. At the Balham Hotel, he admitted to the police that he had deliberately murdered his wife, and his 'suicide attempt' was not a particularly impressive one. There were varying opinions concerning his eyesight: might he have been clever enough to have hoodwinked the doctors, and securing a place at the St Dunstan's Hostel through exaggerating the symptoms of his eye disease? There is no doubt that Meader was a work-shy, drunken fellow, who repeatedly defrauded St Dunstan's, the charity that had done so much to help him. And why was he using three different Christian names interchangeably? It was Meader's good fortune that his wife was twenty times worse than him. Remarkably, in a case where a husband stood accused of having murdered his wife, there was no sympathy at all for the murder victim. The *News of the World* thought the verdict just about right; the immoral Mabel Meader had died as miserably as she had lived.

THE CURSE ON ELMHURST MANSIONS, 1935-36

Even in mid-Victorian times, there was no such thing as a 'flat' in London. Wealthy people lived in houses with their servants, and although many middle-class families took in lodgers to make ends meet, they were still proud to be masters in their own houses. The destitute lower classes were the 'cannon-fodder', lodging in various insalubrious dwellings; sometimes, an avaricious slum lord might put up an entire family in one single room. In late Victorian times, small terraced houses were sometimes subdivided into ground floor and first floor apartments, but one family still owned or rented the house, and the other family were lodgers paying a weekly rent. The first purpose-built so-called mansion flats in London were Albert Mansions and Albert Palace Mansions, constructed in the late 1860s and early 1870s. These large and impressive-looking buildings contained a number of flats, accessed from communal staircases to each 'mansion'. Initially, the better class of people frowned upon the idea of living in flats, but soon, the idea caught on like a house on fire: the mansion flats were large, modern and affordable. They appealed to people from all walks of life: bachelors, unmarried women, and small families.

In late Victorian and Edwardian times, the construction of mansion flats was all the rage: one development was larger than the next, and they rapidly spread from central London into the suburbs. Yet another mansion flat development was Elmhurst Mansions, situated in Elmhurst Street and Edgeley Road, Clapham. Constructed on a large scale, Elmhurst Mansions consisted of more than 200 flats. In these long, three-story terraces, each staircase provided access to six two-bedroom flats, two on each floor. Apart from some attractive stained glass in the entrance-halls, the flats were rather dark and drab, but they were still eagerly snapped up by the Londoners. In the 1930s, the flats in Elmhurst Mansions had become rather tired and down-at-heel, and some of them were inhabited by prostitutes and 'kept women'. In 1935 and 1936, murder would strike twice at Elmhurst Mansions, in rapid succession.

★★★

In December 1935, the ground floor flat at No. 203 Elmhurst Mansions was home to the 35-year-old prostitute Eva Porter, who called herself Eva Markwick or Eveline McGinty. The daughter of a West Bromwich coffee-house keeper, she had left home as a teenager to become an actress. Lacking the talent to succeed on the London stage, she had ended up in Weston-super-Mare, where she met another actor named John Markwick. They once hoped to get married, and Eva gave birth to their daughter Ruby in December 1922, but she left Markwick a few months later, and returned to the bright lights of London. She settled down in Clapham and became a prostitute, keeping the girl Ruby with her. In 1935, she was still walking the Clapham streets, but her downfall had continued: worried about poverty in old age, she accepted all comers, and could entertain four or five 'gentleman friends' in an evening. A newspaper photograph shows her looking unexpectedly elegant and refined, given her dismal position in life. Eva Porter shared the flat at No. 203 Elmhurst Mansions with her 46-year-old boyfriend Arthur Brooks. He was not her pimp, but a chemist who was running the pharmacy at No. 256 King Street, Hammersmith [it still stands]. Brooks was well aware that Eva was a prostitute, but he did not seem to mind much; instead, he was jealous of her former admirer, the Brixton tram driver Charles Rutland.

The girl Ruby Markwick, who still lived with her mother, had her thirteenth birthday on December 2 1935. There was a jolly party at No. 203 Elmhurst Mansions, although the jealous Arthur Brooks was annoyed that the gallant tram driver Charles Rutland came along with a present. After the party, Eva Porter and Arthur Brooks went to the Alexandra public house, Clapham Common, where she had a double whisky. She then went out soliciting, and

2.27 Eva Markwick is found murdered at Elmhurst Mansions, from the Illustrated Police News, December 12 1935.

was cautioned by a police constable. Arthur Brooks went back home to the flat at 10 pm, in an angry temper. He shouted at the girl Ruby that she should go to bed. About half an hour later, all hell broke loose at No. 203 Elmhurst Mansions. Eva Porter, who had just returned to the flat, screamed terribly, and the neighbours called the police. Arriving at the scene, the Clapham constables found Eva Porter dead in her bedroom, with multiple stab wounds. Arthur Brook had two deep stab wounds to the stomach, but was still conscious. He told the police that Eva had returned home with a 'client' at 10.30 pm. All of a sudden, Arthur had heard her scream. Going to investigate, he had encountered a short, partly dressed man, who said that Eva had stabbed him first, and scratched his face. The stranger had then stabbed him twice in the belly, before running off.

Arthur Brooks died in hospital the day after, so the case was now one of double murder, or so at least the police presumed. They published the brief description of the attacker in the newspapers, and began looking for credible suspects. Charles Rutland had an alibi, and so did the shabby former actor John Markwick, who was keeping an amusement pavilion on the pier in Weston-super-Mare. But it attracted notice that no person had seen the attacker either enter or exit the flat. He was supposed to have told Arthur Brooks that Eva Porter had stabbed him first, but no unidentified man with stab injuries had been seen in the days after the murder, in any London hospital. And when Eva Porter saw a 'customer', it was her habit to demand payment in advance, put the money in her handbag, and deposit the bag in the kitchen. But the police found the handbag in her bedroom. Sir Bernard Spilsbury performed the autopsies, concluding that Eva Porter had been murdered by multiple stab wounds. Arthur Brooks had two stab wounds in close proximity, which might be self-inflicted.

The detectives now suspected that Arthur Brooks had murdered Eva Porter, and then stabbed himself, and that he had deliberately lied to the police about the attacker. The coroner's inquest on Eva Porter and Arthur Brooks returned a verdict of murder and suicide against Brooks, the case was closed, and the mystery of Elmhurst Mansions conveniently solved.[24] But suicide through self-stabbing is quite uncommon, and when it does occur, there are often 'hesitation marks': minor injuries nearby. It is rare that a previously sane person stabs himself in the belly twice, through several layers of clothing, and that he then manages to lie to the police in such a convincing manner, sending then on a ten-day wild goose chase after the alleged attacker. And why was a large knife, which was supposed to be the murder weapon, missing from the flat? Brooks, who was mortally wounded, would hardly have been in a position to dispose of it, successfully deceiving the police who searched the flat thoroughly. And what about the 13-year-old Ruby Markwick, who was found sound asleep [or pretending to sleep] in her bedroom, although her mother had been screaming in agony in the room next door, loudly enough to alert the neighbours? She later denied having made any worthwhile observations the evening of the murder, but it might well have been a good idea for the detectives to press her further on this point. The verdict of the coroner's jury may well ultimately have been a correct one, but I suspect that the truth behind this first Elmhurst Mansions tragedy may well have been somewhat more spicy than the official version.

⋆⋆⋆

The mystery of No. 203 Elmhurst Mansions quickly and conveniently solved by the police, calm returned to the drab Clapham mansion flats. But Death would make one more spin of the roulette wheel, and this time, Murder would come calling at – No. 8 Elmhurst Mansions! This flat was home to the 48-year-old prostitute Beatrice Vilna Sutton. She had once been married to the Holland Park tobacconist Frederick Sutton, and had children with him, but he had long since ceased to play any role in her life. Beatrice Sutton was what Eva Porter might well have become if she had been allowed to live for another thirteen years: a prematurely aged, diseased street prostitute. She suffered from advanced syphilis, which had led to heart valve disease and secondary arteriosclerosis, and she had recently had a stomach operation. The doctors had warned her that she could look forward to further surgery to remove a 'growth' from her rear passage. For several years, Beatrice Sutton had a regular boyfriend: a police constable named Bert Audley. When he left her in October 1935, she became very upset, and tried to gas herself. After recovering from the effects of the gas, she moved into the flat at No. 8 Elmhurst Mansions to start a new life, as well as she could.

From her new mansion flat, Beatrice Sutton continued to prostitute herself. Middle-aged and unattractive, she had to accept all callers. But on April 4 1936, she was found strangled to death in her flat. The police presumed that she had been murdered by her latest 'client', but the hunt for this individual made little headway. The Clapham detectives trawled the underworld, but they found no trace of the evening visitor to No. 8 Elmhurst Mansions. But all of a sudden, there was a very promising development, namely that the RAF aircraftman Frederick Field had confessed to a military policeman that he had murdered Beatrice Vilna Sutton.

Five years earlier, Frederick Field had been at the centre of another celebrated London murder: the slaying of the young prostitute Norah Upchurch, who had been found dead in the small empty shop at No. 173 Shaftesbury Avenue [it no longer stands]. A former RAF aircraftman, Frederick Field had worked for a firm of signboard fixers, and he possessed the keys to this shop. He told the police that he had handed over these keys to a tall stranger wearing a plus-four suit and a beige tweed cap. But since no other individual had seen this person, the police suspected that Field was lying. There were two other murder suspects, however: a foolish young sailor who had become engaged to marry Norah Upchurch without knowing that she was a prostitute, and a drunk who had been one of her clients, and the last person to see her alive. In a bizarre twist, this drunk turned out to be Frank Foster, a distinguished former Ashes cricketer who had fallen upon evil times. Foster was tracked down after a dishonoured cheque for £10 with his name on it had been found in Norah's flat, but there was nothing to directly link him with the murder.

At the coroner's inquest on Norah Upchurch, Frank Foster was severely censored for his habit of paying prostitutes with dud cheques. Still the coroner, Mr Ingleby Oddie, made it clear that he felt that Frederick Field was the major suspect, and that he had told the police many untruths. In his memoirs, Oddie described how he had asked Field a number of hostile and searching questions: although "an impudent and self-confident fellow", Field had seemed on the verge of breaking down and confessing, before recovering his sang-froid. The coroner's jury returned a verdict of murder against some person unknown, and Field walked free.[25] He went back to his signposting job, but in 1933, he came into the office of a national newspaper, to confess that he had murdered Norah Upchurch. He gave some degree of detail about how he had taken her to the empty shop for some casual sex, before strangling her to death in a fit of rage. He repeated his confession when remanded at the Great Marlborough Street police station, and was charged with the murder of Norah Upchurch. But when Field was on trial at the Old Bailey, he retraced his confession, and said that he had merely been trying to clear his name. A verdict of Not Guilty was returned, and Field once more walked free.

In June 1935, Frederick Field rejoined the RAF, but he would not last long within its ranks. In March 1936, he stole four cheques at Hendon Aerodrome, and absconded without leave. Importantly, he was on the run at the time Beatrice Sutton was murdered, but he was later recaptured and prosecuted by the military. When he was transported from the Tooting Petty Sessions to the prison cells at Hendon Aerodrome, he told the warrant officer escorting him that he knew something about the recent Clapham murder. When questioned by Detective Inspector Halliday, who led the murder investigation, Field said that after forging the signature on the four cheques, cashing them and spending the money, he had felt fed up with life. Lacking the courage to commit suicide, he had decided to murder the prostitute Beatrice Sutton, at her flat in Elmhurst Mansions, in order to be hanged for her murder. Detective Inspector Halliday, who knew all about Field's confession to the murder of Norah Upchurch, and the dismal outcome of the trial, decided to get maximum detail out of him, about every aspect of the murder, and Field willingly complied. He told all about his sinister visit to the flat at No. 8 Elmhurst Mansions, the victim's little Pekinese dog, and the positioning of her body after he had murdered her. This turned out the be excellent work by this experienced detective, since to be sure, the creature Field once more retracted his confession in May 1936, when he stood trial at the Old Bailey for the murder of Beatrice Sutton. In court, he said that when on the run from the police and the military, he had hidden inside the understairs cupboard at Elmhurst Mansions and gone to sleep in there. He had heard a quarrel inside No. 8, and seen a man exit the flat. Investigating, he saw Beatrice Sutton murdered inside the flat. Dejected and fed up with life, he had made an effort to remember every detail about the flat and the murder scene, in order to be able to be able to describe everything in detail when he confessed to the murder in the hope of being hanged.

But although there had been no eyewitness to the murder of Beatrice Sutton, the police had been able to find a string of witnesses who corroborated many points in Field's confession, and a doctor testified that the body had been positioned exactly like the prisoner had described in his confession. Frederick Field was found guilty of murder and sentenced to death; after an appeal had failed, he was executed at Wandsworth Prison on June 30 1936.[26] The debate has continued concerning his guilt, both with regard to the murder of Norah Upchurch, and the murder of Beatrice Sutton. The police file on the latter murder makes it clear that the case against him was a solid one, and that his confession was supported by a good deal of independent evidence. Either Frederick Field murdered Beatrice Sutton, or the police put much effort into framing him for this murder, and bribing a number of witnesses to perjure themselves. The former alternative seems much more likely. As for the murder of Norah Upchurch, Field is definitely the chief suspect, and the available police files make it clear that the Scotland Yard detectives had a strong belief that he was the guilty man. The similarity with the case of Beatrice Sutton, and its aftermath, certainly provides food for thought.

MURDER IN VOLTAIRE ROAD, 1938

William Teasdale was a young London police constable, living at No. 48 Voltaire Road, Clapham, with his wife Ruby and their young daughter. Teasdale was a competent policeman, but there was nothing to suggest that he would ever achieve promotion. In 1937 and 1938, he was becoming fed up with his job and looked for civilian employment. But the 32-year-old Teasdale had other, more sinister predilections. Apart from the little household in Voltaire Road, he was also 'running' another young lady friend, the secretary Miss Dorothy Maude Boud. He had introduced himself to her as a single man, and after a whirlwind romance, she had accepted his proposal of marriage. The wedding was planned to take place in late May 1938.

Om March 3, William Teasdale took Dorothy to see 'Me and My Girl' at the Victoria Palace. But his wife Ruby, who had started to suspect that her husband was up to no good, had clandestinely followed him there. Teasdale must have received a shock when his wife came up to the guilty pair in the theatre lobby and asked Dorothy 'Are you with him?' After the startled young lady had answered in the affirmative, Mrs Teasdale continued 'Do you know he is a married man, and I am his wife and he has a baby?' Young Dorothy was completely at a loss, but Teasdale turned to his wife and said 'Don't be silly!' before ushering his girlfriend into the theatre. But since Dorothy was very upset by the painful scene in the lobby, they left during the first interval. Constable Teasdale stoutly denied being married, and tried various explanations of the scene in the lobby, but Dorothy did not believe him. William Teasdale left her at 2 am and returned to Voltaire Road, presumably in a far from happy frame of mind.

The following day, the 28-year-old Mrs Ruby Teasdale was found murdered at No. 48 Voltaire Road. She had been felled with a blow and then strangled to death. William Teasdale was of course the obvious suspect, particularly since he had left a note saying that he had got to the end of his tether, and was going to take the coward's way out. But Teasdale was swiftly arrested in his home town of Sunderland, without having made any attempt at self-destruction.

When he was on trial for murder at the Old Bailey on April 28, before Mr Justice Goddard, things were looking far from good for William Teasdale. His mother-in-law provided some very damning evidence about his previous caddish treatment of poor Ruby, and Dorothy testified as to his bigamist tendencies. There was no obvious explanation how a 32-year-old police constable could have behaved in such a foolish and irresponsible manner. All the defence could do was to point out Teasdale's previous unblemished record, and to allege that there had been provocation, and that the killing had not been premeditated. Giving evidence in court, Teasdale said that Ruby had struck him, and said that she would become the mother of another man's child. But the jury found him guilty of murder, although adding a strong recommendation to mercy. Mr Justice Goddard sentenced Teasdale to death, but the Home Secretary reprieved him on May 13.[27] The police file on him at the National Archives is closed until 2038, but the Voltaire Road murderer is said to have been released in the 1950s, and led a honest and law-abiding life for many years.

CHILD MURDER IN BATTERSEA, 1943

Francis Buckley was a young London thief, in and out of prison throughout the 1930s. He later joined the Royal Marine Engineers, but hardly distinguished himself. In 1943, he married Mary Ann Thwaites, the widow of a fellow soldier who had been killed on active service, and moved in with her at No. 6 Cairns Road, Battersea. His wife had two little girls, Christine and Eileen Thwaites, from her previous marriage. In addition, she gave birth to another child in September 1943, presumed to have been fathered by Buckley. A few days later, Buckley deserted from the military and returned to No. 6 Cairns Road, but celebrating becoming a father seems to have given him some very dangerous ideas. The very same evening, on September 22 1943, his wife found him in the lounge with her daughter Eileen, who appeared to be lifeless and still. She cried out 'You've killed my baby! What have you done to her?' On trial for murder at the Central

Criminal Court, Buckley was found guilty and was sentenced to death. According to the police file on the case, they found it unlikely that the Home Secretary would be moved by the plight of such a creature as Buckley, but for some reason or other, he received a late reprieve.[28]

ANOTHER MURDER IN BOUNDARIES ROAD, 1953

In 1953, the little house at No. 165 Boundaries Road, Balham, was home to the middle-aged chef Mr Herman Schreiber, his wife Charlotte and her five-year-old daughter from a previous marriage, Miriam Susan Gray. There were also three lodgers in the house, one of them the 24-year-old furnaceman John Francis Wilkinson. Although Wilkinson was known sometimes to drink to excess, landlord, landlady and lodgers seem to have got on reasonably well.

But on August 15 1953 there was tragedy at No. 165 Boundaries Road. Herman and Charlotte Schreiber slept in the first floor front bedroom, but little Miriam Susan had her nursery downstairs. In the middle of the night, Charlotte Schreiber heard the sound of glass breaking, but she went back to sleep since "She thought it was cats". But a worse marauder that the feline kind was at work that fell night. Early in the morning, Mr and Mrs Schreiber woke up with a start, since their room was full of smoke. Groping their way downstairs, the panic-stricken couple found that their kitchen was well alight, but they managed to put the flames out. But worse things were to come. When Charlotte Schreiber went to look for Miriam Susan, she found her brutally battered to death underneath her blankets.

The police first formed the opinion that burglars had broken into the house, murdered Miriam Susan to prevent her from screaming, cut the telephone wire, and set the kitchen on fire. But when experienced forensic experts were set to work at No. 165 Boundaries Road, they declared that this had clearly been an 'inside job': no burglar had entered the premises. This made the lodger John Francis Wilkinson the main suspect. A nasty piece of work and a confirmed drunkard, he was arrested and charged with the crime. Unwisely and quite possibly inebriately, Wilkinson made a long statement to the police, detailing how he had broken a leg off a chair and gone down to the nursery. When little Miriam Susan had started to toss and turn, he had struck her again and again. Amazed that the battered, blood-soaked little wretch was still alive, he had finally grasped her round her neck and throttled her to death. Wilkinson had been drinking beer and vermouth that night, but he was not blind drunk. Thinking that it might be a good idea to burn down the house to conceal his crime, he had set the kitchen alight, but this stratagem had not worked out as he had planned.

At the coroner's inquest on Miriam Susan Gray, the sordid story of her murder caused widespread horror and distress. Mrs Charlotte Schreiber, described as a slimly built, grey-haired woman in a black suit, detailed how she had found her daughter murdered. There was further outrage when forensic experts testified that the murderer had attempted sexual intercourse with the five-year-old child. Copies of 'Bedside Clubman' and other filthy porn magazines were discovered in Wilkinson's room. His fingerprints matched those found at the crime scene. Considering his ill-judged confession to the police, there could be no other verdict than wilful murder against John Francis Wilkinson, and the young furnaceman was committed for trial at the Central Criminal Court.

On November 3 1953, John Francis Wilkinson stood trial for the murder of Miriam Susan Gray, before Mr Justice Hilbery.

There was no question, from his confession and the detailed forensic evidence, that he had killed the little girl, but his barrister tried the 'insanity defence'. Two psychiatrists confidently stated that although Wilkinson did not suffer from any known disease of the mind, he was an abnormal man with a psychopathic personality. Wilkinson's barrister Mr Rountree replied that some medical authorities did regard psychopathy as a disease of the mind, but Mr Justice Hilbery ruled that there was no evidence of insanity. Mr Rountree said that in view of his Lordship's ruling, he would not address the jury again. Wilkinson was accordingly found guilty and sentenced to death. An appeal was tried, but again there was no sympathy for the kind of creature Wilkinson represented: the Lord Chief Justice dismissed the Boundaries Road child murderer's appeal. The Home Secretary did not find reason to recommend any interference with the course of the law, and Wilkinson was duly executed at Wandsworth Prison on December 18 1953.[29]

THE CLAPHAM DIVAN MURDER, 1955

Patrick Antonio Ross was born in Burma in 1933, and could speak Hindustani since he was educated in India. But apart from his linguistic prowess, he lacked both talent and qualifications. He tried joining the R.A.F., but was rejected for flying duties, and later dismissed from the service after being convicted for stealing a post office savings book. In 1955, when Patrick Ross was 22 years old, his life seemed to hold little promise: he worked as a warehouseman, among other odd jobs, and lived in a second-floor bedsit in a large Victorian house at No. 2 Abbeville Road, Clapham.

On November 2 1955, the 29-year-old Indian student Akon Chandra Dutta arrived in London on a flight from the United

States. The globe-trotting Indian, who had been studying electrical engineering in Canada, was planning to amuse himself in London for a while, before travelling on to Paris. A short, thin, balding cove, he carried with him a large wad of dollar banknotes and travellers' cheques.

On November 5, Dutta chanced to meet Patrick Ross in Piccadilly. When the Indian asked for directions, Ross thought it funny that this silly foreigner did not know where he was. He answered him in Hindustani, and they went to have a few pints of beer in a pub nearby, before sharing a bottle of whisky at Dutta's lodgings. They became good friends, and the following day, the Indian was invited back to the No. 2 Abbeville Road. Exactly how these two had planned to amuse themselves at the flat is not known, but their brief acquaintance certainly ended badly: the brawny Ross knocked the Indian on the head with a large iron bracket, killing him. He relieved the sub-continental traveller of his valuables, and hid the body inside a large divan. He then went to see a local prostitute, paying her £4 for the night. The following day, Sunday November 6, Ross attended the Remembrance Day service at the Cenotaph in Whitehall, in the company of Miss Ann Tilling. The patriotic murderer invited his young lady friend back to his flat, where she was invited to sit on the divan containing the dead Indian, without realizing that anything was amiss.

The good news for Patrick Ross was that the Indian traveller was not missed by any person, particularly by the police. The friendly prostitute had given him some useful advice about how to cash traveller's cheques and exchange dollar banknotes, which he made use of to fill his wallet with £400 in cash. The bad news was that he did not have any good idea how to dispose of the body. He lacked the skill to dismember it, and did not have access to a motor vehicle; nor was it entirely straightforward how to smuggle the corpse downstairs from his second-floor flat. Driven to desperation after the body had started to decompose, Ross offered the workmates John Deacon Nicholl and David Hyler £50 if they could help him dispose of a dead body. He asked Hyler if he could drive a car, telling him that he had killed a man, and needed transportation to dump the body somewhere. The two workmen turned out to be honest people, and after turning down his offer, they went to the police. Since the desperate Ross had approached strangers in the street, asking for help to dispose of a dead body, the police had already got a tip from one of their informers.

The Clapham constables acted with commendable determination: without any further ado, they called at Flat 2c at No. 2 Abbeville Road, at a time when Ross was not at home, and 'sniffed out' the decomposing body inside the divan. The following morning, Ross could read all about the sensational 'Clapham Divan Murder' in the newspapers. The Abbeville Road murderer could still have made his escape from the Metropolis, but Ross lacked the cunning and determination of 'Acid Bath' Haigh and various other cool customers who occupied the Murder Houses of London. He meekly telephoned the police to give himself up, saying 'I'm the man you want for this job!' When examined by a psychiatrist, he showed little remorse for his crime, and appeared callous and immature, although fully sane and fit to plead.

When Patrick Ross was on trial for murder at the Central Criminal Court on January 30 1956, he pleaded Not Guilty. Mr Christmas Humphries outlined what appeared like a very solid case for the prosecution. There was no doubt that Ross had taken Dutta back to his flat, that Dutta had been murdered in there, or that Ross had been seeking advice about how to dispose of his remains. Giving evidence, Ross said that he had gone berserk after Dutta had made some offensive remarks about the Royal Family. It took the jury three and a half hours to find him guilty of murder, and he was sentenced to death. After awaiting execution for more than a month, he received a late reprieve from the Home Secretary.[30] He is said to have spent nearly two decades in prison, before being released, and is rumoured still to be alive today. The large and impressive murder house at No. 2 Abbeville Road still stands today, although it remains subdivided into a number of flats. The divan was later purchased from the police by a collector of criminal curiosities, and also still exists today.

MURDER AND SUICIDE IN AMNER ROAD, 1962

Edwin Moore worked as a civilian clerk in the R.A.F. for many years. He married his wife Cynthia in the early 1940s, and they had a son named Derek, but the couple separated permanently in 1948. Edwin Moore left the R.A.F. in 1962 and settled down at a farm in Norfolk with his mother. In early June 1962, he received a divorce petition from his estranged wife, who was planning to remarry. His mother noticed that he seemed more gloomy and brooding than usual, but he did not tell her the reason.

On June 4, Edwin Moore went to No. 15 Amner Road, Clapham, where Cynthia was living with her mother and the son Derek. He brought with him a loaded shotgun from the farm, which he made use of to shoot and kill his estranged wife. Derek was an eyewitness to the murder. And as he and his grandmother ran out of the house to seek help, they heard Edwin Moore commit suicide with the shotgun.

Since there was a scarcity of news in June 1962, the sordid story of the murder and suicide in Amner Road hit the tabloid headlines. The plight of the 17-year-old schoolboy Derek, who had lost both his parents, was of course the 'human interest' of the story. 'I saw Mother Murdered!' exclaimed the headline of the

Daily Mail, and the *Daily Express* praised 'The Bravery of Derek Moore'.[31] Derek was a prefect at the Bec School for Boys at Tooting Bec, and the reporters were amazed that the day after the murder, he sat and passed his exams at this school. Before this extraordinary schoolboy joined the ranks of yesterday's newspaper celebrities, a further article stated that he was living with his grandmother in the murder house, and that he was planning a month's cycling trip in continental Europe.[32]

THE MURDER OF DIB FIELD, 1962

There are two files on Dib Field in the National Archives. One of them, open to the public, contains his medal card from his service as a private soldier in the Royal Welsh Fusileers during the Great War. The other one, closed until 2053, has the details of his murder in 1962.

Due to his uncommon name, it is possible to follow Dib Field's obscure life in some detail, using online genealogy tools. After his wartime service, he settled down as a shopkeeper and tobacconist in South London. He married a woman named Emily Shrosbree in 1923 and they may well have had children. Dib Field moved from shop to shop, often in the Brixton area. A short, thin man, he lived in the flat above the shop with his wife, leading a humble life without any extravagances.

In 1962, when Dib Field was 68 years old, he kept a small newsagent's shop at No. 110 Acre Lane, Brixton. On July 14, an awkward-looking youth came into the shop, asking for a sixpenny chocolate bar. When Dib Field turned his back to the customer to get the chocolate, the youth seized up a heavy bottle of mineral water from the counter and struck him a hard blow on the head. Dib Field lurched forward and struck his head hard against the

2.28 A postcard showing Acre Lane, Brixton. The murder shop at No. 110 can be clearly seen in the second row of three-story houses on the right.

floor. The youth leapt over the counter, stole £12 10s. from the till, and made his escape without being spotted by any witnesses.

When Mrs Field came downstairs from the flat to serve her husband some tea and sandwiches, she discovered him lying on the floor with serious head injuries. Dib Field was taken to hospital, where he expired three days later, and the case was now one of murder. The Acre Lane murder remained a mystery until July 20, when it was featured by the *South London Press*. The article was read by the 19-year-old warehouse boy James Heron, who was aghast to find that he had in fact murdered the old man he had 'coshed' to get his hands on the £12 10s. He confessed to his mother and sister in Camberwell, and they advised him to give himself up to the police.

James Heron told the detectives that he had been very hungry, and that after he had spent his last sixpence on a chocolate bar, he suddenly got the idea to knock the old man down and rob the shop. Although he had struck Dib Field hard, and seen his head bounce when it hit the floor, he had not even checked that the old man was alive. When James Heron was on trial for murder at the Old Bailey on September 14, before Mr Justice Roskill, his barrister Mr Norman Skelhorn conceded that the prisoner had caused Dib Field's death under tragic circumstances. No one could feel anything but indignation and anger at the thought of a harmless, inoffensive old man being struck down in his shop, he went on.

Giving evidence, Heron said he had no idea why he had suddenly attacked the old shopkeeper. Two psychiatrists testified for the defence, stating that Heron was below average intelligence, that he was withdrawn and isolated, and that he suffered from an abnormality of the mind that would impair the responsibility for his acts. The jury found Heron guilty of manslaughter on the grounds of diminished responsibility, a not uncommon verdict at the time the death penalty was being debated, and he was sentenced to life imprisonment.[33] The only memorials to Dib Field's humble and blameless life are two files in the National Archives, some assorted internet scraps in the genealogy databases, and the murder shop at No. 110 Acre Lane.

MURDER BY A PORNOGRAPHER, 1969

Michael John Muldoon, a young Soho crook, made pornography his business in the 1960s. More clever and enterprising than his fellow pornographers, he supplied many porn shops with naughty films and photographs, and easily made a living from his profession. He set up his own photography business and described himself as a company director. Muldoon had more than one run-in with the Porn Squad detectives, who he alleged wanted bribes as 'protection money'. When he refused to pay, he claimed that these bent coppers made sure that he served 18 months in Pentonville Prison for breaking the Indecent Publications Act. In prison, he met a violent criminal named Gerard Hawley, a former soldier in the Parachute Regiment, and they became good friends.

After Muldoon had emerged from prison, he continued his pornography business just like before. He married one of his models and had two children with her. In May 1969, they lived in a flat at No. 126 Stockwell Road, Lambeth. A friend of theirs, the young film salesman Kenneth Charles Eighteen, lived in the flat next door. On the evening of May 20, Muldoon and his wife invited Eighteen and Hawley for a party. The men drank excessively, and according to Muldoon, they also took LSD. The volatile, much-tattooed Hawley soon kicked up a row, but this would be the last time he was ever seen alive. Some days later, his dead body was retrieved from a ditch in Epping Forest.

Muldoon was soon the prime suspect for the murder of Gerard Hawley. He did not deny that the ex-soldier had been partying at his flat, or that there had been a lot of drink and drugs about. He claimed that all of a sudden, a strong man with a goatee beard, whose name might have been 'Tony' appeared in the flat, and began fighting Hawley with knives. The police found no evidence that 'Tony' existed, however. A tyre print near the ditch where the body was found matched the tyres on Muldoon's Lancia car, and this finding was used to put pressure on the pornographer.

On trial at the Central Criminal Court for the murder of Gerard Hawley, Muldoon claimed that Hawley had attacked him with an ornamental carving knife, and that he had acted in self-defence. This version was not believed, since Muldoon had been untruthful before, and since Hawley had been stabbed not less than 89 times. Still, injuries to Muldoon's hands indicated that some time during the fracas, he had grabbed hold of a knife blade. Mrs Muldoon and the man Eighteen were both charged as accessories. The latter provided some damning statements in court, namely that he had seen Muldoon with a knife in each hand, and that he had struck him a karate blow to the neck to drag him away from his victim. Eighteen had wanted to phone for an ambulance, he claimed, but Muldoon had promised to take Hawley to hospital in his own car.

Although there was some evidence to indicate that Muldoon had really been attacked with a knife, the pornographer was found guilty of murder and was sentenced to life imprisonment. Mrs Muldoon and the man Eighteen were acquitted of murder, but they were found guilty of acting with intent to impede Muldoon's arrest; she got three years' probation, and he was jailed for three years. These were harsh sentences, particularly when compared with the lenience shown to the hippie Robert Lipman, the Walpole Street killer of 1967. But then Lipman's wealthy family could afford a crack legal team, whereas the exertions of Muldoon's defenders were wholly unsuccessful.

Michael John Muldoon served ten years behind bars, narrowly escaping being assaulted by friends of Hawley who were also serving time. Once he had been released, the pornographer set up a new studio and produced more hard-core porn. Clever enough to realize that the consumers of pornography would be keen to enjoy his art from the safety of their own houses, rather than in some smelly Soho cinema, he founded the company Videx Ltd and became one of Britain's leading purveyors of porn videos. He clashed with the moral campaigner Mary Whitehouse, with the feminist movement, and with that ludicrous figure, the seventh Earl of Longford, also known as 'Lord Porn'. He privately published his multi-volume autobiography *I, Pornographer*, under the name Michael J. Freeman. He claimed to have been 'framed' for the murder of Hawley by his old enemies in the corrupt Porn Squad.[34] The murder flat at No. 126 Stockwell Road still exists, over a William Hill betting shop in this busy street.

CHAPTER 3

LEWISHAM, DEPTFORD AND GREENWICH

On every lip a speechless horror dwelt;
On ev'ry brow the burthen of affliction;
The old Ancestral Spirits knew and felt
The House's malediction.
Such earnest woe their features overcast,
They might have stirr'd, or sigh'd, or wept, or spoken,
But, save the hollow moaning of the blast,
The stillness was unbroken.

This chapter will deal with the murder houses in a large part of Southeast London, consisting of Lewisham, Deptford, Greenwich, and various south-eastern suburbs south of the Thames. For many years, the most famous murder house in Greenwich was Mr Bird's house in London Street [it had no number], where this wealthy gentleman was murdered, along with his housekeeper, in 1818. Burglary was clearly the motive, and later a highwayman named Charles Hussey was convicted for the double murder, and executed, on some dangerously feeble evidence. The ghost of Mr Bird was said to be haunting his old house, and no person dared to live there for decades to come.[1]

Awful Tragedy at Deptford.

3.1 Edward Callaghan murders Mary Ann Evenden and her daughter in Copperas Square, Deptford, from the Illustrated Police News, June 12 1897

No. 155 Church Street, Deptford, where the mysterious Deptford Poisonings occurred in 1888, no longer frowns upon the passer-by. No older houses remain in Copperas Square, off Bronze Street, Deptford, where Edward Callaghan murdered his married sister Mary Ann Evenden, and her oldest daughter Ann, in 1897. No. 21 Baildon Street, Deptford, where James Botton murdered his wife Catherine in 1901, no longer frowns upon the passer-by. The house of horrors at No. 38 Batavia Road, New Cross, where Frank Cavilla murdered his wife and four children in a bloodbath in 1902, no longer stands, although some remaining older houses in this road show what it must have looked like. Many older houses survive in Gosterwood Road, Greenwich, but not No. 49, where Edward Harrison murdered his married daughter Elizabeth Jane Rickus in 1904.[2]

Even the relatively modern murder houses of southeast London have been severely decimated. No. 192 Edward Street, Deptford, where Henry Vanner murdered Martha Elisa Barber in 1928, and then committed suicide, no longer stands. Nor does No. 180 Edward Street, where the middle-aged homosexual William Brown stabbed his teenage lover to death in 1938. No. 213 Maxey Road, Plumstead, where Mrs Alice Stamp was murdered by the 16-year-old burglar B.N. Rose in 1969, has been lost underneath a huge modern development. No. 1 Glenforth Street, Greenwich, where the illegal immigrant Prem Dhande murdered the four children of a relative who had disowned him in 1975, has suffered the same fate, as judged by comparison between a contemporary photograph of the murder house and the present-day nondescript housing.[3]

But although the extensive development of southeast London had meant the end of the line for many a historic murder house, many are still standing. Read the amazing story of Greenwich's oldest murder pub and its poetic resident ghosts, ponder the mysterious murder of Mrs Tyler in Kidbrooke Park Road, and have a look at the nondescript little shop in Deptford High Street, inside which the earliest use of fingerprint technology led to the arrest and conviction of two brutal murderers. In 1912, a man named Arthur J. Miller killed his wife at No. 19 Doggett Road, but this obscure suburban tragedy was given very little newspaper attention. The same is not true for another house in the terrace, No. 27 Doggett Road, site of the unsolved murder of Maxwell Confait in 1972. It is said to be haunted, and thus should be approached with caution.

GREENWICH'S OLDEST MURDER PUB, 1822

In the County of Wicklow I was born'd
but now in Maidstone die in scorn

3.2 Greenwich Hospital, from an old postcard.

I once was counted a roving blade
but to my misfortune had no trade
women was always my downfall
but still I liked and loved them all
a hundred I have had in my time
when I was young and in my prime...

These doggerel verses were written by John Smith, a 78-year-old former sailor who had become a Greenwich Pensioner, as he was awaiting execution at Maidstone Gaol. A strong, vigorous old fellow, hale and hearty in spite of his years, he had always been very fond of female company. When Old Jack, as he was called, met an ageing floozie named Catherine Jones in a London brothel, he persuaded her to join him at Greenwich Hospital, where he got her a job as helper in one of the wards. She was known as 'Jack Smith's Wife' and the old man hoped she would remain true to him.

A woman from London to me came
she said with You I would fain remain
if you'll be constant I'll be true
I never want no man but You…

But 'Catherine Smith' did not adhere to her unconventional 'marriage vows'. After residing with Old Jack at the Hospital for 18 months, she started 'going out' with a younger and more attractive Pensioner. This made Jack furious, and on October 4 1822, he sneaked out to the 'Cricketers' public house in central Greenwich. He asked the barman if he had seen his faithless Catherine, but was answered in the negative. Still, old Jack remained at the pub, swigging from a jug of ale and clutching a sharp knife in his pocket. And indeed, his brazen 'wife' soon came sauntering into the pub with her admirer, ignoring old Jack and ordering two glasses of gin. 'You know I take it with peppermint!' she admonished the barman, but as he was reaching for the peppermint-bottle, Jack sneaked up to his 'wife' and ended her life, as he expressed it:

then to the Cricketers he did go
to see if he could find her out or no
not long been there before she came in
with this same fellow to fetch some Gin
then with a Knife himself brought in
immediately stab'd her under the Chin
and in five minutes she was no more
but there laid in her purple gore…

'You have killed me! You have killed me!' poor Catherine screamed. Rather callously, the landlord of the Cricketers, who clearly was no proto-Samaritan, advised her to run to the

THE NEW
NEWGATE CALENDAR,
CONTAINING THE
REMARKABLE LIVES AND TRIALS OF NOTORIOUS CRIMINALS, PAST AND PRESENT.
SATURDAY, JANUARY 30, 1864.
[One Penny.

THE MURDER AT THE "CRICKETERS," GREENWICH.

3.3 John Smith murders his 'wife', from the New Newgate Calendar.

Infirmary nearby, but she only got forty paces before dropping dead. 'You wicked old man, how could you do so rash an act?' the landlord cried, seizing hold of Jack. 'She had been with that fellow all night!' the tough old Pensioner replied.

On trial for murder at the Kent Assizes, Jack Smith told the court about his 'wife's' unsatisfactory behaviour. He had challenged her when she came into the pub with her 'lubber', and ordered her favourite peppermint gin. Her only response had been to put her foot down hard on one of his corns. Infuriated, he had stabbed her in a fit of anger, and he hoped the court would show him mercy. The verdict was one of 'Guilty', however, and Jack was sentenced to hang.

Awaiting execution, Jack wrote his own 'Ballad of Maidstone Gaol', the doggerel history of his life. It was rightly considered "truly astonishing that the mind of a man nearly fourscore years could, by any possibility, under circumstances so peculiarly awful, for a moment be so abstracted from his situation as to admit of so extraordinary a production." The *Morning Chronicle* published Jack's poem in its enterity, as did the *Newgate Calendar*. But still, old Jack was executed at Maidstone Gaol on December 23. He did not recite his poem on the scaffold, but merely remarked that women had always been his downfall.[4]

The Cricketers pub at Greenwich lived on for many years after Jack Smith, the murderer poet, had been launched into eternity. Remarkably, the old pub was still up and running as late as 2004, described as a popular watering-hole for local old men, who liked its cask ales on tap, and did not want to frequent the 'touristy' pubs. But since the old pub was not making a profit, it was closed a few years later. For a while, the murder pub was a glitzy gay bar, and it then became a 'tiki bar', although neither reincarnation lasted very long. It is now a rather tacky-looking fish and chips shop. Although admitting that the fish and chips on sale are not bad, Greenwich conservationists want the historic Cricketers to be converted back into a pub again, but this does not look like happening, since money tends to speak louder than conservationists.

If we are to believe a mysterious character who calls himself 'the People's Poet', the spectres of Jack and Catherine Smith are still haunting the old Greenwich fish and chips shop. They agree fully with the Greenwich conservationists about the sad fate of their favourite watering-hole. One night, when the Poet was passing by the former Cricketers, having 'had a few' at another establishment, he heard a croaking male voice exclaim"

Alas, my ghost now haunts this shop
'Midst 'taters, chips and fritter,

Instead of having one last drop
of good old John Smith's Bitter!

At first, the Poet though he might be hallucinating, but a quivering female voice joined in:

Alack, old Jack, you murdered me,
to end my life in sin!
And now I must teetotal be
without peppermint gin!

The voices of the two ghosts then declaimed, at a very sorrowful note:

Our spectres quite transparent are,
we long even for Hell;
Instead of our nice saloon bar,
that dreadful fishy smell!

THE STRANGE TALE OF JEREMIAH TOOMEY, 1868

In 1868, the two Irish labouring men Patrick Desmond and Jeremiah Toomey lodged together at King Street, Deptford. In August 23 that year, they had an angry quarrel at the Navy Arms public house in New King Street, about four shillings and sixpence Toomey thought Desmond had stolen from his pocket. Toomey left the pub and went back to his lodgings. Another workman saw him take up a knife and wave it about in a threatening manner. When asked what he was about to do, he said "I mean to put three inches of this into Patsy before I go to bed to-night!" The other man tried to dissuade him, but Toomey walked to the Navy Arms, ran up to the bar, and stabbed Desmond hard, before making his escape. Patrick Desmond, who was just 24 years old, died at Guy's Hospital two days later. Several witnesses had seen Toomey at the Navy Arms, and the coroner's inquest on Patrick Desmond returned a verdict of wilful murder against him. The hue and cry was on for Jeremiah Toomey, but he had left London, for good.

In June 1870, Jeremiah Toomey was discovered at No. 8 Harleston Street, Openshaw, near Manchester, where he had been working as a forgeman. Although absconding to Lancashire, and assuming the name of John Williams, he had kept up a correspondence with his elderly mother in Deptford, and one of these letters had fallen into the hands of a police sergeant named Watson, who took it to Chief Inspector Clarke at Scotland Yard. Clarke went to Openshaw, where he and Inspector Rowbotham of the Lancashire Constabulary arrested the suspect, who was still in bed when they tracked him down. He at first denied being Jeremiah Toomey, but later admitted being the wanted man, although he firmly denied murdering Patrick Desmond. Chief Inspector Clarke had brought with him one of the witnesses from the inquest, a woman named Helen Coates, who thought the suspect was very like the Jeremiah Toomey she had seen.

'Murder will out!' exclaimed the newspapers, and there was general rejoicing that one of London's many murder mysteries would be solved. The suspect was brought to London and confronted with three witnesses from the Navy Arms, but they all said 'This is not the Jeremiah Toomey who stabbed Patrick Desmond.' The Openshaw mystery man was released, and the police had to give him his return fare. The murder of Patrick Desmond remains unsolved to this day.[5] Although New King Street has few older buildings remaining, the Navy Arms still stands, although it has been converted into flats.

3.4 A drawing of the murder house at No. 67 Kidbrooke Park Road, from Lloyd's Weekly Newspaper, August 21 1898.

THE BLACKHEATH MYSTERY, 1898

The 60-year-old Mrs Arabella Charlotte Tyler was the widow of Mr William John Tyler, the late Secretary of the India-rubber and Gutta-percha Telegraph Works Company Ltd, of Silvertown. After her husband had died in early 1897, she lived on in their elegant detached villa at No. 67 Kidbrooke Park Road, Blackheath, just opposite St James's Church. On one side of No. 67 was a similar villa, on the other the Manor Park Farm. The large rear garden overlooked the Kent County Cricket Ground. Mrs Tyler lived in comfortable affluence, with her spinster daughter Maud and her recently widowed daughter Mrs Violet Huxham. They normally had two domestics, but the housemaid had just left, and Mrs Tyler was waited on by her general servant Ann Gusterson.

3.5 The mystery servant Mary Ann Gusterson, from Lloyd's Weekly Newspaper, August 21 1898.

On Sunday August 13 1898, Mrs Tyler had seemed uncommonly energetic, saying that she would rise at 5 am the next morning, to do some hard graft in the garden. Both her daughters were away, and Ann Gusterson was the only other person who slept in the large house. On Monday morning, Ann Gusterson woke up at 6.30. She was surprised to see that the doors from the kitchen to the garden were open, and looked if her mistress was working out there, but Mrs Tyler was nowhere to be seen. She lit the stove and prepared the glass of hot water that her mistress liked to drink each morning. But when the domestic entered Mrs Tyler's room, carrying her frugal repast, she saw her mistress lying on the floor at the foot of the bed, wearing her night clothes. Her face was quite livid, and her head thrown back. Realizing that she was dead, the servant girl ran out into the road and screamed for assistance. Two workmen came to her aid, one of them going for the police and the other guarding the house, as Ann Gusterson herself went for the doctor.

Dr Clifford, the local practitioner, declared that Mrs Tyler had been dead for several hours. Her neck had strangulation marks from powerful fingers, her face was blue, and her eyes were starting from the head. This was clearly a case of murder by strangulation. The police made a thorough search of the murder house. They saw marks that might indicate that the murderer had tried to force the large French doors to the dining room. There were also signs that the intruder had entered the house through climbing up some trellis work leading from the porch to Mrs Tyler's bedroom window. Ann Gusterson said that her mistress used to leave her window open about a foot, due to the August heat; thus the intruder would have found it easy to enter the room. But Mrs Tyler had woken up and confronted the intruder, who had strangled her to death. There were some open drawers in the bedroom, and also signs that some of the downstairs rooms had been searched, but nothing valuable had been stolen. The police suspected that the intruder had intended to burgle the house. Rather adventurously, they presumed that the reason he had not stolen more was that a large hayrick at nearby Manor Park Farm had mysteriously caught fire the very same night, and that the intruder had been alarmed by the sound of people running along Kidbrooke Park Road to extinguish the flames. In the garden, several footprints were found, indicating that the murderer had opened the kitchen doors to the garden and fled through the flower beds. The Scotland Yard detectives were busy making plaster casts of these footprints.

Mr E. Negus Wood, the deputy coroner for West Kent, was communicated with, and the inquest on Arabella Charlotte Tyler begun on August 17, in the Kidbrooke Mission Room. Mrs Tyler had told friends that she was fearful of burglars, since the house was quite isolated, and annoyed at local youths stealing fruit from the garden. Her son-in-law Samuel Childs said that the house at No. 67 Kidbrooke Park Road had contained plate valued at £220, although he was not sure whether Mrs Tyler's jewelry was worth much. Ann Gusterson seemed quite distraught and had to sit down while giving evidence. Mrs Tyler had had only one visitor the day before the murder, the neighbour Mrs Georgina Jackson. The police surgeon Dr Cooper agreed with his fellow practitioner that Mrs Tyler had been strangled by a powerful intruder.

The inquest was adjourned until September 15, and then until October 12. Chief Inspector Conquest, who was in charge of the police investigation, told the jury that further time was needed, since the Blackheath Mystery was an extremely complex case. A writer in the *Illustrated Police News* commented that "Nothing transpired as to the nature of the evidence which will then be forthcoming, but rumour has that it will be of an extremely interesting character." But when the inquest was finally resumed on October 12, the result was a damp squib. The coroner announced that Chief Inspector Conquest had given him a full account of the murder investigation, and that he had decided that there was not significant evidence to make out a prima facie case against any person. The jurymen were not happy about this. One of them said that many a crime had been traced through the detective work of jurymen: they were not dummies, but should be allowed to question the witnesses themselves. The coroner reluctantly agreed. The juryman insisted that he must ask the servant Ann Gusterson, about whom many rumours had been abounding, some probing questions. She denied having been visited by any sweetheart while residing at No. 67 Kidbrooke Park Road. The only person who had come to see her there had been a female cousin. She had been surprised to see the kitchen doors to the garden open the morning after the murder, she said. But clearly not surprised enough to investigate whether a burglary had occurred before she brought her mistress her breakfast, the suspicious juryman retorted. Nothing more came of this attempt to incriminate Ann Gusterson, however: the coroner had his way, and the jury returned a verdict of wilful murder against some person or persons unknown.[6]

It is possible to discern three different murder scenarios in the Blackheath Mystery. The first one agrees with the police hypothesis: a burglar intends to rob No. 67 Kidbrooke Park

3.6 A photograph of the Blackheath murder house, from Harmsworth's Magazine, December 1898.

Road and misadvertently enters Mrs Tyler's bedroom. To prevent her from giving the alarm, he strangles her, before ransacking the house. But would a burglar really choose the hazardous route up to the first-floor bedroom, without knowing who was there? Why go to the extremes of murdering Mrs Tyler, instead of just knocking her on the head? And why did the intruder make sure it looked like the house had been burgled, through opening drawers and cupboards, while not stealing anything valuable? In Mrs Tyler's bedroom, two valuable rings were kept in an open drawer, but neither was stolen. And was it not a remarkable coincidence that when the 'burglar' struck, none of Mrs Tyler's daughters were in the house, and only one of the domestics?

The second scenario involves an old enemy of Mrs Tyler coming to settle the score with her, before doing his best to make the murder look like a burglary gone wrong. Mrs Tyler's daughters and remaining son-in-law denied that she had any enemies, but would they have known everything about her past? In the third scenario, Mrs Tyler's son-in-law hires an assassin to murder her, to make sure that, through his wife, he gets a share of her wealth. The burglary was a cover-up and Ann Gusterson an accomplice. In her will, Mrs Tyler left a total of £5,869. But the son-in-law in question, Mr Samuel Childs, who had married young Margaret Mary Tyler in 1891, appears to have been a respectable gentleman, who stayed away from criminal conspiracies, and earned his income by more conventional means than murdering his mother-in-law. Mrs Tyler had changed her will in September 1897, to leave the bulk of her estate to the three daughters. What had the earlier will contained, and why did she change it? Might it have had anything to do with George Trevor Huxham, who died from what was supposed to be diabetes in 1895, aged just 33, after being married to Violet Tyler for just two years? And why did Samuel Childs, when interviewed by a journalist just after the murder, claim that the cause of death had been heart disease?

The Blackheath Mystery would have been a match even for Sherlock Holmes. It is quite an interesting and anomalous crime, which I would suspect has a more adventurous solution than the 'burglar' hypothesis favoured by the police. It is a great pity that the police files on the case, which should have been kept at the National Archives, have been lost or stolen. The murder house at No. 67 Kidbrooke Park Road still stands, just opposite St James's Church at the crossing with Wricklemarsh Road. The large house has been subdivided into several small flats. There is no longer any trellis work near the porch, leading to the first floor bay window.

MASS MURDER IN CHARLTON, 1901

In 1858, the ancient Irish barony of Cahir became dormant. A certain Joseph Lawrence Butler, of Lewisham, claimed the title, but without success. This individual had two sons, of whom the second, Thomas Butler, became a quartermaster-sergeant in the Army Service Corps. He served with distinction in India and Egypt, before settling down at a small semi-detached house at No. 63 Charlton Lane with his wife Sarah Lilian and their six children. Butler had always been fond of his offspring, whose age varied from a lad of eighteen to a babe in arms. He was employed at the War Office, but also did duty at Dover. In May 1901, the 45-year-old Butler was ordered to South Africa, with a company of the Army Service Corps.

3.7 Thomas Butler guns down his children at No. 63 Charlton Lane, from the Illustrated Police News, May 25 1901.

On Sunday May 19, gunfire was heard from No. 63 Charlton Lane. Mrs Butler came running into the house of her neighbour, carrying her baby. All of a sudden, her husband had gone mad, she explained, and opened fire at his children with his heavy army revolver. A police constable was summoned, but after hearing that an armed maniac was at large at No. 63, he prudently awaited the arrival of two colleagues before entering the house to investigate. But when Thomas Butler saw the constables approach the house, he meekly handed over his revolver and submitted himself a prisoner. On the floor lay six of his children, all bleeding from serious injuries. The teenage son Laurence and the young daughters Clara, Hilda, Grace and Vera were all stone dead. Only the 14-year-old Lily was breathing, and she was taken to the Seaman's Hospital in Greenwich. Thomas Butler could provide no explanation for this sanguinary outrage, and his wife was prostrate with grief. His elder brother Laurence, who told the journalists that he was by right Baron Cahir, but that he had not claimed the title, explained that Thomas had sent him a telegram on Sunday afternoon, with the text 'Come by next train. It will be to your great advantage and fatal to me.' Alarmed by the sinister wording, the 'Baron' had made haste to Charlton, but when he arrived the five children had already been murdered.

At the inquest on the five murdered children, Mrs Butler and the 'Baron' gave evidence as to the prisoner's antecedents. Throughout his long army career, the quartermaster-sergeant had been a honourable, popular man, who had never committed any dishonest or criminal act. When questioned, Thomas Butler looked quite insane, with unnaturally bright and sparkling eyes. In answer to the charge, he exclaimed "I only grieve, indeed, that my daughter Lily suffered for a moment! In all the other cases I know that it was instantaneous death, and no suffering!" His wife, who could imagine the horrible scene when the madman gunned down his terrified children, probably disagreed. Thomas Butler had made a will back in 1897 leaving everything to his wife, but he had scrawled an alteration on it, dated May 13, namely that if his wife and all his children died, he would leave everything to his brother the 'Baron'. This had not happened as planned, however, due to Mrs Butler's hasty retreat with her baby, and the fact that Lily was progressing favourably in the hospital.

When Thomas Butler was on trial at the Old Bailey for five counts of murder, and a sixth of shooting at Lily Butler with intent to murder her, the alienist Dr Maudsley and the prison doctor James Scott gave evidence as to their opinion of the prisoner's fitness to plead. They had both interviewed the Charlton mass murderer, and were amazed to find that he was quite jolly and proud of what he had achieved. He had seen his wife speaking to a certain Mr Pye in the road opposite his house, and instantly knew that she had been unfaithful to him, or at least intended being so. He prayed to God, and decided to kill all his children, since their

3.8 A postcard showing Charlton Lane, stamped and posted in 1907. The murder house at No. 63 is further down the road.

mother was not a suitable person to look after them. He had intended to shoot himself as well, but now he was looking forward to dying on the scaffold instead. Thomas Butler's father had been confined in an asylum with 'mania' and it was clear to the two doctors that the Charlton Lane mass murderer was far from sane. Mrs Butler had always been a good and faithful wife to him, and the suspicion that she had an affair with Mr Pye was wholly unfounded. The jury found him guilty but insane, and he was detained at Broadmoor during His Majesty's pleasure; he died there in 1923.[7] The murder house at No. 63 Charlton Lane still stands.

THE FATAL FINGERPRINT, 1905

Thomas and Anna Farrow were an elderly couple who tended Mr George Chapman's oil and colour shop at No. 34 Deptford High

3.9 A drawing of Chapman's Oil Shop at No. 34 Deptford High Street.

3.10 A photograph of the Chapman murder shop.

Street. Although Thomas was 71 years old in 1905, and Anna 65, they both beavered away with commendable industry, keeping the small shop open from 8 am until 9.30 pm, helped by their younger assistant William Jones.

On the morning of March 27 1905, when William Jones came trudging to work as usual, he found the shop door locked. He walked over to one of Mr Chapman's other shops nearby, returned with another assistant, and entered the shop through the back door. To his horror, he found Thomas Farrow lying dead in the parlour, murdered by a series of heavy blows to the head. Mrs Farrow was lying in bed, unconscious and badly injured by a couple of hard knocks to the head. The rifled cash-tin of the shop, which had obviously been handled by at least one of the murderers, was carefully examined for fingerprints by the police.

Aside from the lack of forced entry, it was clear that the Farrows had been attacked separately. The discovery of two black masks fashioned from stockings, left at the scene, indicated that [at least] two men were involved. Since the Farrows were in their night clothes, the police had speculated that Thomas Farrow had been deceived into opening the door in the middle of the night. He was immediately attacked, but was still able to pursue after the robbers, but they knocked him down again. His assailants went up to the upstairs flat, attacked Mrs Farrow, located the cash box, and fled with the money.

For a while, there were hopes that Mrs Farrow would recover consciousness, and be able to describe her assailant, but the harmless old lady died on March 31. Instead, the police got hold of some important leads. Two independent witnesses had seen the brothers Albert and Alfred Stratton in Deptford High Street the night of the murder. These two were well-known local young roughs, certainly capable of violent crime. They were both prostitute's bullies, living off the earnings of their 'lady friends'.

3.11 Two unflattering drawings of the murderous Brothers Stratton.

It turned out that Alfred had been 'running' a certain Hannah Cromarty, who claimed to be pregnant with his child. This state of affairs had not prevented him from taking a generous proportion of her immoral earnings, or disciplining her using his fists. When Hannah was questioned by the police, she sported a black eye, administered by Alfred the day before the murder. At midnight, she had heard Alfred speaking to some person outside, saying 'Shall we go out tonight, or leave it for some other night?' The following day, after the murder, he had cleaned his trousers using paraffin, and put blacking on his brown boots. All of a sudden, Alfred also had plenty of money, purchasing food, coal, and even a daily newspaper.

When the two Strattons were arrested, they seemed as tough as ever. After being 'nabbed' in Deptford High Street, Albert calmly said 'Is that all?' when he was charged with the murder of the Farrows, and the theft of their savings of £13. The idea that a fingerprint could be useful to identify a murderer seemed very droll to the two Strattons, but the print on the cash-box matched Alfred's thumb exactly. As the police kept accumulating evidence against the two young ruffians in custody, Albert became apprehensive. Fearful of a long prison sentence, he asked the assistant gaoler what he thought of his chances, but this individual did not hazard a guess. After checking that his brother was not listening, Alfred then said, rather callously, 'I reckon *he* will get strung up, and I shall get about ten years!

This unwise blabbering to the gaoler did not do the Stratton brothers any good when they were on trial at the Old Bailey for the wilful murder of Thomas and Anna Farrow. The evidence against them, which included the thumb-print on the cash-box, seemed rock solid: they were found guilty, sentenced to death, and executed at Wandsworth Prison on May 23 1905. Not many people know that the rather nondescript shop at No. 34 of the busy Deptford High Street is a memorial to a sordid murder for profit, which led to the first murder trial in Britain where fingerprint evidence played a crucial part.[8]

As for poor Hannah Cromarty, who had bravely given evidence against the two murderous ruffians, she turned out to be pregnant with Alfred Stratton's child. After she had suffered a miscarriage, there was a good deal of newspaper sympathy for her, and George R. Sims made an appeal to the charitable Londoners to have her sent to Canada to start a new life. Sims was later dismayed to find that Hannah had quickly returned to Deptford, where she was arrested by the police after making a disturbance outside the murder house at No. 34 Deptford High Street.[9]

MURDER IN BOVILL ROAD, 1905

Albert Edward Thompson was a house-painter living at No. 96 Bovill Road, Forest Hill, with his wife and four children. He was fond of having a drink or two, but respectable and hard-working. In 1904, the Thompsons took a lodger, a respectable woman named Alice Fisher. Mrs Florence Thompson became good friends with her lodger, and they often went out together, shopping and amusing themselves. In early February 1905, the 41-year-old Bert Thompson had had enough. He sternly reminded Florence that the right place for a wife was at home, and not at the music halls. She responded that she should go out when she liked, and an angry quarrel ensued. A few days later, when Bert was at work, both Florence and Alice Fisher moved out of No. 96 Bovill Road, for good.

Bert must have regretted his harsh words to his wife when he realized that she had deserted him and the children. He had their 18-year-old daughter Rose deliver some pathetic letters to his wife, care of Alice Fisher, to persuade her to return to No. 96 Bovill Road. Their three younger sons were badly ill, lying in bed and sobbing 'Mummy, please come home!', and even the family cat was mourning her absence. But Florence Thompson, who was making a career as a professional nurse, did not reply to these letters. But when Bert claimed that their son Frederick was in fact dying, she did return to No. 96 Bovill Road when Bert was at work. Being a competent nurse, she could see that although the boy was in bed, there was nothing much wrong with him. When Bert came home from work, the elegantly dressed Florence told him that she would never return to the humdrum life at No. 96 Bovill Road: she would make her living by nursing, and sue for a separation without maintenance. With the outcry 'If that is so, then my life is ended!' Bert ran into the kitchen, fetched a knife, and stabbed Florence hard in the neck, killing her instantly. Their daughter Rose, an eyewitness to the murderous attack, ran out of the house screaming.

Rose managed to attract the attention of Police Constable Alfred Aldridge, who took Bert Thompson into custody. The pathetic wife-killer signed and exclaimed "It is quite true what my daughter has told you. I have cut my wife's throat and now she is settled with; I do not care what becomes of myself." When Bert Thompson was on trial for murder at the Old Bailey, before Mr Justice Darling, there were further painful scenes when the Thompson children gave evidence against their father. Alice Fisher delivered some very damning evidence, saying that Bert had been a drunkard who had ill-treated his wife with regularity. The defence barrister Mr Lawless recalled the children, who completely denied these allegations. Their father had always been very fond of their mother, and also kind to themselves; he drank only sparingly, and ate very little food after their mother had left. Mr Lawless further shook Alice Fisher's credibility by exposing that prior to moving into No. 96 Bovill

Road, she had lived with a man who was a convicted thief. There was a fair amount of newspaper publicity about this obscure suburban murder, due to the prisoner's pathetic exhortations, and the various spicy revelations in court. The *Penny Illustrated Paper* even reproduced a grainy photograph of the murder house, looking very much like it does today.

To save Bert Thompson from the gallows, Mr Lawless asked the jury to consider a charge of manslaughter, but the stern Mr Justice Darling reminded him that he was asking the jurymen to deliberately violate their oath. The charge was one of murder, and this was quite a monstrous address to a jury. The jury accordingly found Albert Edward Thompson guilty of murder, but with the strongest possible recommendation to mercy. Mr Justice Darling sentenced him to death, but when he said that he would himself support the recommendation to mercy, the prisoner exclaimed 'Thank you, my lord!' Albert Edward Thompson was duly reprieved by the Home Secretary, disappearing into a prison cell, and obscurity.[10]

THE LEWISHAM MYSTERY, 1908

Just where Loampit Vale, Lewisham, changes its name to Loampit Hill, there is a small terrace of four narrow houses, probably a good deal older than the surrounding ones. In 1908, the 40-year-old repairing tailor George Hume lived in one of these little houses, No. 3 Loampit Hill, with his 27-year-old wife Bertha and their young son. He had been a soldier, serving in India and South Africa, but had been invalided out of the army after suffering sunstroke. Hume had opened a tailor's shop in Hither Green Lane, but it had failed miserably. In 1908, Hume gave up the lease and moved his tailoring utensils back home to No. 3

Loampit Hill, where he opened a makeshift tailor's shop in the front room.

After his tailoring business had failed, George Hume became increasingly dejected and morose. He had always been a heavy drinker, but now he spent more time in the public houses than in his humble little tailor's shop at Loampit Hill. Although he had made sure that the front of No. 3 was adorned with signs saying 'G. Hume, Repairing Tailor', he often deserted the shop to go drinking, leaving his wife Bertha in charge. She of course objected to his drunken habits, and there were several quarrels. On November 13 1908, Mr David Sterry, one of George Hume's few remaining customers, came to No. 3 Loampit Hill to deliver a coat he wanted to have mended. George was complaining that his wife had been away all afternoon, and that he had not had any tea. Just as Sterry left, she arrived home. Two days later, the neighbour Fanny Willcox, living at No. 5 Loampit Hill, saw George and Bertha with their little boy. The next day, she again saw George sweeping the doorstep up to his shop. She asked him 'How is the missus?' and he replied that she was poorly and that he had just given her some medicine. Later the same day, the concerned Mrs Willcox again approached her neighbour, but this time he told her his wife had gone away.

Mr Sterry met George Hume in the street on November 16, asking him if his coat was ready. Hume replied "No, I've done my bloody lot in! Come and have a drink, and I'll tell you something that will surprise you." Seeing that Hume was already quite inebriated, Sterry declined this invitation. Later the same day, the off-duty police constable John Smith saw Hume walking down Lewisham High Street, quite drunk and leading his little son by the hand. When asked what he was doing, Hume replied 'I'm going to give the little bugger a wash!' Constable Smith thought Hume quite unfit to look after a child, and took him into custody.

On the way to the police station, the impoverished tailor made various more or less confused utterances, one of them being 'I suppose you think you have got a decent job?' directed at the policeman. He several times pointed at the opposite pavement, saying 'Look at them; they are making dumb motions at me!' although there was no person to be seen. At the police station, Inspector Cornelius Garner thought Hume quite insane, and he was sent to the Mental Ward of Lewisham Infirmary. At the Mental Ward, the attendant John McArdell noted that George Hume smelt strongly of drink and seemed quite confused. When his pockets were searched on arrival, two gold rings were found.

But as George Hume sat gibbering in the Mental Ward, his father-in-law William Curtis came to No. 3 Loampit Hill to see his daughter. Since there seemed to be no one at home, he broke down the ramshackle front door. In the front room, used as Hume's workshop, there were cuts in the linoleum carpet, and some of the floorboards seemed quite loose. There was a very unpleasant smell in the room. When Mr Curtis called at the police station, Inspector Garner remembered the drunken tailor George Hume who seemed to have lost his reason. He went to see Hume at the Mental Ward, and although the lunatic himself had nothing worthwhile to contribute, the attendants told him about the gold rings found in Hume's pocket. Furthermore, Hume had been making incoherent statements about the fidelity of his wife and the paternity of his child. Inspector Garner returned to No. 3 Loampit Hill, where he removed the linoleum carpet and lifted the floorboards. Underneath them was the fully clothed body of Bertha Hume. She had been strangled with a piece of string tied tightly around her neck. Remarkably, the police file on Hume at the National Archives contains a mounted photograph of this horrid spectacle, the body lying next to the lifted floorboards. When arrested by the police at the Mental Ward, for the suspected

3.12 The discovery of the body of Mrs Hume underneath the floorboards, from the Illustrated Police News, November 28 1908. Note the drawing of the murder house.

murder of his wife, Hume seemed quite surprised, saying 'I almost forgot all about it! If I had not been jealous of her it would not have happened, but I could not stand the disgrace. I knew I had done something and I was going to give myself up.'

The trial of George Hume at the Old Bailey for the murder of his wife was not a lengthy affair. The various witnesses described his activities the days around the murder, the police

3.13 The discovery of the murder, and another image of the murder house in Loampit Hill, from the Illustrated Police Budget, November 28 1908.

3.14 A postcard of Loampit Hill, stamped and posted in 1904, clearly showing the murder house at No. 3 in the small terrace to the left.

inspector gave an account of how the body of the murdered woman had been found, and the medical officer of Brixton Prison, who had kept Hume under observation, gave his opinion that the prisoner had genuine insane delusions, and was not responsible for his actions. George Hume was duly detained at Broadmoor, but was released eleven years later.[11] Hopefully, he did not return to the house at No. 3 Loampit Hill, to dispose of another wife underneath the floorboards. The murder house is still standing, and its external aspect is virtually unchanged since 1908, apart from the windows being replaced and the signs of 'G. Hume, Repairing Tailor' removed.

MURDER BY A LEWISHAM LUNATIC, 1919

Mr John William Prickett, a respectable Lewisham journeyman carpenter, lived at No. 25 Blagdon Road, with his unmarried son John George and the middle-aged lodger Mrs Priscilla Bacon. Mrs Bacon, a widow, counted as a family friend. Young John George Prickett was something of a weirdo, however. He had suffered from a disease suspected to have been syphilis, and this had made him 'odd in the head'. During a brief period of military service in 1918, he had spent much time in various hospitals with headaches and influenza. Demobilized in January 1919, he returned to his old job as an assistant clerk at Somerset House, but not for very long: unspecified after effects of the influenza forced him to give up his job in July. Mr Prickett noticed that John seemed very gloomy and morose. After he had gone to bed and refused all meals, a doctor was called in, and the invalid was removed to Greenwich Infirmary for two weeks of bed rest.

John George Prickett returned home on August 6, but his mental state had not improved. Two days later, he left home, leaving a note for his sister Florence, who was a nursing sister at the Bermondsey Military Hospital, that he intended to drown himself. Florence Prickett and her brother Harry searched the Thames embankments, but without finding John George. But the following day, the invalid was found at Sundridge Infirmary, where he had been taken after drinking acid. On August 20, he was discharged back home to No. 25 Blagdon Road, awaiting trial for attempting suicide. On the following morning, Mr Prickett went to work at 5.30 am, leaving John George in the house with Mrs Bacon.

When Mr Prickett returned home, he saw that water had been leaking from the bathtub upstairs. Going up to investigate, he found the body of Mrs Bacon in the bath. She had been hit hard five times with an iron bar, before being drowned. When Detective Inspector James Pulle came to No. 25 Blagdon Road, along with Dr Robert Donnellan, it was clear to them that this was a case of murder. The obvious suspect was of course the unbalanced John George Prickett, and it turned out to be far from difficult to find him: an hour earlier, he had walked into Blackheath police station and confessed the murder to the sergeant on duty. His shirt was stained with blood, and the murder weapon, a heavy iron bar, was found on a rack in the kitchen.

"Dead Woman in Bath! Mysterious Crime in Lewisham!" exclaimed the headline of the *Daily Express* when reporting on the inquest on Priscilla Bacon, but there was really little that was mysterious about this sordid crime in a quiet South London back street. John George Prickett was clearly far from sane, and he freely admitted murdering the family lodger, although he failed to provide a credible motive, apart from that he had been aiming to destroy himself afterwards. The inquest returned a verdict of wilful murder against young Prickett, but before he went on trial at the Old Bailey, on September 10, he had been thoroughly examined by the medical officer at HMP Brixton, Dr G.B.

Griffith. It was clear to the doctor that John George Prickett was suffering from deep depression. He took no interest in his present precarious position; in fact, he wanted to be hanged. He said that after the painful experience of drinking acid, he had been fearful of making any further rash attempts at suicide; the best way was instead to murder some person, and then he would be executed himself! When Dr Griffith said that this was rather hard on the murder victim, Prickett replied that she had been a nice old woman, and that he had gone to church with her. The outcome of the trial was that John George Prickett was found guilty but insane, and he was incarcerated in Broadmoor.[12] Old Mr Prickett remained in the murder house well into the 1920s. He was still alive in 1930, when his son was released from Broadmoor, without causing any further criminal mayhem.

THE NEW CROSS GATE SHOP MURDER, 1934

In 1934, Mr Robert James Venner had been the manager of Henry Cohen's Tailor Shop at No. 187-9 New Cross Road for not less than 26 years. A tall, pipe-smoking, 55-year-old man, he kept long hours tending the shop, but was paid a less than impressive salary. Although he had money enough for his daily needs, he was unable to save money, or to afford purchasing anything interesting or valuable.

On the evening of July 6 1934, Robert James Venner was working at the tailor's shop as usual. At 6.20 pm, when the shop was still open, a passer-by saw him staggering about inside the shop, his head covered with blood. He had been hit repeatedly over the head, presumably with an iron bar. Five days later, he died from his injuries at the Miller General Hospital, Greenwich, without regaining consciousness, and a murder investigation

3.15 A postcard showing New Cross Gate.

began. The motive was supposed to have been robbery, since around £7 had been stolen from the shop till. There was newspaper speculation that the mark of 'X' in blood inside the shop had some sinister significance, or that the last thing Venner had done before the assault had been to measure his killer for a suit, meaning that his measurements were entered into the shop ledger.

The murder shop was (and still is) situated just by busy New Cross Gate, where there were several tram and omnibus stands, and plenty of people about. One witness had seen a man leave Venner's shop, hiding something underneath his coat; another had observed three men, one of whom was exceptionally pale, exiting the shop. A light-blue saloon car observed nearby might well have been the murderers' getaway car. Numerous other witnesses had seen mysterious men lurking about, but their descriptions varied wildly. The police believed the murder of Robert James Venner was a robbery gone wrong. One or two men had entered the shop to steal the contents of the till, and when

3.16 Venner is found murdered, and a sketch of the murder shop at No. 187-9 New Cross Gate, from the Illustrated Police News, July 19 1934.

Venner tried to intervene, they had 'coshed' him hard enough to kill, and brought the murder weapon with them. Another man had been the lookout outside the shop, and yet another accomplice might well have been driving the getaway car. The local detectives tried to put pressure on their police informants, but these mischievous individuals had little worthwhile to contribute, except to 'squeal' on various old enemies to 'frame' them for the 'New Cross Job'.

The police soon found their main suspect. A 'spiv' and racing tipster named Joseph Neale had turned up with an amazing story of seeing three men leaving the murder shop, and blood seeping under its door. He had tried to sell this story to the newspapers before contacting the police. Neale was soon a suspect himself, since he was a known thief and violent criminal, who associated with all kinds of unsavoury types. He had spoken to his estranged wife about being 'the outside man' in the New Cross Gate 'job', and threatened her with violence if she went to the police (as she later did, nevertheless). The police informant Frederick Evans was not surprised that Neale had been involved in the Venner case. He named Neale's two accomplices as 'Flash Joe' and 'Charlie the Navvy', also known as Joseph Gibbons and Charles Nougher. All these three were hardened criminals, certainly capable of planning and carrying out an armed robbery. Neither of them had an alibi, although Lougher had tried to persuade a fellow lodger to give him one. Neale's account of seeing blood running underneath the shop door was impossible, since the doorway was lower than the pavement. The measurements in the shop order book fitted Neale, but they also fitted thousands of other Londoners, and if Neale had been inside the shop, then his ex-wife's story of him admitting to being the 'outside man' was a fabrication.

All three suspects were taken into police custody, and a series of identity parades were carried out, but none of the ten crime scene witnesses could pick them out. No bloodstains were found on their clothes, or in Neale's car, and there was no other worthwhile technical evidence against the three suspects. The all stoutly denied any involvement in the murder of Robert James Venner, and the 'squealer' Evans refused to make an official statement against them, perhaps indicating that his original account had been less than truthful. After all, Evans was himself a thief with nine convictions against him. And if Neale had been the mastermind behind the robbery turned murder, then why would he have gone blabbering about it to his estranged wife, and to some complete strangers? In the end, although the police detectives remained convinced that Joseph Neale and his two associates were involved in the murder, they lacked sufficient evidence to prosecute them.

The police file on the New Cross Gate murder was kept open for several years to come. A prisoner named Pearson implicated a thief named Alfred Arthur Bailey, who had made various allusions to the 'New Cross Job' while serving a sentence at Pentonville Prison. Since Bailey was a serious villain, another set of identity parades was arranged, again with a negative result. In 1935, a police informant pointed the finger at the Welsh labourer Sammy James, a native of Treforest. He had a long list of convictions for assault and petty crime, but was able to clear himself with regard to the murder of Robert James Venner. As late as 1941, a Watford police informant claimed that an old charwoman had implicated that the young labouring man Rodney Pharoah had been involved in the New Cross shop murder, but this tip proved entirely unreliable, and the police file on the case was finally closed, for good.[13] Today, the former tailor's shop at No. 187-9 New Cross Road, the only memorial to this unsolved murder mystery from 1934, is home to the 'Costcutter' supermarket.

THE MURDER OF SHEILA WILSON, 1942

Sheila Margaret Wilson was an eleven-year-old girl, living at No. 67 Leahurst Road, Lewisham, with her parents and younger brother. She had been evacuated to Dorset for a while in 1941, but moved back home in May 1942. Her father was away working in a demolition project in Wiltshire, but Sheila's mother looked after her. In spite of the war, the children were out playing in the street. Sheila was old enough to look after herself, her mother reasoned, and she was allowed to run errands, and to play with her various friends. But on July 15 1942, Sheila disappeared. She had been out playing earlier in the day, and then made an expedition to buy sweets, from which she did not return. Her mother, Mrs Edith Margaret Wilson, called in the police a few hours later. A posse of neighbours and A.R.P workers made a search of bombed houses nearby, but found nothing.

In spite of there being a war on, there was much newspaper interest in the 'Girl in Green' case, so called because Sheila had been wearing a green dress at the time she disappeared. According to a newspaper description, Sheila was four feet five inches tall, with fair hair, rosy cheeks, and blue eyes. One of her playmates told a journalist that Sheila had said that she would be visiting a man in Greenwich, but the police were sceptical. They thought the solution to the disappearance lay closer to home, and undertook door-to-door searches of the humble little Lewisham terraces near Leahurst Road. There was much uproar locally, and all children were kept indoors. On July 20, Detective Inspector Chapman and a party of police went to search a small lodging house at No. 19 Leahurst Road, just 23 doors away from the Wilson family home. They were told that one of the lodgers, the 38-year-old former A.R.P. stretcher bearer Patrick William Kingston, had moved out just after Sheila had disappeared. This sounded promising, they thought, and Kingston's room was thoroughly searched. Underneath the floorboards were the remains of little Sheila, who had been raped and then strangled to death.

The owners of the lodging-house, Mr and Mrs Hyder, faced some searching questions from the detectives, but they were able to prove that they had known nothing about their lodger's sinister activities. Instead, the police issued a description and a photograph of the main suspect Patrick William Kingston, a dodgy-looking cove with dishevelled dark hair. He walked with a limp and lacked part of his left index finger, after being blown up while on duty with the A.R.P. He was likely to be wearing a shabby dark brown pinstripe suit. Sheila's father returned from Wiltshire and personally took part in the hue and cry, scouring the London streets all day for the fugitive. But it was one of the regular policemen who collared Kingston when he inexplicably returned to Leahurst Road on July 23. When arrested, he blurted out 'I strangled her, and then I got scared and went away!'

Patrick William Kingston, who was considered sane and fit to plead, stood trial for the murder of Sheila Wilson at the Central Criminal Court on September 14 1942, before Mr Justice Hallett. The trial would become famous for being one of the shortest murder trials on record, lasting less than five minutes: Kingston willingly pleaded guilty, and was sentenced to death. There was neither pity nor mercy for the kind of creature he represented, and he was hanged at Wandsworth Prison on October 6.[14]

The *Sunday Pictorial*, a low-quality sensation newspaper that flourished at the time, provided a distasteful postscript to this sad instalment in London's annals of murder. They wanted to investigate whether little Sheila could communicate from the Great Beyond, and poor Mrs Wilson, who had a liking for spiritualism, took them up on their offer. The medium Estelle Roberts soon made contact with Sheila's spirit. The murdered girl described how she had been strangled, said goodbye to her friends, and asked what had happened to her favourite shoes. And indeed, Mrs Wilson had just given Sheila's red dancing shoes away! 'Cor blimey!' many a reader of the *Pictorial* must have exclaimed at this startling revelation from the spiritual world.[15] But today, the sole memento of this forgotten murder and outrage is the little house at No. 19 Leahurst Road.

MAN OF 78 ON MURDER CHARGE, 1942

Samuel William Elbra was born in Blackfriars in 1864. He became a labouring man in the Woolwich district, married his wife Annie in 1886, and may well have had offspring. In 1900, he was an inpatient in Cane Hill Asylum, receiving treatment for 'mania'. The year after, he deserted his family and went to New Zealand to join his mother. He worked as a gold miner for quite some time, before joining the Otago New Zealand Infantry in 1914. He served in Egypt and France, but his conduct was extremely poor, and his military record marred by constant drunkenness and insubordination. He was eventually invalided out of the army due to 'mental stupor and debility' and granted a pension of ten shillings a week. Throughout the 1920s and 1930s, Elbra drifted in and out of various hospitals, asylums, and institutions for the unemployed. He worked as a jobbing gardener when he felt like it, which was not particularly often, and sometimes 'busked' in the street with his banjo.

In 1941, when Samuel Elbra was 77 years old, he was still in good shape physically, and very strong. In December that year, he moved into the ground floor front room in a small lodging-house at No. 9 Rippolson Road, Plumstead. It was kept by the 68-year-old Mrs Elizabeth Jane Buckenham, a sturdy, cantankerous woman with a great fondness for drinking beer and gin. Elbra soon became the lodging-house bully, intimidating the drunken old men who lived there, and once giving Mrs Buckenham a hard knock in the face when she came asking for the weekly rent. At night, he sometimes marched around in the house, playing his banjo and singing in a stentorous voice. The police were called to No. 9 Rippolson Road on at least two occasions: after the assault on Mrs Buckenham, and after one of Elbra's nocturnal concerts, but they thought the drunken old soldier a harmless eccentric, and took no further action. Since Elbra had more than once threatened to murder her, and since the police had not been of any help, Mrs Buckenham gave him notice that he had to leave.

On July 2 1942, Mrs Buckenham caught Samuel Elbra pilfering food in the larder. 'You there again!' she cried out, and tried to give him a knock, but since she was much the worse for drink, Elbra dodged her blow. He seized up a large broom and began hitting her on the head with a hearty goodwill, until she collapsed in a heap on the floor. He then proceeded to cut her head off with a sharp kitchen knife, dismember the body, and bury the remains in the kitchen garden. He stole all the food and drink in the house, and enjoyed a hearty meal in his room. Since he had lit a fire in the grate to burn Mrs Buckenham's clothes and some other incriminating evidence, the police soon came calling after they had seen smoke emanating from the front window. Elbra was at his best behaviour, however, apologizing for his over-exuberance in stoking the fire, and the police once more left the house without taking any action. When Mrs Buckenham's son-in-law came calling on July 3, he found Elbra asleep in his room, having eaten and drunk well. The old man said that Mrs Buckenham might well have gone away for a few days, but his manner seemed odd. One of the other lodgers had seen Elbra digging in the garden, and when the son-in-law went to inspect the kitchen plot, he saw Mrs Buckenham's thighbone sticking up between the carrots and cabbages.

When charged with murdering Elizabeth Jane Buckenham, Samuel Elbra showed no remorse whatsoever: indeed, he exclaimed 'I was proud to get rid of such rubbish from the streets!' The brutality of the Rippolson Road murder, and the age of the presumed murderer, meant that there was some degree of newspaper interest: 'Man of 78 on Murder Charge!' exclaimed the headline of the *Evening Telegraph*. But Samuel Elbra never made it to the Central Criminal Court. He seemed quite insane, and after the doctors at Brixton Prison had seen evidence of his 42-year history of psychiatric disease, he was found insane and unfit to plead.[16] The Rippolson Road murderer died at Broadmoor in 1947, aged 83.

THE CERES ROAD MATRICIDE, 1957

In 1954, the middle-aged Woolwich Arsenal workman Mr Absalom Chesson married Mrs Marie Frith, a widow with two adult children. One of these children, Thomas Frith, was himself a married man with a family of his own, but his brother Albert was a weirdo who was still living with his mother at the age of 37. He could not hold a job for more than a month or two, and had a mania for walking. He could walk 30 miles in a day to go visiting his brother, of whom he was very fond. When Albert went on the tramp, he travelled even further, sleeping rough in parks and gardens, before returning home very tired and footsore. Even though Albert had his own bedroom in the family flat at No. 97 Ceres Road, Plumstead, he preferred sleeping in the garden, weather allowing. His eccentric manner, excessive pedestrianism, and reluctance to wash, must have made him quite a cross to bear for the Chessons, but nevertheless, his mother was very fond of him.

On August 27 1957, Mr Chesson went to work as usual at 6.20 in the morning. Just as he left home, Albert came lurching in from the garden to have his breakfast. Mr Chesson had noticed that recently, his wife had been more worried that usual about Albert's strange behaviour, although the weirdo seemed his usual truculent self. A few hours later, Mr Frederick Davies, who owned the house at No. 97 Ceres Road, and sub-let three rooms to the

Chessons, could hear Mrs Chesson and Albert quarrelling angrily. He heard Albert raving about needing new shoes, since his excessive walking had worn out all his other pairs. Then there was a series of heavy thuds, the sound of a falling body, and silence from Mrs Chesson. Albert came running downstairs, out through the front door. Fearful that Albert had injured his mother, Mr Davies made his way upstairs. To his horror, the landlord found Marie Chesson lying dead on the floor, with extensive head injuries. Then the door opened and Albert stood there staring at him. Not having time to appreciate that he might well be looking at a murderer intent on eliminating a key witness, Mr Davies told Albert to fetch a doctor, but the weirdo just ran away. Dr Bertha Roche was eventually called in, but all she could do was to declare Mrs Marie Chesson, a large and sturdy woman, dead from severe trauma to the head. The murder weapon, a blood-stained flatiron, was found nearby.

It was clear to the police detectives that Albert Frith must have beaten his own mother to death. They issued a description of him, illustrated with a distinctively unflattering photograph: the Ceres Road suspect was a dirty, unshaven cove looking very much like a tramp, and wearing a raincoat, an old hat, and a pair of very worn shoes. A number of tramps and raincoated 'flashers' were rounded up by the police, but remarkably, there was no trace of Albert Frith. For a person believed to be of mediocre intelligence, Albert was dodging the police with surprising success: more than two weeks after Marie Chesson had been murdered, he was still on the run. Before the murder he had spoken confusedly about joining the French Foreign Legion, or of purchasing a small boat and sailing it to Africa, but the police did not think the penniless fugitive capable of such ambitious endeavours.

On September 12 1957, a young police constable saw a dodgy-looking cove approaching the Tooting Slipper Baths. He was wearing a dirty raincoat, and his shoes were extremely worn. The canny constable waited outside the baths, and when the suspect came out, he was asked to identify himself. The tramp produced a sicknote with the name 'Herbert Frederick Till', but the constable did not believe him. When challenged that he was Albert Frith, the suspect broke free and ran away, but only to be recaptured by two other constables in a police car.

With the main suspect safely behind bars, the search for a motive for the brutal murder of Marie Chesson began. Mr Chesson said that in order to curb her son's fondness for walking, she had refused to buy him new shoes, something Albert had resented very much. Looking into Albert's antecedents, a psychiatrist found that he had been diagnosed with schizophrenia already after a brief military career in 1941. He had been an inpatient in Bexley Mental Hospital in 1954-5 after an unprovoked assault on a coffee stall owner. But when examined by the psychiatrist, Albert Frith was considered fit to plead. On trial for murder at the Old Bailey, it was obvious that Albert Frith was far from sane, but on the other hand, he had shown impressive cunning and fortitude while on the run, and had not been far from hoodwinking the inquisitive Tooting constable. His crime had not been premeditated, but was the product of a sudden rage, but on the other hand, he had murdered his own mother in a very brutal manner. In the end, Albert Frith was found guilty of manslaughter, and sentenced to seven years in prison.[17] He served his time, emerged from prison, and eventually died in Greenwich in 1970.

THE MURDER OF MAXWELL CONFAIT, 1972

Back in 1972, the household at No. 27 Doggett Road, Catford, was a very queer one. The owner of the house, the West Indian metal worker Winston Goode, had quarrelled with his wife, and taken up permanent residence on the lower ground floor. His estranged wife lived on the ground floor, with their five children. On the first floor lived the lodger, the 26-year-old homosexual transvestite Maxwell Confait, who called himself 'Michelle'. The bisexual Winston Goode had met him in a gay club and invited him back to No. 27. Mrs Goode cooked for herself and the children, but she wanted nothing to do with the other two inhabitants of the house; after a long day at the metal works, Winston Goode had to share some cheap junk food with Michelle in his basement flat.

Whereas both the Goodes were hard-working people, Michelle was no friend of hard graft. He sat all day in his tiny room, listening to the squalling of the Goode children, and the endless rumble of the trains going back and forth to busy Catford Bridge Station, and perhaps dreaming that this evening, he would meet the man of his life. But each day, this dream became increasingly distant, particularly after he had resorted to prostituting himself. The blokes he picked up on his night-time prowls in central London were not particularly nice: sometimes, he was beaten up by 'rough trade', and at other times, he was arrested by the police for being a street pest. Michelle's hair and teeth were falling fast, but in his wig he could still impersonate a reasonably pretty woman. In contrast, his landlord Winston Goode cut such a ludicrous figure in female attire that most of his cross-dressing activities were confined to the lower ground floor premises at No. 27 Doggett Road.

In the wee hours of April 22 1972, smoke was emerging from No. 27 Doggett Road. The Fire Brigade acted with its usual efficiency, extinguishing the flames that were emanating from the stairs, and from Maxwell Confait's tiny first floor room. On the floor of the smoke-filled room, the firemen stumbled on the dead body of its inhabitant, strangled to death with some wire flex. Medical examination showed that the cause of death had been asphyxia. Crucially, the rectal temperature of the body was not measured, allegedly to preserve evidence of recent sexual activity, meaning that the exact time of death could not be determined.

Initially, the main suspect in the murder investigation was Winston Goode. When first questioned by the police, he claimed to have been woken up by the crackling of the fire at about 1 am. He had dashed upstairs to save his wife and children, before calling the Fire Brigade from a telephone box. But here he was lying, since the Fire Brigade had in fact been called by a neighbour roused by Mrs Goode. And why, if Goode had dashed upstairs in a great hurry, was he fully dressed when the firemen arrived? Both Mrs Goode and the Fire Station Officer thought his behaviour at the scene very odd indeed, like if he had just been through something much worse than finding his house on fire. Earlier the day of the murder, Mrs Goode had heard a voice scream 'I've a good mind to gas all of you and leave you!' in the downstairs flat. Had the volatile Winston Goode murdered his boyfriend, after the faithless Michelle had decided to leave him for another man? Goode was harshly questioned by the police, but made no admission of guilt. A few days later, he was admitted to Bexley Psychiatric Hospital, in a very confused state.

As Winston Goode was languishing in the Bexley asylum, the police investigation of the murder of Maxwell Confait took an entirely different turn. A gang of teenage hooligans had been starting fires in the neighbourhood of Doggett Road. The 18-year-old Colin Lattimore had been observed near one of these fires. When routinely picked up and questioned by the police, he admitted not just starting the fires, but also murdering Maxwell Confait! His two accomplices had been the 15-year-old Ronald Leighton and the 14-year-old Ahmed Salih. They had got into

No. 27 Doggett Road 'through the side door' [there was none accessible], ran upstairs, murdered Maxwell Confait just for the fun of it, lit a fire using paraffin [it had been done with petrol] and then extinguished it [the fire had been burning merrily when the firemen arrived]. Although Colin Lattimore was quite feeble-minded, with a mental age of eight, and although Leighton was an under-age dullard, the police kept on grilling the boys, without the presence of a parent or solicitor, until confessions had been extracted from all three. The boys later alleged that they had been struck and pushed around to make them confess.

Winston Goode now quite forgotten, all three boys were charged with the murder of Maxwell Confait. When they were on trial at the Old Bailey, Mr Justice Chapman described the murdered man to the jury with the remarkable words: "he was an odd creature, and indeed it may even be your view that he has been no great loss to this world." This far from bonhomous judge was also quite hostile to the three accused boys in his summing-up. He made it clear that he regarded the arguments incriminating Goode as little more than a defence ploy, and obtusely commented that if this decent, hard-working man had recently taken out an insurance policy for No. 27 Doggett Road, then why would he want to burn it down? In the end, Colin Lattimore was found guilty of manslaughter and arson, and confined to a mental hospital without a time limit. Ronald Leighton was found guilty of murder, arson and burglary and sentenced to imprisonment for life. Ahmed Salih was found guilty of arson and burglary, and sentenced to serve four years in a juvenile prison. Harsh sentences indeed, on some very flimsy evidence.

As the three boys were rattling the bars of their prison cells, Colin Lattimore's father started a campaign against what he perceived as an unparalleled miscarriage of justice. He knew that his son was not capable of committing wilful murder. In May

1974, the troubled Winston Goode committed suicide by drinking a massive dose of cyanide, taking the secrets of the Doggett Road murder mystery with him to the grave. The following year, Mrs Goode spoke out in the media, saying that Goode had once tried to kill her, and that she was certain that he had started the fire and murdered Maxwell Confait. In October 1975, Mr Lattimore finally succeeded in getting the case reheard in front of a Court of Appeal. The absence of a good estimate of the time of death proved a crucial point. The two distinguished forensic specialists Keith Simpson and Donald Teare suggested that Confait might well have been murdered much earlier than previously presumed, at a time when the boys had solid alibis. Accordingly, they were all freed, and considerable odium was heaped upon the Catford detectives, Detective Chief Superintendent Alan Jones in particular, and on the overly severe Mr Justice Simpson.[18]

The Confait case was everything that a police-bashing 1970s 'leftie' journalist could have asked for, and its reverberations would continue for many years to come. In 1978, the former High Court Judge Sir Henry Fisher chaired a commission that looked into the handling of the case. Controversially, he stated that despite being freed by the Court of Appeal, two of the boys were still "guilty on balance of probability".[19] But in the meantime, the police investigation had resumed, led by Detective Chief Superintendent John George. In a report submitted to the Director of Public Prosecutions, he identified a man named Douglas Franklin as Confait's murderer and another man, Paul Pooley, as a witness to the murder. These two had confessed to being present when Confait was murdered, although they denied committing the crime themselves. One of them was already serving a ten-year prison sentence, and Franklin committed suicide soon after being questioned by the detectives, meaning that he was never prosecuted. Importantly, John George proposed that Confait had been dead for more than 48 hours when found, implying that both the early police investigation and the medical report on the corpse had been deeply flawed. In 1980, another inquiry led by the Attorney General, Sir Michael Havers, proclaimed the three boys to have been wholly innocent of the murder. The following year, they received a total of £65000 in compensation.[20]

The murmurations from the Catford detectives continued, however, since they remained convinced of the guilt of the three boys. They disbelieved John George's story of the two men, and thought it quite suspicious that the main suspect was a dead man. As for Sir Henry Fisher, he stubbornly refused to concur with the Havers report, although being tarred with the same brush as the detectives in the press. In 1980, the journalists Jonathan Caplan and Christopher Price, who had criticized the police in their spicy book *The Confait Confessions*, had to apologize to Alan Jones for the book's contents. As late as 1983, another senior detective, Commander Graham Stockwell, took considerable damages off the left-wing *New Statesman*, one of whose journalists had been too cheeky when trying to blame him for the Confait fiasco.[21]

So, who murdered Maxwell Confait? The case against the three boys does not appear strong, and it is reasonable to suggest that the police extracted confessions from the foolish, suggestible youngsters, perhaps using questionable methods in doing so. But according to a 1985 newspaper report, the now 32-year-old Colin Lattimore gave evidence how a fire had started in his brother's flat, killing one of his nephews and badly burning another.[22] Although he was not criminally prosecuted, this story certainly provides food for thought: had the Catford detectives been right all along, or was Lattimore just abnormally accident-prone? The story about Franklin and Pooley is hard to evaluate, but reading between the lines, it seems reasonable to suggest that these two were also homosexuals, and that Confait may well have died as the result of a bondage sex game going wrong. Nor is there any reason to exonerate Winston Goode, who had both motive and opportunity to murder Confait. He lied about his activities on the night of the murder, and his wife believed him to be the guilty man.

As for the murder house at No. 27 Doggett Road, there have been rumours that Confait's first-floor room was haunted. Groans and bumps in the night were regularly reported by the next inhabitants of the house. In 1985, a team of paranormal investigators is said to have stayed at the premises overnight, and photographed 'orbs' in the murder room. But today, No. 27 Doggett Road looks like an ordinary Catford house. With the railway on one side and a busy road on the other, and aeroplanes flying past above, any self-respecting ghost must have been exorcised long ago.

S1-1 No. 13 and 14 Addington Square, Camberwell, where Mary Gorman Watson was murdered by an unknown assailant in 1863.

S1-2 The former bakery at No. 151 Borough High Street, site of the unsolved murder of Jane Soper in 1875.

S1-3 The side door to the shop at No.151 Borough High Street has been firmly secured, 139 years after the murderer bolted.

S1-4 No. 81 [today No. 49] Grosvenor Park, where James Banbury murdered Emma Oakley in 1891.

S1-5 The former Crown public house at No. 213 Borough High Street, where George Chapman murdered Maud Marsh in 1903.

S1-6 No. 70 Camberwell Church Street, where James Robert Vent murdered Clementina Balchin in 1924.

S1-7 The former Greyhound public house at No. 336 Kennington Park Road, where the publican Ernest Mace murdered his wife Violet in 1932, before committing suicide.

S1-8 No. 19 Southey Road [today No. 1A Cranworth Gardens], South Lambeth, site of the unsolved murder of Gertrude Rose in 1945.

S1-9 No. 20 St Stephen's Terrace, Lambeth, site of the unsolved murder of Agnes Jones in 1967.

S1-10 The betting shop at No. 25-27 Bagshot Street, Walworth, where the gangster Ahmet Abdullah was gunned down in 1991.

S1-11 The Bell public house at No. 51 East Street, Walworth, where David Brindle and the bystander Stanley Silk were murdered by masked gunmen in 1991.

S1-12 The Royal Hotel [today Royal Inn on the Park], where Jimmy Moody was murdered in 1993.

S2-1 The Priory at No. 225 Bedford Hill, Balham, site of the unsolved murder of Charles Bravo in 1876.

S2-2 No. 10 Stanmer Street, Battersea, where Frederick St John was killed in 1896.

S2-3 No. 8 Colestown Street, Battersea, where William Sutton murdered Mary Ann Donoghue in 1896, before committing suicide.

S2-4 No. 14 Linom Road, Clapham, where Henry Brown went on a rampage in 1897, murdering his wife Fanny and severely injuring his mother-in-law Elizabeth Locke.

S2-5 No. 44 Water Lane, Brixton, site of the unsolved murder of Mary Kate Waknell in 1900.

S2-6 No. 17 Clifton Gardens [today Prince of Wales Drive], Battersea, where the actor Weldon Atherstone was murdered in the first floor flat in 1910.

S2-7 No. 21 Comyn Road, Battersea, where Ada Annie Williams killed her illegitimate son John Patrick Dunn in 1913.

S2-8 No. 21 Boundaries Road, Balham, where Arthur Alfred Meader killed his wife Mabel in 1923.

S2-9 No. 203 Elmhurst Mansions, Clapham, where Arthur Brooks murdered Eva Porter in 1935, before committing suicide.

S2-10 The entrance door to No. 8 Elmhurst Mansions, Clapham, where Beatrice Vilna Sutton was murdered by Frederick Field in 1936.

S2-11 No. 48 Voltaire Road, Clapham, where the police constable William Teasdale murdered his wife Ruby in 1938.

S2-12 No. 165 Boundaries Road, Balham, where John Francis Wilkinson murdered the little girl Miriam Gray in 1953.

S2-13 No. 2 Abbeville Road, Clapham, where Patrick Ross murdered the Indian Akon Chandra Dutta in a second floor bedsit in 1956, and hid the body inside a large divan.

S2-14 The murder shop at No. 110 Acre Lane, Brixton, where James Heron killed Dib Field in 1962.

S3-1 The former Cricketers public house at No. 22 King William Street, Greenwich, where John Smith murdered his common-law wife Catherine in 1822.

S3-2 The former Navy Arms public house in New King Street, Deptford, site of the unsolved murder of Patrick Desmond in 1868.

S3-3 No. 67 Kidbrooke Park Road, Blackheath, site of the unsolved murder of Arabella Tyler in 1897.

S3-4 The shop at No. 34 Deptford High Street, where the brothers Stratton murdered Thomas and Anna Farrow in 1905.

S3-5 No. 3 Loampit Hill, where George Hume murdered his wife Bertha in 1908.

S3-6 The former tailor's shop at No. 187-9 New Cross Road, site of the unsolved murder of Robert James Venner in 1934.

S3-7 No. 19 Leahurst Road, Lewisham, where Patrick William Kingston murdered the little girl Sheila Wilson in 1942.

S3-8 No. 27 Doggett Road, Catford, site of the unsolved murder of Maxwell Confait in 1972.

S4-1 No. 10 Alma Villas [today No. 23 Rosemont Road], Richmond, site of the Smethurst mystery of 1859.

S4-2 No. 2 Vine Cottages [today No. 9 Park Road], Richmond, where Kate Webster murdered Martha Thomas in 1879.

S4-3 No. 75 Second Avenue, Mortlake, where Charles Robert Earl murdered Margaret Pamphilon in 1902.

S4-4 No. 51 Clifton Park Avenue, Raynes Park, where Ernest Partridge murdered his wife Mary in 1910.

S4-5 No. 5 Chestnut Road, Raynes Park, where Ernest Churchman killed his sister-in-law Emma in 1912.

S4-6 Winkfield Lodge at No. 54 Parkside, Wimbledon, where Arthur de Stamir murdered Captain Edward Tighe in 1917.

S4-7 No. 51 Cliveden Road, Wimbledon, where Reginald Wilkinson murdered his mother Eva in 1934.

S4-8 No. 29 Queen's Road, Richmond, where Maurice Odell Tribe murdered his sister Dr Naomi Dancy in 1937, before committing suicide.

S4-9 No. 35 Lindisfarne Road, Wimbledon, where Ted Chaplin killed Percy Casserley in 1938.

S5-1 No. 34 Forbes [today Mosslea] Road, Penge, where Harriet Staunton was murdered by her husband and brother-in-law in 1877.

S5-2 No. 4 [today No. 10] Quadrant Road, Croydon, where James Peckham murdered his wife Sophia in 1893.

S5-3 The terrace of houses in Fountain Road, Tooting.

S5-4 The house of horrors at No. 12 [today No. 159] Fountain Road, Tooting, where Frank Taylor murdered his wife and six of his children in 1895, before committing suicide. The wider house to the left is Lee's old shop at the former No. 11.

S5-5 No. 18 Oakwood Road, Thornton Heath, where George Dawes murdered his wife Sarah in 1897.

S5-6 No. 32 Churchill Road, Croydon, where Richard Brinkley murdered Richard and Anne Beck in 1907.

CHAPTER 4

WIMBLEDON, RICHMOND AND KINGSTON

Deserted rooms of luxury and state,
That old magnificence had richly furnish'd
With pictures, cabinets of ancient date,
And carvings gilt and burnish'd.
Rich hangings, storied by the needle's art,
With scripture history; or classic fable;
But all had faded, save one ragged part,
Where Cain was slaying Abel.

This chapter will deal with the murder houses of Wimbledon, Raynes Park, Kew, Richmond, Mortlake and Kingston. These parts of London were relatively spared from the attentions of the Luftwaffe, and have also suffered relatively little from the wrecking-balls and bulldozers of the post-war developers. Many of the solidly built old houses still stand today, from the handsome mansions of Richmond to the humble Wimbledon terraces. A notable exception is Wimbledon's Murder School, Blenheim House at No. 1-2 St George's Road, where Dr George Henry Lamson poisoned his invalid brother-in-law Percy John in 1881. When Lamson had studied medicine, he had heard that aconitine was an undetectable poison, but unfortunately for this calculating

4.1 Dr Lamson's murder school at No. 1-2 St George's Road, Wimbledon, from Famous Crimes Past & Present.

murderer, toxicological science had advanced in the meantime: the poison was detected, and Dr Lamson convicted of murder and hanged.[1] Blenheim House School still stood in the early 1900s, and quite possibly longer than that, but no trace remains of it today.

Richmond is home to some long-forgotten domestic tragedies. On April 30 1904, Reginald Hedley, of No. 27 Onslow Road, shot his nearly two-year-old son Alfred Thomas through the head with a revolver, before committing suicide. On September 22 1914, Charles Henry Weston cut the throat of his wife Jane with a razor at No. 7 Montague Road. He was found guilty but insane, and was committed to Broadmoor. On September 12 1917, Mrs Sarah Paynter, who lived at No. 83 Ennerdale Road, returned home from a holiday to find that Patrick Cleary, a 49-year-old man with whom she had been cohabiting, had gassed himself and his daughter Doris. Since he had suffered from delusions for some time, the inquest returned a verdict of murder followed by suicide whilst of unsound mind.[2]

But although Wimbledon's infamous murder school no longer stands, there is still much to read in this chronicle of Southwest London's topography of capital crime. Shudder at the sight of Richmond's House of Horrors in Park Road, and do not forget to visit the residences of two quite peculiar doctors in its immediate vicinity. Read about how the Victoria Road shop murder was solved, and ponder the sad tale of Mrs Casserley's lover.

THE STRANGE CASE OF DR SMETHURST, 1859

Thomas Smethurst was born in Cheshire in 1803, into a relatively well-to-do family. His father Mr William Smethurst was described as a 'gentleman', and Thomas and his two brothers appear to have been well provided for. Thomas Smethurst studied medicine in London, making slow but steady progress. In 1828, the 23-year-old Smethurst married the 42-year-old Mary Durham, who was in possession of independent means. According to rumour, she had previously been the kept mistress of a wealthy gentleman who had two separate 'families' in London, and was the mother of an illegitimate son.

In 1834, Smethurst qualified as a doctor, in his third attempt, and opened a surgery in Clapham Street, Stockwell. A man of some intelligence and ambition, he travelled to Germany with his wife, and took an interest in the hydrotherapeutic institutes of Bavaria. A believer in the 'water cure' for various diseases, Smethurst published a treatise on this subject, and founded his own hydrotherapeutic clinic in Ramsgate, with considerable success. He then moved back to London for a while, before opening another hydropathic establishment at Moor End Park,

4.2 Dr Smethurst, from the Penny Illustrated Paper, August 12 1876.

Farnham, again with good success. Smethurst and his wife lived in some style, and kept three servants. In 1855, he sold his practice and retired from medical practice, preferring to travel on the continent with his wife. Dr Smethurst had a good deal of money invested in property, and could lead a comfortable life.

In June 1858, the 53-year-old Dr Smethurst and his now 72-year-old wife were living in a Bayswater lodging house. Another resident was the 42-year-old spinster Miss Isabella Bankes. She suffered from some obscure internal complaint, but came from a wealthy family and was in possession of independent means. She became very friendly with Dr Smethurst, and in November, she was asked to leave the lodging-house because of 'improprieties' with the lecherous doctor. Smethurst set Miss Bankes up in lodgings, and the following month he married her bigamously. The good doctor later explained that although he knew that bigamy was frowned upon, he was reluctant to spend any money on divorcing his elderly wife, who could not be expected to last much longer.

The bigamous newly-weds took lodgings in Richmond, moving on to No. 10 Alma Villas, Rosemont Road. Isabella was not in the best of health, suffering from persistent sickness and diarrhoea. A local practitioner named Dr Julius was consulted, but although he dosed her with various tonics and medicines, the invalid did not improve. She was ill both when Smethurst was in residence and when he was away, and Dr Julius and his partner were both completely non-plussed.

4.3 Dr Smethurst overlooking the sickbed, from the Illustrated Police News, September 23 1882.

Dr Smethurst prevented Isabella's sister from having another doctor called in, and his meanness in spending the most paltry sum on his 'wife's' comforts soon attracted adverse comments. A furtive-looking, bald-headed man with a large belly and a bushy reddish moustache, Smethurst was a far from prepossessing specimen of humanity, and Dr Julius found him particularly disagreeable. On April 30, Smethurst made haste to have Isabella's will executed by a Richmond solicitor: in this document, which described her as a spinster, she left everything to her dear friend Dr Smethurst, with the exception of a brooch.

Isabella Bankes died in great agony on May 3 1859, and since Dr Julius and his partner immediately made their suspicions known, Dr Smethurst was soon in serious difficulties. He was summoned before the Richmond magistrates already on May 4. The medical men were adamant that her symptoms had been those of poisoning, and the police soon discovered about the bigamous marriage, and the last-minute will leaving everything to him. The autopsy showed that Isabella Bankes' stomach and intestines were inflamed, the terminal part of the small intestine being particularly badly affected. The medical experts debated which poison had been made use of, since chemical analysis proved inconclusive. Dr Taylor, of Guy's Hospital, presumed that Isabella Bankes had been dosed with antimony and arsenic in small doses, and at intervals, but he had no evidence to support this. Nevertheless, since the local doctors were very much against

Dr Smethurst, and since the medical experts declared themselves certain that Isabella Bankes had been murdered through the administration of an irritant poison, the good doctor was committed for trial at the Old Bailey.

When the trial of Dr Smethurst began on August 15 1859, there was very considerable newspaper interest. For months, the medical journals had been debating the case, some writers siding with Dr Smethurst, others with the Richmond practitioners accusing him of murder. The case for the prosecution made much of the bigamous marriage, the late will, and Dr Smethurst's general avarice and mean-spiritedness. But then again, the medical witnesses against Dr Smethurst were far from convincing: Dr Julius and his partner were no leading lights within their profession, and their knowledge of the pathophysiology of arsenic poisoning left much to be desired. Dr Taylor had to admit that the test for arsenic he had conducted had been worthless, since the assay had been contaminated. And the autopsy had revealed that Isabella Bankes had been six weeks pregnant when she died.

The defence called a number of medical witnesses, who did what they could to confound the jury: Isabella Bankes might have died from chronic bowel disease, from dysentery, or from complications to pregnancy. The money left in her will was tied up in a mortgage. There was no evidence upon record that Dr Smethurst had been purchasing poison, unless he had stockpiled some medical supplies from his period in practice. But when the five-day trial of Dr Smethurst ended on August 19, the summing-up of Chief Baron Pollock was very much against the prisoner. After deliberating for forty minutes, the jury found Dr Smethurst guilty of murder, and he was sentenced to death. With his usual coolness, Smethurst spoke to assert his innocence, accusing Dr Julius of perjuring himself in court.

The date for the execution of Dr Smethurst was set to August

31 1859. But in spite of his unfriendly and mean-spirited attitude, the plight of Dr Smethurst had found him many friends within his own profession. Not without reason, many doctors found it disgraceful that one of their own number would be executed for murder, on such feeble evidence. The doctors bombarded the newspapers and medical journals with letters objecting against the conviction of Dr Smethurst. Even Mrs Mary Smethurst contributed a letter to complain about her dear husband's fate. This unprecedented newspaper assault from the medical profession angered Charles Dickens, who for some reason or other was certain that Smethurst was guilty, but the Home Secretary Sir George Cornewell Lewis, whose grasp of the Smethurst mystery may well have exceeded that of the rabble-rousing novelist, was becoming seriously worried that he was presiding over a great miscarriage of justice. He asked the celebrated surgeon Sir Benjamin Brodie to confidentially examine the evidence in the Smethurst case, and the result was that the Queen was recommended to grant Dr Smethurst a free pardon, since there were serious doubts concerning his conviction.[3]

Having been saved from the gallows, with a narrow margin, the dismal Dr Smethurst had to return to the Old Bailey on a charge of bigamy. This time, there was no pardon for him, and he was sentenced to twelve months in prison, with hard labour. But Smethurst emerged from prison as mean-spirited as ever. He returned to court in 1861, to claim the £800 left to him in Miss Bankes' will, and after the case had dragged on for almost a year, Smethurst had success. This extraordinary doctor then insinuated himself back in favour with his elderly wife, and they lived together for a year before she died, allegedly from natural causes, in 1863, and the doctor cashed in yet another inheritance. In 1865, when Dr Smethurst was sixty years old, he married a 26-year-old woman and lived with her in various London lodgings; he did not work, and seems to have spent the money he had earned from his matrimonial adventures relatively quickly. When he finally expired in 1873, Dr Smethurst was only good for £100.

If Dr Smethurst had been on trial for being a howling cad, the only possible verdict would have been one of guilty. Even on a charge of murder, there are some obvious suspicious circumstances: why did this outwardly respectable doctor marry bigamously, why did he behave with such unseemly meanness, and why was he in such a hurry to have the will drawn up? The doctors were right that many of the symptoms suffered by Isabella Bankes, like the excessive diarrhoea and vomiting, were consistent with an irritant poison having been administered. It is true that the doctors found no arsenic in the body, and only small amounts of antimony, but surely Dr Smethurst would have sufficient toxicological knowledge to be able to select a poison that would be more difficult to trace? Mr Serjeant Ballantyne, who led for the prosecution at the Old Bailey, was of course most unsatisfied with the outcome of the case. He suggested that the cunning Dr Smethurst must have dosed his wife with chloride of potash to invalidate Reinsch's test for arsenic. The bold Serjeant also suggested, from hearsay evidence, that Smethurst and his chemist brother had committed murder by poison before. Dr L.A. Perry, who edited the Smethurst volume in the Notable British Trials, also thought the good doctor a very lucky man to get away with murder.[4]

But then, on the other hand, there is evidence that Miss Bankes was unwell already before making the acquaintance of Dr Smethurst. The autopsy findings are quite consistent with her suffering from Crohn's Disease, a form of inflammatory bowel disease with affliction mainly of the terminal ileum. Some, but not all, of her symptoms, are also typical for this condition: the persistent diarrhoea in particular. It should be noted that the Richmond doctors dosed Miss Bankes with liberal amounts of various tonics and restoratives, and some of her symptoms may well have been side effects from this polypharmaceutic approach. The presence of arsenic in one of her stools, and the presence of small amounts of antimony in her bowels, is of questionable significance, since both these substances were widely used in tonics in Victorian times. Thus the conclusion must be that Sir Benjamin Brodie was right: there is not sufficient evidence that Miss Bankes was poisoned at all, and it remains quite possible that she died from disease. The Old Bailey jury made too much of the biased testimony of the Richmond doctors, and both Sir Benjamin Brodie and the Home Secretary deserve praise for saving Dr Smethurst from the gallows.

As for murder house detection aspects on the strange case of Dr Smethurst, there is no Alma Villas today, and the murder house has been presumed to be lost. But perusal of the Post Office directories for 1888 and 1894 shows that in the intervening years, No. 1-No. 20 Alma Villas had become No. 5-No. 43 Rosemont Road. Dr Smethurst's house at No. 10 Alma Villas is the present-day No. 23 Rosemont Road, and it still stands today.

A RICHMOND HORROR STORY, 1879

In 1879, two semi-detached small cottages in Park Road, Richmond, were owned by a certain Mrs Ives. This old lady herself lived at No. 1 Vine Cottages, as she called it, and rented the other cottage to Mrs Julia Thomas, a 60-year-old former schoolteacher who had been twice widowed. After the death of her second husband in 1873, this rather eccentric and pernickety old lady had moved into No. 2 Vine Cottages, a two-storey semi-detached villa built in grey stone with gardens at the front and back. The difficulties of the Victorian postman, with all these

4.4 Kate Webster and the Richmond murder house, from the Penny Illustrated Paper, July 5 1879.

'Rows', 'Terraces' and 'Cottages' in every road, was further aggravated by the fact that before Mrs Ives had moved in, the two houses had been known at No. 1 and No. 2 Mayfield Cottages, and the names were used interchangably. The area around Park Road was not heavily populated at the time, although Vine Cottages were close to a public house called The Hole in the Wall.

Mrs Thomas' short temper and high demands of cleanliness meant that her servants usually did not remain at No. 2 Vine Cottages for very long. In late January 1879, she employed yet another general servant, the 30-year-old Irishwoman Kate Webster, This strong, brutal-looking woman brought a good reference with her, forged by a friend of hers. She was fortunate that Mrs Thomas did not know about her background, since not only did she have a long history of drunkenness and dishonesty, she had also been imprisoned for theft, and given birth to a son born out of wedlock.

It did not take long before mistress and servant were at serious loggerheads at No. 2 Vine Cottages. The pernickety Mrs Thomas scolded Kate for her incompetence, sloth and lack of cleanliness, and the sturdy, hard-faced Irishwoman more than once answered her back. Mrs Thomas made sure that Kate's term of employment would end by the last day of February. But still, as the weeks went by, the relationship between mistress and servant kept deteriorating. The nervous Mrs Thomas was becoming fearful that Kate would injure or murder her. When Kate asked to be allowed to remain in the house until March 2, Mrs Thomas did not dare to refuse her this favour.

On March 2, there was an angry quarrel between Mrs Thomas and Kate, after the latter had returned to No. 2 Vine Cottages quite drunk. Kate, who had a vocabulary that would have graced a Billingsgate fishwife, damned and blasted her employer with a hearty goodwill. A respectable, religious former schoolmistress like Mrs Thomas is unlikely to have heard such horrid words from a woman before. The shaken old lady went to church, and several people saw that she looked very worried and upset, although they did not inquire what was the matter.

In spite of the terrible scene earlier in the day, Mrs Thomas, whose instinct of self-preservation appears to have been quite defective, returned to No. 2 Vine Cottages. Kate was waiting for her there, with murder in mind. Mrs Thomas tried to take refuge in her bedroom, but Kate followed her upstairs. She seized hold of her employer and flung her headlong down the stairs. Mrs Thomas landed with a heavy thud, and Kate seized her by the throat and throttled her to death. The Irish virago then dragged the limp body of her mistress into the kitchen, where she made use of a saw, a chopper and a knife to dismember it. She lit a roaring fire underneath the large kitchen copper, and as soon as the water boiled, she loaded various body parts into it. This was

4.5 Portraits in connection with the murder of Mrs Thomas, from the Illustrated Police News, May 17 1879.

hot work, and Kate had to go to The Hole in the Wall pub to refresh herself at regular intervals, leaving what remained of her mistress boiling in the copper.

With admirable coolness, Kate Webster cleaned the murder house and the kitchen. She put the bones and some flaps of skin in a wooden box and a Gladstone bag. She answered the door to visitors and delivery boys, and seemed to be her regular truculent self. There is even a – hopefully apocryphal – story that Kate went round the neighbourhood offering two tubs of lard for sale, declaring them to be the best drippings; this was the residue left by her recent 'cookery' in the kitchen copper. With the help of a singularly unsuspicious boy, she managed to throw the box and the Gladstone bag into Thames. The box and its contents did not sink like she had expected, but was found washed up in shallow water next to the riverbank the very next day. It was spotted and recovered by a coal porter driving his cart past the Barnes Railway Bridge. After the discovery had been reported to the police, the remains were examined by a doctor, who found that they consisted of the trunk (minus entrails) and legs (minus one foot) of a woman. Around the same time, a human foot and ankle were

4.6 More vignettes from the Kate Webster case, from the Illustrated Police News, July 12 1879.

found in Twickenham. Crucially, the incompetent doctor who examined these body parts erroneously attributed them to a young woman with dark hair, and nobody thought of old Mrs Thomas. The newspapers dubbed the unexplained murder the Barnes Mystery, and speculated that the body might have been used for dissection by some medical students.

Kate Webster stole everything valuable in the murder house, but before escaping to Ireland, she also wanted to sell the furniture. Passing herself off as Mrs Thomas, she contacted a former publican named John Church, who agreed to buy it. But when Church came to No. 2 Vine Cottages, he was spotted by Mrs Ives. She told him that since Mrs Thomas was in arrears with her rent, her furniture was not going anywhere. From her description of the original householder, it became clear to Church that the woman who had passed herself off as Mrs Thomas was in fact her servant Kate Webster. When he went through the clothes in the delivery van, he found a letter addressed to the real

4.7 Kate Webster, from the Illustrated Police News, May 3 1879. The bottom right panel depicts the attempt to steal Mrs Thomas' furniture from the murder house.

Mrs Thomas. The police were called in and searched No. 2 Vine Cottages. They discovered bloodstains, burnt finger-bones in the hearth, and fatty deposits behind the copper, as well as a letter left by Kate Webster giving her home address in Ireland. They immediately put out a 'wanted' notice giving a description of Kate and her son. She was arrested at her uncle's farm at Killanne near Enniscorthy, and taken back to Richmond via Holyhead.

The murder of Mrs Thomas caused a great sensation in London: when the news broke, many people travelled to Richmond to look at the murder house. Kate Webster went on trial at the Old Bailey on 2 July 1879, before Mr Justice Denman. The prosecution was led by the Solicitor General, Sir Hardinge Giffard. and Kate was defended by the prominent London barrister Warner Sleigh. Over the course of six days, the court heard a succession of witnesses piecing together the story of how Mrs Thomas had met her death. Kate attempted to implicate the publican Church and her former neighbour Porter, but both men had solid alibis and were cleared of any involvement in the

4.8 Kate Webster the night before her execution, a fanciful drawing from the Illustrated Police News, August 9 1879.

murder. Kate's defence counsel sought to emphasise the circumstantial nature of the evidence and highlighted his client's great devotion to her son as a reason why she could not have been capable of the murder. A particularly damning piece of evidence came from a woman who told the court that Kate had visited her a week before the murder and had said that she was going to Birmingham to sell some property, jewellery and a house that her aunt had left her. The jury interpreted this as a sign that Kate had premeditated the murder, and convicted her after deliberating for about an hour and a quarter.

Hoping to avoid the death penalty, Kate pleaded that she was pregnant. Eventually the Clerk of Assize suggested using the archaic mechanism of a jury of matrons, constituted from a selection of the women attending the court, to rule upon the question of whether Kate was 'quick with child'; it turned out that she was not, and accordingly she was sentenced to death. Kate

4.9 The execution of Kate Webster, from the Illustrated Police News, August 2 1879.

Trial Sentence & Execution of

KATE WEBSTER

For the Murder of Mrs. Thomas, at Richmond.

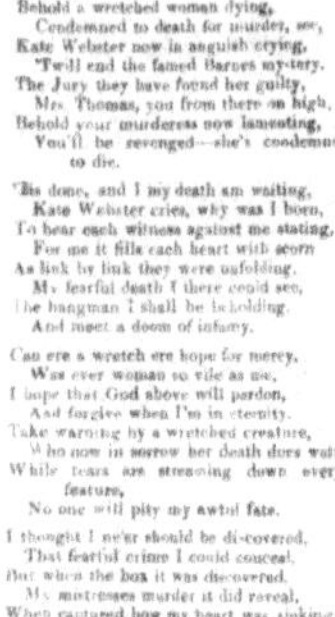

Behold a wretched woman dying,
Condemned to death for murder, see,
Kate Webster now in anguish crying,
'Twill end the famed Barnes mystery.
The Jury they have found her guilty,
Mrs. Thomas, you from there on high,
Behold your murderess now lamenting,
You'll be revenged—she's condemned to die.

'Tis done, and I my death am waiting,
Kate Webster cries, why was I born,
To hear each witness against me stating,
For me it fills each heart with scorn
As link by link they were unfolding,
My fearful death I there could see,
The hangman I shall be beholding,
And meet a doom of infamy.

Can ere a wretch ere hope for mercy,
Was ever woman so vile as me,
I hope that God above will pardon,
And forgive when I'm in eternity.
Take warning by a wretched creature,
Who now in sorrow her death does wait
While tears are streaming down every feature,
No one will pity my awful fate.

I thought I ne'er should be discovered,
That fearful crime I could conceal,
But when the box it was discovered,
My mistresses murder it did reveal,
When captured how my heart was sinking,
That boy Porter the truth did say,
From guilt and death I now am shrinking,
In a murderer's grave I must lay.

Farewell to all, my child, my father,
For me the solemn bell will toll,
Oh, would a child I had died rather,
May God have mercy on my soul.
Oh, mistress dear, while you in heaven
Your pity pray and pardon give,
And may I hope to be forgiven,
When on earth I no longer live.

4.10 A broadside hawked in the streets on the day of Kate Webster's execution.

Webster was hanged at Wandsworth Prison on July 29 1879, and buried in an unmarked grave in one of the prison's exercise yards.[5] The old crime writer Guy Logan had a journalist colleague who was once imprisoned at old Wandsworth gaol for the non-payment of rates. When he complained that his cell was particularly uncomfortable and spooky, the warder exclaimed "Why, you ought to be honoured, you did! Blow me if they ain't been and given you Kate Webster's condemned cell!"[6] There has been speculation among afictionados of South London ghosts that the "Grey Lady of Wandsworth', a ghost still haunting Wandsworth Prison, is the apparition of Kate Webster.[7]

The day after the execution, an auction of the property of Mrs Thomas was held at the murder house. John Church, the publican, managed to obtain the furniture after all, along with numerous other personal effects including her pocket-watch and the knife with which Mrs Thomas had been dismembered. The copper in which the body of Mrs Thomas had been boiled was sold for five shillings, and a woman bought the chopper that had been used with such gusto for two shillings. Other visitors contented themselves with taking small pebbles and twigs from the garden as souvenirs. Since nobody would live there, the murder house remained unoccupied until 1897. But when the 'ghost-hunter' Elliott O'Donnell corresponded with the lady who had gone to live at No. 2 Vine Cottages in 1897, she assured him that there had been no ghostly manifestations, although the servants had been reluctant to work at such a notorious murder house. Guy Logan was always keen to point out that he had more than once passed the pretty little murder cottage in what was now Park Road. He even wrote that "The majority of houses which have been the scenes of murder seem ever after to be under a cloud, and to shudder, as it were, from the public gaze, but this cannot be said of the neat and pretty little villa at Richmond, which was the locale of Kate Webster's horrid crime. I have passed it many times in the course of years, and anything less like the popular conception of a 'murder house' it would be hard to imagine."[8] Elliott O'Donnell, who edited the *Trial of Kate Webster* in the Notable British Trials series, did not share Guy Logan's murder house detective skills, since the careless ghost-hunter reproduced an alleged 'contemporary print' that clearly does *not* depict the murder house at what is today No. 9 Park Road. This valuable and well-kept house is in good repair and looks very much like it had done at the time of the horrible events back in 1879.

The horrible details of the brutal murder of Mrs Thomas caused an immediate sensation and were widely reported in the press. Such was Kate Webster's notoriety that within only a few weeks of her arrest, and well before she had gone to trial, Madame

Tussaud's created a wax effigy of her and put it on display for those who wished to see the 'Richmond Murderess'. When a friendly aunt took Guy Logan to Madame Tussaud's, he shocked her by demanding an immediate descent to the Chamber of Horrors. As Guy himself later expressed it, "My depraved interest in the models of the notorious criminals was such, I have been told, that it was with difficulty I was persuaded to return to the 'central transept', where the waxen Kings, Queens, and other celebrities held court. I could not be induced to come away from Kate Webster, whose image I regarded with fascinated horror. There, in front of me and as large as life, was the waxen counterfeit of the dread woman whose crime had caused such a stir, and who looked capable, in my youthful imagination, of boiling half a dozen mistresses in as many choppers."[9] There was also a popular song about the Richmond Murderess:

The terrible crime at Richmond at last,
On Catherine Webster now has been cast,
Tried and found guilty she is sentenced to die.
From the strong hand of justice she cannot fly.
She has tried all excuses but of no avail,
About this and murder she's told many tales,
She has tried to throw blame on others as well,
But with all her cunning at last she has fell.

It is quite uncommon that women commit murder with dismemberment, but the fierce, coarse-looking Kate Webster was not particularly feminine. Elliott O'Donnell described her as "not merely savage, savage and shocking... but the grimmest of grim personalities, a character so uniquely sinister and barbaric as to be hardly human". Her appearance and behaviour were seen as key signs of her inherently criminal nature. Her callous lying in court, and attempt to 'frame' Church and Porter also caused revulsion. Many Victorians who came to gawp at her statue at Madame Tussaud's viewed Kate Webster as the ultimate murderess: strong, ugly and brutal, and capable of every crime. The anti-Irish sentiments of the time were also fuelled by her crime; the demonisation of Kate Webster was a part of the public perception of the Irish as innately criminal.

So, the *flesh* of Mrs Thomas was boiled in the copper, and her *bones* were dumped in the Thames. But what about her *head*? Well, the story goes that in 1952, the celebrated naturalist Sir David Attenborough bought a house situated between Vine Cottages and the Hole in the Wall pub. The old pub closed in 2007 and fell into dereliction but was bought by Attenborough in 2009 to be redeveloped. On 22 October 2010, workmen carrying out excavation work at the rear of the old pub discovered the skull of a woman. It had been buried underneath foundations that had been in place for at least 40 years, on the site of the pub's stables. It was immediately speculated that the skull was the missing head of Julia Thomas, and the coroner asked the Richmond police to carry out an investigation into the identity and circumstances of death of the skull's owner. Carbon dating indicated that it was dated between 1650 and 1880, but it had been deposited on top of a layer of Victorian tiles. The skull had fracture marks consistent with Kate Webster's account of throwing Mrs Thomas down the stairs, and it was found to have low collagen levels, consistent with it being boiled. It entirely lacked teeth, something that is of importance, since we know that Kate Webster stole Mrs Thomas' 'snappers' which contained a gold plate, to have them sold. In July 2011, the coroner concluded that the skull was indeed that of Mrs Thomas, and it was decently buried.[10] Although the evidence for the skull's authenticity is far from conclusive, one can almost see the brutal Kate Webster exclaiming 'Begorrah!

Good riddance to yer!' and giving the head of Mrs Thomas a mighty kick, sending it into the hole she had dug in the rear yard of the pub.

NO REPRIEVE? GOOD JOB TOO! 1902

The French immigrant George Pamphilon was employed as a salesman at Clark's Nursery, Putney, and lodged with his wife Margaret in the ground floor flat at No. 75 Second Avenue, Mortlake. Their neighbour at No. 83, the 56-year-old retired baker Charles Robert Earl, befriended them in April 1900. In the evening, he was often invited to their flat for a game of dummy whist. But the following year, Earl took a firm dislike to the Frenchman and his wife. He accused George Pamphilon of spreading lies about him, and Margaret of gossiping to his own wife about his various demerits.

Several times, Charles Robert Earl blackguarded Pamphilon in the street, calling him a dirty Frenchman, a drunkard and a thief. Earl thought it particularly blameworthy that Pamphilon was not 'keeping' his wife, and that she had to work as well. On March 1901, Pamphilon was again shouted at in the street by his unbalanced neighbour: Mrs Pamphilon's gossip had ruined his wife, he screamed, but now he would mark Pamphilon for life, and ruin him! The following month, Earl sneaked up to No. 75 Second Avenue and broke all the ground floor windows. In July, he threatened to murder both the Pamphilons. Since George Pamphilon was becoming seriously worried what his demented neighbour might be capable of, he took out a summons against Earl and asked for police protection. The police could not waste resources on some bickering neighbours, however.

Charles Robert Earl thought it great cheek that Pamphilon

had taken out a summons against him. A fortnight later, he stood screaming abuse outside No. 75 Second Avenue, until the infuriated Frenchman armed himself with a stick and went out to trash him. Later the same evening, Earl returned and broke all the windows. This time, Earl charged Pamphilon with assault, and Pamphilon Earl for abusive language and criminal damage; the former summons was dismissed, but the second one confirmed, and Earl fined accordingly.

For several months, peace returned to Second Avenue. But Charles Robert Earl thought it a great affront, which cried out to Heaven for vengeance, that his devious neighbour had dared to prosecute him criminally. He sat drinking hard at No. 83, brooding over his misfortunes, and telling his neighbour that he was plotting revenge against the Pamphilons. On March 6 1902, Earl went sneaking up to No. 75 Second Avenue, protected by a heavy fog. He knocked at the front door, and when Margaret came to open it, he pulled a revolver and fired three shots at her, screaming 'Take that! Take that!' betweend the rounds. The demented killer ran the length of Second Avenue, to reach the White Hart, a large pub situated at Barnes Terrace, for some refreshments. He then went on to Hammersmith, quite possibly hoping to escape from London. But the police had been promptly summoned to No. 75 Second Avenue by the upstairs lodger blowing a police whistle. A doctor had declared Mrs Pamphilon dead, from several close-range revolver shots. Since Earl was known to have a grudge against the Pamphilons, and since he had been observed running away from the murder scene, his description was issued to every police station in West London. Two police constables saw Earl in King Street, Hammersmith, and promptly seized hold of him. The loaded revolver was taken from his inside pocket, and he was removed to the Hammersmith police station.

Charles Robert Earl made no secret of having murdered Mrs Pamphilon: he gave the police a full confession, and expressed much satisfaction that she was dead. 'She won't ruin another man's house!' he exclaimed. When Earl was on trial for wilful murder at the Old Bailey, his defender faced a hopeless task. His client's vengeful and mean-spirited nature was exposed in court, as was his unreasonable hatred for the Pamphilons. His movements the evening of the murder were traced by a number of witnesses. The medical officer at Holloway Prison found nothing to suggest that Earl had been suffering from insane delusions or homicidal mania, but declared him fully sane. The Vicar of Fulham gave the prisoner a good character, but the kindly clergyman's intervention could not save the Second Avenue murderer: the jury unanimously found him guilty as charged. Earl then exclaimed 'I shot the woman because she was fifty times worse than a common street harlot, and her husband knows it, and he is a bigger liar than I am! I am guilty, my Lord!' After Mr Justice Grantham had sentenced him to death, the unrepentant Earl shouted 'Thank you, my Lord; I will go there with pleasure!'

Charles Robert Earl's defender tried an appeal, but it fell through. His client exclaimed, when informed of this, 'No reprieve? Good job too!' He was hanged at Wandsworth Prison on April 29 1902.[11] Both the murder house at No. 75 Second Avenue and Earl's house at No. 83 still stand; after inspecting them, the reader can follow the murderer's route to the still extant White Hart, an impressive Thames-side Victorian public house.

A SWIMMER'S DESPAIR, 1906

Carl Maximilian Reyndl, a young man of German descent, became a London waiter at an early age, advancing to become bar-tender at Hotel Cecil. In 1905, when he was 23 years old, Reyndl became a minor newspaper celebrity after staging a number of spectacular swimming stunts. He swum from Charing Cross to Gravesend in five hours and three quarters, and would have set a new record from Dover to Ramsgate, had he not been impeded by cramp. The *Daily Mirror* and other newspapers published some favourable notices of his activities, and this made Carl Maximilian's confidence in his own ability grow out of proportion.[12]

But the management of Hotel Cecil objected to their bartender neglecting his duties to take part in various swimming races, and he was unceremoniously sacked from his post. A tall, burly cove with a bushy moustache and a large Stetson hat, Reyndl thought the time had come for him to become a professional swimmer. To save money, he moved in with his uncle, the grocer Adolf Anspach, at No. 14 Salisbury Road, Richmond.

Reyndl had long been interested in Anspach's young daughter Alma, and to begin with, she had been flattered by his attentions. She had written him some letters couched in affectionate terms, and the amorous swimmer had believed that they were engaged to marry. But Mrs Anspach pointed out to her daughter that Carl Maximilian's prospects in life were not particularly bright, having been fired out of Hotel Cecil in disgrace, and not managing to secure another job. He had failed to win any swimming races, and an attempt to swim the English Channel had resulted in dismal failure.

As a result of her mother's gossip, Alma Anspach told Carl Maximilian that she had had enough of him. When the swimmer tried to change her mind, angry quarrels resulted, and Mrs Anspach told him to find lodgings elsewhere. In early September 1906, the once-confident Carl Maximilian was becoming quite desperate: he was without a job, without a roof over his head, without success as a swimmer, and now also without his beloved Alma. He wrote a letter to the *Daily Mirror*, containing the words:

I am determined to claim my fiancée and to commit suicide in consequence. I wished to attempt to swim the Channel last year, but, not having the necessary help and advice, I had a good failure, and only spent all my savings and also lost my employment.

My young lady, under the influence of her mother, threw me over, and I think she deserves punishment. I would kill her mother too, but I hope she will be more punished by living to see the misery she has caused.

Now I am to be thrown away like a sucked-out orange. I will do my utmost to make sure that I kill her.

Bringing with him a loaded revolver, Carl Maximilian went to Richmond, and was admitted into No. 14 Salisbury Road. Mrs Anspach allowed him to see Alma, and she left them alone after saying that she hoped they would not quarrel again. But then there was the sound of gunfire. The demented Carl Maximilian had shot Alma dead with three shots, and then sent two more bullets

4.11 The desperate swimmer Reyndl guns down his sweetheart and then commits suicide, from the Illustrated Police News, September 15 1906.

through his own head. The coroner's jury later returned a verdict of wilful murder against Carl Maximilian Reyndl, and found that he had committed suicide whilst of unsound mind. The *Daily Mirror* published his letter under the heading 'Swimmer's Despair: Pathetic Farewell of German who Shot Himself and his Sweetheart in Richmond!'[13]

MURDER IN RAYNES PARK, 1910

Ernest Partridge was a 44-year-old antique furniture dealer, living at No. 51 Clifton Park Avenue, Raynes Park, with his wife Mary and daughter Ethel Maud. He also had a son, Ernest Jr, who had left the parental home after getting married. Ernest Partridge had once been relatively successful, but in 1909 his business went bankrupt. He had to close his shop and move his remaining antiques back to No. 51 Clifton Park Avenue. His brothers helped him with money, since the Partridge family was becoming quite destitute. Young Ethel, who worked as a dressmaker, was the family breadwinner. Ernest tried his hand at making carved tables, which he tried to sell through the door-to-door trade, but with little success. Sometimes, when he came home tired and footsore after having trudged round the neighbourhood all day, he would smash the tables to pieces in a paroxysm of rage.

And his table-smashing antics were not the end of Ernest Partridge's unbalanced behaviour. He sometimes woke up in the middle of the night, and insisted on throwing stones and flower-pots into the garden, aiming at non-existent 'intruders' He kept a number of sharp knives hidden under the bed, for use against burglars. Once, he lit a newspaper and walked round the house with it. Since Mary Partridge was fearful that he would burn the house down, she made sure that in the future, all matches should be kept hidden.

On May 12 1910, Ethel Partridge saw her father behaving as oddly as ever: he kept running up and down stairs, mumbling to himself. She decided to stay with her brother for a few days. Two days later, Ernest Partridge came into the Kingston police station, where he told the officer on duty that he had murdered his wife at No. 51 Clifton Park Avenue. He had cut her throat with a razor and then stood and watched her die. He had intended to drown himself in the Thames, he said, but like many other murderers in this book, he had become much more squeamish when it came to taking his own life. When a party of police constables went to No. 51 Clifton Park Avenue, they found a sign on the stairs, saying 'Don't go upstairs. I have cut your dear mother's throat. Fetch a Policeman. My body will be found in the River near Putney.' In the first floor bedroom, the body of Mary Partridge was on the blood-soaked bed, with a large gash in her throat.

On trial at the Old Bailey for the wilful murder of his wife, Ernest Partridge seemed as mad as a hatter. He had told the medical officer at Brixton Prison that he had gone into the bathroom to shave, when he suddenly got the impulse to murder his wife, making use of a large razor to cut her throat. He then remembered nothing until a milkman knocked on the door, with the shout 'Milk, threepence a quart!' Ernest remarked to the doctor that if the milkman had made use of this outcry just a few moments earlier, his wife would still have been alive. Coming to his senses and realizing what he had done, Ernest was desolate, or so at least he claimed. He pawned three paintings for two shillings and sixpence, using the money to buy himself some final drinks before he would destroy himself, but he did not have the courage to plunge into Thames. Ernest Jr testified that his father had not been kind to his family, and that he himself had more than once recommended his mother to apply for a separation order. Ethel Partridge, who also gave evidence at the trial, was blamed for not equipping her father with safety razors, with which he would not have been able to murder people. She and her late mother should also have made sure that he was examined by a doctor, since he should have been certified insane years ago, the harsh Brixton Prison medical officer added. The jury found Ernest Partridge guilty but insane, and he was committed to Broadmoor.[14] He was released in the 1920s and died at Wandsworth in 1926, aged 60.

SHOCKING CRIME AT WIMBLEDON, 1912

Robert Churchman was a well-to-do London publican, who held the Woodbine public house at Finsbury Park, and the Green Gate in Tottenham. He was fond of a drink or two himself, and so was his wife Emma. She had a furious temper, and made her husband's life quite miserable. Her mental health left much to be desired, and she made several dramatic suicide attempts, through cutting her throat, setting her clothes on fire, leaping out of the window, and drinking carbolic acid. In his forties, Robert Churchman fell ill, and was no longer up to keeping a pub: they went to Merton Park, where Robert took a confectioner's shop. As Robert lay ill, Emma twice tried to murder him by stuffing a large pocket handkerchief into his mouth, but his sister Mrs Henrietta Matthews managed to save the ailing ex-publican.

After Robert Churchman had died in November 1909, Emma moved in with his widowed brother Ernest, another former publican, at No. 5 Chestnut Road, Raynes Park. Ernest Churchman, a timid and assuming middle-aged man, soon realized his mistake. Emma ruled the household with an iron hand.

In her fits of fury, she threw plates and glasses at Ernest and his daughters, and kept a sharp knife in her pocket, to threaten them with. Emma had brought with her two angry little terrier dogs, and when she was drunk, she liked to set these animals on Robert's children. In early February 1912, Emma went on a proper drinking bender, ending up in a police cell. The Wimbledon Police Court fined her ten shillings for being drunk and incapable.

On February 26 1912, Ernest Churchman's sister Mrs Henrietta Matthews received a cryptic telegram:

H. Matthews, Sawston, Cambs. – Come quickly or murder out. Ernest.

She replied 'Come at once' and he did come, later the same day. After she had said she was pleased to see him, the following extraordinary conversation took place:

'You won't be pleased to see me when I tell you.'

'Whatever is the matter?'

'I have done Emma in.'

'What have you done?'

'I have cut Emma's throat.'

Mrs Matthews persuaded Ernest to give himself up to the police. The same evening, some officers raided the house at No. 5 Chestnut Road. In the ground floor front room, they found the body of Emma Churchman, the head nearly severed from the body. Her two dogs kept watch over the body. At the inquest on Emma Churchman, her brother-in-law Owen Churchman outlined all her demerits, and so did Henrietta Matthews. Mildred Annie Churchman, Ernest's sixteen-year-old daughter, testified that she and her younger sisters had been very frightened of the termagant Emma. Once, she had seized up two knives, with the words 'I will put one through you and one through your father!' The landlord at No. 5 Chestnut Road testified that due to the

4.12 Emily Churchman is found murdered at No. 5 Chestnut Road, from the Illustrated Police News, March 9 1912.

many angry quarrels taking place at the premises, the Churchmans had received notice to evacuate the premises. Ernest had removed his furniture to Epsom, but with her usual stubbornness, Emma had refused to go, even though Ernest had offered her £50 to leave. When asked to explain himself, all the pathetic Ernest Churchman had to say was "It is quite true – I have had a terrible life with her. She used to drink and swear at my children… she had been rowing all morning, and took a knife up to me, but I got it away from her. When I went in she came for me, and I suppose the continual worry overcame me at last, and I lost myself." A witness had seen Ernest standing at the front room window after the murder: the ex-publican had "presented a peculiar appearance, as he appeared to be half-demented by the way he was grinning."

The coroner's jury returned a verdict of wilful murder against Ernest Churchman, adding that the act had been committed under extreme provocation. At the Old Bailey, Ernest pleaded guilty to manslaughter, and this plea was accepted by the prosecution. Stating that he had "evidently submitted to a long course of provocation", Mr Justice Horridge sentenced him to five years' penal servitude.[15]

THE MURDER OF CAPTAIN TIGHE, 1917

Edward Tighe, a wealthy landowner whose family held an estate in Co. Kilkenny, Ireland, became an officer as a young man, serving with the Rifle Brigade in the Burmese War. After unsuccessfully attempting to become an M.P., he settled down at his Irish estate, and became High Sheriff of Kilkenny and West Meath. Although his health was indifferent, the Captain rejoined the army at the advent of war in 1914. He was detached to the Rifle Brigade depot, but due to his severe asthma, he was invalided out of the army a few years later.[16] In 1917, Captain Tighe took the lease of Winkfield Lodge, a fine villa near Wimbledon Common. Mrs Viola Tighe joined him there on November 9, and they kept a full staff of servants in the large, elegant house.

On November 12 1917, Mrs Tighe attended a lecture in London. She returned to Winkfield Lodge in the evening, and when she went to bed at 10.30 pm, she left her husband in the billiards room. He was presumed to have gone to bed as usual. The following morning, a housemaid heard a groaning noise from the Captain's bedroom. She found him on the floor, with severe head wounds. Beside him was a heavy poker, blood-

4.13 Captain Tighe is found beaten nearly to death, from the Illustrated Police News, November 22 1917.

stained and bent. Some petty objects, including an oxidised watch and an old mackintosh, had been stolen. The police concluded that a burglar must have broken into Winkworth Lodge, that Captain Tighe had woken up and disturbed the intruder, and that he had been struck down from behind. At first, the task of finding this burglar was a daunting one. He had not left any evidence behind, and London was full of thieves and burglars, to whom were added various deserters and other military riff-raff from America and the Colonies. Captain Tighe died from his wounds on November 17, without regaining consciousness, so the investigation now concerned a murder. Colonel Sir Francis Younghusband, the celebrated explorer, identified the body of his old friend Edward Tighe, brutally done to death in the presumed security of his own house.

For a few weeks, little progress was made in the hunt for the murderer of Captain Tighe. But in mid-December, when the lodgings of a known burglar and deserter named Arthur Henry de Stamir were searched by the police, the mackintosh and the oxidized watch were found, and identified by Captain Tighe's domestics as some of the items stolen at the Winkworth Lodge burglary. The foolish burglar had not had the wits to 'lose the swag'! Equally imprudently, de Stamir did not deny being present during the Winkworth Lodge burglary, although he claimed that it had been his partner in crime, the Australian deserter Reginald Fisher,

4.14 A drawing of the Parkside murder house.

who had struck down Captain Tighe. The police found no evidence that this individual even existed, however. The burglar de Stamir, who had an impressive criminal record of repeated thefts, burglaries and various military misdemeanours, was duly tried, sentenced to death, and hanged at Wandsworth prison on February 12 1918.[17] He did not die instantaneously, and the prison doctor blamed the hangman John Ellis for not giving him enough rope. The veteran executioner retorted that de Stamir had fainted on the scaffold, just before the trapdoor opened, possibly because he had not been given a glass of brandy to strengthen his resolve.[18]

The stately, elegant Winkfield Lodge was owned by Joseph Hood M.P. in the 1920s, before being acquired by the Apostolic Nunciature in 1938. It is now No. 54 Parkside. Popes John Paul II and Benedict have both stayed there, without feeling the need for an exorcist to be called in. Unlike the spectre of his namesake Hamilton in *The Ingoldsby Legends*, which haunted his murderers carrying its severed head, Captain Tighe's ghost seems to have behaved itself with suitable decorum when the Pontiff came to visit.

4.15 A postcard showing houses in the Parkside.

MURDER OF A WIMBLEDON WIDOW, 1934

The middle-aged Mrs Eva Wilkinson lived at No. 51 Cliveden Road, Wimbledon, with her son Reginald. From an early age, Reginald had been a very difficult boy. Born in Brentford in 1910, he had been educated at the Friends' School in Saffron Walden. He had done reasonably well academically, but was a gloomy and morose boy who often complained of ill health, although doctors found nothing wrong with him. He had worked as an optician's assistant for a while, but suffered a nervous breakdown in 1929, and largely led a vegetating existence after that time. He blamed all his misfortunes on excessive masturbation leading to degeneration of his nervous system. His father had died when he was just two years old, and his mother and uncle had found masturbation such a painful subject to discuss that they had not warned him against its lethal effects. For not providing him with appropriate advice about this delicate subject, Reginald much resented his mother and uncle, and the family doctor as well. In the summer of 1933, after Reginald had kicked and struck his mother, the doctor certified him insane. But after he had spent three weeks at Netherne Mental Hospital in Coulsden, he was discharged since a supposedly more competent doctor at the asylum did not agree to certify him. Reginald seemed far from sane to the people who knew him, and he still had occasional violent outbursts.

On May 29 1934, Dr Joseph Harvey, who had once declared Reginald Wilkinson insane, received a letter with some very insulting and libellous remarks added on the back of the envelope. He thought he could recognize Reginald's handwriting. The doctor went to see Reginald's uncle, and together they went to No. 51 Cliveden Road to confront the lunatic. But Reginald was nowhere to be seen. Instead, they found Mrs Wilkinson lying dead in a pool

4.16 Mrs Wilkinson is found murdered, and a drawing of the murder house at No. 51 Cliveden Road, from the Illustrated Police News, June 7 1934.

of blood, with her head in a basin full of water. Her head was battered with a blunt instrument, and she had a stab wound in the throat, and by her side was a letter suggesting that she had committed suicide. The doctor told the police all about the weirdo Reginald sharing the house with his mother, and regularly threatening her with violence. Since Reginald could not be found locally, his description was sent all police forces in the Home Counties. It did not take long for a message to come from Saffron Walden that Reginald had been apprehended there. He had visited his old headmaster Mr Charles Brightwen Rowntree at the Friends' School there, carrying with him a suitcase full of knives, hammers and other implements. When the headmaster asked what he wanted to do with these, Reginald told him that he had used the hammer to stun his mother, before murdering her with one of the knives.

Reginald Wilkinson was taken back to Wimbledon to attend the inquest on his mother. At the Wimbledon Police Court, Dr Harvey and others gave evidence against him, and he was committed for trial at the Surrey Assizes. A photograph of him in the *Daily Mirror* shows a very rum-looking cove with an over-large, misshapen head. But at the Assizes, the only witness called was Dr Grierson, the Brixton prison doctor, who had examined Reginald and who found him unfit to plead. For murdering his mother, the only person who cared about him, he was committed to Broadmoor for an indefinite period of time.[19] It is likely that he was eventually released, or perhaps transferred to another asylum, since he died in Newark, Lincolnshire, in 1986.

MURDER OF A TWICKENHAM RECLUSE, 1936

The 60-year-old widow Laura Mordaunt-Chapman was a well-known Twickenham recluse. Although owning a large house at

4.17 Mrs Mordaunt-Chapman's body is found, and a sketch of the murder house, from the Illustrated Police News, July 16 1936.

No. 126 Hampton Road, she lived only in a few basement rooms and kept no servants. Mrs Mordaunt-Chapman was the widow of a Captain in the Royal Navy, she claimed, and they had both been very wealthy when they enjoyed a grand society wedding. She owned several other houses which she rented out, and kept much of her cash savings in the house, since she did not trust banks. Her neighbours advised her to get a watch-dog, but the reclusive lady did not approve of these animals.

One of Mrs Mordaunt-Chapman's few acquaintances was the 69-year-old Albert Hadfield, who carried on business as a confectioner at No. 14 Nelson Road, Whitton [the shop no longer stands]. He helped to maintain her houses, and made himself useful in helping the reclusive lady with her various contacts with the outside world. On Thursday July 9 1936, Hadfield came to No. 126 Hampton Road to receive some instructions about the houses. He knocked at the door but nobody opened it. Hadfield was aware that Mrs Mordaunt-Chapman sometimes did not feel like answering the door, but he saw that a note he had left behind the previous day was still there. This was against the recluse's habits, so Hadfield had a look inside the lower ground floor window. The house looked even more untidy than usual, and he thought it must have been ransacked by thieves. Hadfield called the police, saying that he thought someone had entered No. 126 and that 'there might be a body'. The police constable who took the call advised Hadfield to have a look inside himself, but the old confectioner said he was too frightened to attempt anything of the kind.

Arriving at the scene, the police swiftly forced the door to No. 126. They found Mrs Mordaunt-Chapman lying dead on her bed. She had been stunned by a blow to the head, and then stabbed not less than 47 times by the frenzied attacker. The murderer had gathered 200 newspapers, hoarded by his eccentric victim, to build her a funeral pyre, but it had not caught fire as planned. A great quantity of empty whisky bottles were found on the premises, and there was speculation that Mrs Mordaunt-Chapman had been in the habit of consuming at least three bottles of whisky per week, among a liberal supply of other alcoholic beverages. It attracted suspicion that although Hadfield had told the police constable answering his call that there might be a dead body on the premises, he exclaimed 'My God!' and seemed quite affected when he saw the corpse on the bed. The police also found that there was a good deal of malicious gossip about the old confectioner locally. He lived apart from his wife, a crippled old woman, and was said to be more than friendly not just with Mrs Mordaunt-Chapman, from whom he had borrowed a considerable sum of money, but also with a certain Mrs Gander.

Detective Chief Inspector Donaldson, who led the murder investigation, did not think the murder was committed for plunder. There had been no attempt to search for money or valuables. Either the killer had been a lunatic on a rampage, or an old enemy of the murdered woman, he speculated. Mrs Mordaunt-Chapman had probably been murdered on Monday July 6, since her *Daily Express* for that day had been read, but not the issue for the following three days. Sir Bernard Spilsbury, who performed the autopsy on Mrs Mordaunt-Chapman, thought her murderer a homicidal maniac. The timid old Albert Hadfield looked the very opposite to a maniac, however: short, quite deaf, and peering at the world through a pair of powerful spectacles. Giving evidence at the coroner's inquest, Mr Albert Henry Davies of 'The Knoll', Usk, had testified that his sister Laura Mordaunt-Chapman had been a strong, sturdy woman. Still, there was a steady flow of incriminating evidence against the harmless-looking confectioner. He was well-known in Twickenham, riding around on his bicycle dressed in old-fashioned garments. He had denied being at No. 126 Hampton Road on Monday or Tuesday the week of the murder, only on Wednesday and Thursday. But a man had seen his bicycle parked at the premises on the Monday, and a woman claimed to have seen him in Mrs Mordaunt-Chapman's bedroom on the Tuesday! On early Thursday morning, a milkman had seen a shadowy figure on one of the windows of No. 126, but he could not tell if it had been Hadfield, or even if it was a woman or a man. The finding of a thumbprint in a bloodstain on a postcard in the murder room excited the police. It was too blurred to be compared with Hadfield's, but if clearly had the mark of a scar, as did Hadfield's thumb.

On trial at the Old Bailey for the murder of Mrs Mordaunt-Chapman, on September 23, Hadfield looked as harmless as ever. What the prosecution could prove was, at the very most, that he had perhaps not been entirely truthful about his movements on the week of the murder. He only possessed two pairs of trousers: both were free from bloodstains, and had not been recently washed. The confectioner denied any involvement in the murder, and the police had to admit that he had seemed perfectly frank and honest, and helped them with their investigations as well as he could. He had borrowed £500 from Mrs Mordaunt-Chapman, but kept up perfectly with the repayments. His daughter, and various other witnesses, provided him with a moderately solid alibi. After hearing the evidence against Hadfield, Mr Justice Greaves-Lord formally asked the prosecuting counsel 'whether it was safe on this evidence to put anyone in jeopardy'? Equally solemnly, Mr Eustace Fulton, prosecuting, replied 'My view is that it is not safe. It would be very dangerous in my view on such evidence as this.' The jury duly found Albert Hadfield not guilty.[20] There was jubilation among his supporters outside the Old Bailey. Old Mrs Hadfield had been unable to attend the final day of the trial, due to her crippled state, but Mrs Gander rushed up to kiss the trench-coated little man as he was led away by his daughter

Phyllis and her fiancé Bandsman Sergeant Williams, of the Royal Military School of Music. 'Wedding After Her Father is Vindicated!' exclaimed the *Daily Mirror* when Phyllis and the military musician were married a few days later.[21]

After his acquittal, Albert Hadfield became a minor newspaper celebrity. He and his daughter freely gave interviews to the press, something that seems to have annoyed his wife, Mrs Julia Hadfield, whom he had deserted many years earlier. She summoned him before the South Western Police Court for failing to pay her maintenance money. In court, she alleged that the lecherous confectioner had buried a woman, with whom he had been cohabiting, under her own name, at Twickenham Cemetery! In an interview with a *Daily Mail* journalist, Hadfield said that after leaving his wife, he had for many years been cohabiting with Mabel Lucy Hammond, the daughter of a Tooting builder. She had been the love of his life, and they had a daughter alive. She had lived with him as Mrs Hadfield, and had also been buried under that name. Phyllis Hadfield, who was also interviewed, generously said that in spite of old Hadfield's marital peccadilloes, no child could have had a better father. In the end, Hadfield was ordered to pay his wife 12 shillings per week maintenance.[22]

Albert Hadfield wrote the CID several angry letters, complaining about the obstinacy and stupidity of DCI Donaldson, and the general incompetence of the Scotland Yard detectives. He pointed out that Mrs Mordaunt-Chapman had once gone to Haslemere to see a man named Edward Alexander Apted, but this man had already been written off as a suspect. Hadfield kept pestering Scotland Yard with his impertinent letters for more than a year, although the exasperated detectives advised him to leave well alone and concentrate on his business. After disappearing into obscurity, he may well have been the Albert Hadfield who died in East Glamorgan in late 1952, aged 85.

Why were the police so convinced that Hadfield was the guilty man? The case against him, as presented in court, was woefully inadequate. The police learnt it the hard way that although it is easy to find some gossipy old women to blacken the character of the accused, this kind of evidence does not go far in court. It does not seem likely that such a timid little man like Hadfield could have inflicted such terrible injuries on his tall, sturdy victim, or kept such a cool head when pressed by the police. Even DCI Donaldson had to admit that "Hadfield is a cool calculating individual, who obviously has given the position very great consideration." But the stubborn detective could not think up a credible motive, except that the annoying Mrs Mordaunt-Chapman may well have got on his nerves. It was speculated that Hadfield had wanted to steal the deeds for the loan of £500, but since the loan had been set up by solicitors, this suspicion also fell through.

So, if Albert Hadfield did not murder Mrs Mordaunt-Chapman, who did? It is strange and blameworthy that according to the police file on the case, the only other serious suspect was the man Apted, a strange character with an interest in opium dens and spiritualism, but he was able to clear himself by some unspecified stratagem. In the initial reports of the murder of Mrs Mordaunt-Chapman, a sighting of two men spotted outside her house was mentioned, but it does not seem to have been adequately followed up after Hadfield had become the prime suspect.

When making some inquiries, I found some interesting leads, which appear to have been unknown to the detectives at the time. Algernon Mordaunt Chapman was born in Guildford in 1852, the son of a coachman. He became a commercial traveller, and was twice heavily fined for travelling on the railways without a ticket, although he could well afford to purchase one.[23] He later became a moneylender and capitalist, building up a portfolio of houses in Brighton and Haslemere. He married Laura Eliza Davies in 1905, under the name Algernon Mordaunt-Chapman, and the 1911 Census lists them as being 'of Private Means', and living at No. 58 Eltham Road, Lee, with their two servants. Mrs Mordaunt-Chapman was born in Llancayo, near Usk, and her two brothers were said to be among the richest men in Monmouthshire. In 1917, Algernon Mordaunt-Chapman made himself odious by evicting a poor man and his wife and ten children from a house in Haslemere, because they had fallen behind with the rent.[24] He died in 1922 aged 68, leaving in excess of £7 418 to his wife. She had, in turn, left £14 635 to the farmers Albert Henry and John Oliver Davies [her brothers?] and £1960 to the farmer Arthur Owyn Davies and the spinster Phyllis Mary Davies.

This information sheds some much-needed new light on the mystery. Since Algernon Mordaunt Chapman had not been some gentlemanly naval officer, but a mean-spirited usurer and slum lord, might some old enemy of his have taken revenge on his widow? How much of a scoundrel had he been, and to what degree had his wife assisted in his business dealings? We also now know who benefited from the death of Mrs Mordaunt-Chapman, but it would seem highly unlikely that some of the richest men in Usk would arrange to murder their own sister. Still, it would have been interesting to know more about the testamentory arrangements of Mrs Mordaunt-Chapman: had she changed her will, or threatened to do so? It might well be that she was murdered by some random madman or burglar, but there is also the possibility that it was a murder for hire, caused by some discreditable incident in her own past or that of her husband, or possibly by a threat from Mrs Mordaunt-Chapman to make some drastic changes to her will.

MURDER AND MYSTERY IN RICHMOND, 1937

John Horace Dancy, a young doctor, graduated just before the Great War. After serving in the Royal Army Medical Corps, he returned home in late 1916. In 1921, he married a fellow practitioner, Dr Naomi Tribe. The daughter of a clergyman, she had been employed in various menial doctoring jobs since 1909. Physically, the two doctors were very much unlike. The tall, thin, bespectacled John Dancy was a far from prepossessing specimen of humanity, but Naomi was very beautiful, with abundant light brown hair, regular features and large blue eyes.

The two Dr Dancys set up practice together over a boot shop in Shepherd's Bush. Since neither of them had the connections needed to succeed in London's nepotistic medical world, they had to rely on competence and hard graft. John was a very ordinary doctor, but Naomi had her fair share of professional ambition. She lectured on sociology and hygiene, and held appointments at various hospitals, becoming the assistant medical officer to the Hammersmith child welfare clinics. The two doctors gradually improved their positions in life, saving money and bringing up three children. In 1936, they purchased a large detached house at No. 29 Queen's Road, Richmond. Although John was by then semi-retired due to some nondescript malady, the two doctors were very comfortably off.

The same could not be said for Naomi Dancy's brother Maurice Odell Tribe. On active service as an officer in the trenches in the Great War, he had sustained a severe head wound in 1916, when helping to rescue seven men who had been buried by shellfire. He was awarded the Military Cross for bravery, but lost an eye and was invalided out of the army. An intelligent, educated man, he had socialist ambitions and started a club for underprivileged children, as well as helping to rehabilitate criminals recently released from prison. But his life hit the rocks in the early 1930s, when he became the victim of alcoholism and depression. Due to his excessive drinking and smoking, he was losing the sight in his remaining eye. A stint in a mental hospital in 1935 did not have the desired effect, and his wife left him since he had become impossible to live with. The unbalanced Maurice Tribe often spoke of committing suicide, or alternatively threatened to murder his sister Naomi. He envied her comfortable life at No. 29 Queen's Road, with her eyesight and all her faculties intact, whereas he himself was quickly developing into the wreck of a man. John Dancy, who regularly saw Tribe as a patient, was becoming increasingly worried what the demented ex-officer was capable of, particularly since he had retained his service revolver, and a supply of ammunition.

In November 1937, the drunken Maurice Tribe was hit by a car when bumbling about in the West End. Since he had injured his knee and could not cope on his own, the Dancys reluctantly took him in as a resident patient at No. 29 Queen's Road. It did not take long for Tribe to show the more sinister aspects of his personality. He quarrelled angrily with his sister about her life insurance, and threatened to murder her. Although incapacitated by his knee injury, he could still hobble about the house. John Dancy decided to stay awake as long as Tribe was up and about, to make sure he was not up to any mischief. The invalid kept limping about well into the wee hours, frequently visiting the toilet. The doctor kept an eye on him, something that Tribe seemed to resent; he retreated to the upstairs lavatory and locked himself in. Moments later, two revolver shots rang out. At first, John Dancy thought that his brother-in-law had committed suicide, but then he saw Tribe emerge from his wife's bedroom, which communicated with the lavatory. 'What have you done, Maurice?' the startled doctor exclaimed. But Tribe came hobbling straight at him, with his still smoking revolver aimed at the doctor's head.

John Dancy quickly retreated to his own bedroom, but Tribe followed him. To confound his half-blind adversary, the doctor turned off all the lights, but Tribe nevertheless fired at him. The canny doctor gave a groan and pretended to fall to the ground, intending to trick the madman into believing he had been hit. And this simple strategy worked a treat: after standing peering at Dancy for a while, Tribe hobbled off to the lavatory. Strangely, considering that he was dealing with an armed lunatic, the doctor then followed Tribe to the lavatory, rattled the door and shouted 'Give me that gun, Maurice!' 'Stand aside or I will shoot you like a dog!' the madman retorted, and Dancy quickly followed his advice. But after this threatening outcry, Tribe fell silent. The doctor recovered his sang-froid, went upstairs, and forced the lavatory door open, to find that his brother-in-law had cut his throat with a razor. He then belatedly ran into his wife's bedroom. She lay dead on the bed, shot through both eyes while still asleep.

When the police arrived at No. 29 Queen's Road, John Dancy gave them a blow-by-blow account of the tragedy. Albeit sad to have lost his wife of many years, he seemed surprisingly sprightly, and proud of his stratagem to 'fox' the madman. Nor were the police entirely convinced by his story; in particular, how could an unarmed man who had just narrowly avoided being shot by a madman actually have the courage to pursue this individual to the lavatory where he had entrenched himself. But there was a wealth of evidence in favour of Maurice Odell Tribe being as mad as the proverbial hatter, and full of hatred against his sister and brother-in-law. Once, this strange man had complimented his sister for her beautiful eyes; now, he had wilfully destroyed them. The weapon used had been Tribe's old service revolver, and technical

4.18 Scenes from the murder of Dr Naomi Dancy and suicide of her brother Maurice Odell Tribe at No. 29 Queen's Road, Richmond, from the Illustrated Police News, December 2 1937.

evidence spoke in favour of some person firing this weapon into John Dancy's bedroom. The post-mortem findings were consistent with Tribe committing suicide.

At the inquest on his wife, the journalists were much impressed by the coolness shown by the tall, bespectacled John Dancy: 'Facing Armed Madman, Doctor 'Foxes' and Lives' exclaimed the headline of the *Daily Mirror*. But the police were still not quite convinced. How could an invalid like Maurice Odell Tribe, whose body hardly contained a single healthy organ, be able to go on a rampage through the house, murdering his sister and nearly accounting for his brother-in-law as well? When Tribe's belongings were ransacked, several pornographic postcards were found, and John Dancy admitted supplying these to him. Several people wrote anonymous letters to the police, pointing the finger at the doctor, claiming that he wanted to get his hands on his wife's life insurance money. Had John Dancy shot his wife, fired at the panelling in his bedroom, and cut the throat of his invalid brother-in-law? An astounding letter arrived from Dorothy Sayers, the celebrated author of crime fiction. She had been contacted by John Dancy, who had offered her a guided tour of the Queen's Road murder house! In a long telephone call, this weird doctor had been most persistent, hinting that she might benefit from purchasing the rights to his amazing story, for use as the plot of one of her books, but she had fobbed him off. She told the police she found his offer quite unnatural and inexplicable.

But in the end, the police had to admit that although the murder at No. 29 Queen's Road was surrounded by many suspicious peculiarities, the case against John Dancy was not a strong one. He was a respectable, middle-aged doctor, well supplied with money, and seemingly devoted to his wife. Although Dancy might not have been unhappy to see the last of the parasite Tribe, murdering his wife was simply not in character.

Although there is no evidence that he was a habitual drunkard, he may well have had a few 'snifters' before getting what he perceived as the bright idea to contact Dorothy Sayers. At any rate, John Dancy collected his inheritance and the life insurance money and lived happily ever after. He remained in the murder house until 1966, when he retired to Bournemouth, expiring there in 1976 at the age of 85.[25]

MURDER OF A SURBITON JEWELLER, 1938

Mr Ernest Percival Key was a respectable, 64-year-old jeweller with his shop at No. 74 Victoria Road, Surbiton. A native of Hull, he had been in business at Surbiton for 22 years. On Christmas Eve 1938, which was a Saturday, the shop was open as usual, but that particular day, Mr Key did not return home. He was found in the shop with extensive slashing injuries to the head, and died on his way to hospital. When interviewed by a journalist, his son

4.19 A postcard showing shops at Victoria Road, Surbiton.

and daughter both expressed their opinion that Mr Key must have fallen over in the shop and striking his head on a gas stove, but the police were treating it as a case of murder. They wanted to interview a woman dressed in grey, who had been seen entering the shop at 11 am the day of the murder. Mr Jack Key, the son, said that he had found his father dead in the shop's back room, but he had not noticed any signs of a struggle.

Ernest Key had been a prominent Freemason, and a leading member of the Surbiton Lodge. Earlier in 1938, he had been photographed in full Masonic regalia. He was also a spiritualist, and the local mediums were soon in touch with the police. One of them reported that Assam, Mr Key's spirit guide, had sent the message 'Do not go to the shop!' the day after the murder. There was no explanation why this normally reliable spirit guide had mixed the days up so badly. Another medium reported that Assam had transmitted a message from the dead man, namely 'Take care of mother. Everything will be all right.' They were awaiting another message from the spiritual world, in which Mr Key would name his killer.

The police preferred to work with more down-to-earth clues, however. A garage proprietor had gone into Key's shop on Christmas Eve. He had heard noises from the back room, but since nobody came to serve him, he went out again. He had been in a hurry, and the noises had not seemed suspicious. Several people had seen the murderer on his way from the shop: a shabbily dressed man with dark hair and ruddy complexion. He had left his hat behind in the murder shop, but instead he had stolen Mr Key's overcoat, which was retrieved from a taxi in which the killer had travelled. The police suspected that there had been a quarrel between Mr Key and the killer, over some stolen jewelry the man had offered for sale, but Jack Key denied that his respectable father had ever been a receiver of stolen goods. The murderer had stolen £15 in pound notes, a gold watch and chain, and a baby's silver rattle.

The police soon received some very encouraging news about the Victoria Road murderer's later activities. The day of the murder, a shabbily dressed man had called at an outfitter's shop not far away from the murder scene, and bought a bowler hat. Although they only had one that was too small, he had purchased it. He had then taken a cab to the Kingston County Hospital, where Mr Key had also been taken, to have a deep cut on his hand dressed. He told the porter he had cut himself when working with a wood-cutting machine, and the doctor that he had been run over by a motorcycle combination. He had given the name 'Charles Jackson' and an address in Norbiton, but there was no such person there, indicating that the killer had shown some much-needed caution and given a false name and address.

On December 30, the police arrested the 29-year-old unemployed motor driver William Thomas Butler, who had a police record for burglary, and who fitted the description of the killer very well. He had a cut on his hand, recently bandaged, and the stolen silver rattle was found in the house where he lodged with his mother. He had told her he had been run over by a bicycle when he came home with his wounded hand and blood-stained clothes on Christmas Eve. A pawnbroker picked him out as the man who had recently pawned a gold watch and chain, and several pound notes were found in his wallet. Still, Butler stoutly denied murdering Mr Key, or even being in Surbiton on Christmas Eve. After a number of witnesses had picked him out as the man they had seen near Mr Key's shop, he changed his statement. A man he knew only as 'Detective Reeves' had kidnapped him on Christmas Eve, and forced him to drive to Surbiton. The 'Detective' had entered Mr Key's shop and later emerged wearing another coat. He had forced Butler to drive him to a lonely road, where he had been knocked down, cut on the hand, and forced to put the 'Detective's' blood-stained clothes and stolen coat on. But 'Detective Reeves' existed only in Butler's imagination, the police asserted.[26]

On trial for murder at the Old Bailey on February 16 1939, Butler had had time to think up another story. He now stated that after becoming unemployed, he had taken to burgling houses. He had a wife and two children, and his daughter had fallen ill and been taken to hospital. Butler had known Mr Key very well, and that he had more than once sold the Surbiton jeweller stolen goods from his burglaries. On Christmas Eve, he had gone to the shop to pick up £15 that Mr Key owed him, but the jeweller refused to give him the money. After they had started to quarrel, Mr Key had picked up a knife and attacked him. After receiving a cut to his hand, Butler had overpowered the old man and stabbed him to death. The 'honest' Butler had then taken some money from Key's trouser pocket, as well as some jewelry, but only just enough to cover the amount he was owed. Since his own overcoat had been badly stained with blood, he had taken Mr Key's coat instead. When Jack Key was in the witness-box, Butler's barrister asked him if there had been some trouble earlier the same year, when stolen rings worth 15s. had been found in Mr Key's shop, but Jack could not recall such an incident, and again stoutly denied that his father had been a receiver of stolen goods.

In spite of Butler's last-ditch attempt to plead self-defence, the jury returned after fifty minutes with a verdict of Guilty.[27] Mr Justice Singleton said that Butler had been convicted on the clearest possible evidence of a brutal murder, and sentenced him to death. A petition for his reprieve was organized by his wife Mrs Evelyn Butler and her friend Mr Ernest George Thurloe, but without many people bothering about such a brutal miscreant. An appeal was turned down, and Butler was hanged at Wandsworth Prison on March 29 1939.[28] Less than two months later, the *Daily*

Express could announce that a 'Two-Month Widow of Murderer is to Marry Again!' And indeed, young Evelyn Butler married her much older friend Ernest George Thurloe, who had once helped her to organise a petition for her murderous husband's reprieve, after such an unconventionally short period of mourning.[29] As for Butler's knife, it was sent to Scotland Yard's Black Museum, and it may well still be there today. As for the murder shop at No. 74 Victoria Road, it is today the Surbiton Flight Centre.

MRS CASSERLEY'S LOVER, 1938

Percy Casserley was a wealthy brewer who rose to become director and secretary of Watney's, the well-known Wandsworth brewers and distillers. In 1927, when he was 48 years old, he married the 25-year-old Georgina Mary Stenning, and settled down in a comfortable detached house at No. 35 Lindisfarne Road, Wimbledon. But after a few years, Mrs Georgina Casserley found Percy a most unsatisfactory husband. An alcoholic of long standing, he was a moody and taciturn fellow, and practically impotent. In the 1930s, Percy several times voluntarily entered various asylums and alcoholic's homes, but once he had been discharged back into the world of pubs and liquor stores, he soon went back to his old ways, frequently drinking himself into a stupor. In 1937, during one of now 56-year-old Percy's stints in an alcoholic's home, the 35-year-old Georgina Casserley met a handsome young builder's foreman named Edward Royal Chaplin, who was working on some houses nearby. These two soon became close friends, and lovers. When Percy emerged from the sanatorium, Georgina asked him for a divorce, but the alcoholic sullenly refused: she was *his* property, and he would not allow her to go to another man!

To Mrs Casserley, the contrast between the dismal Percy and

her beloved Ted could not be greater. Although he had once been a celebrated athlete, Percy was the wreck of a man, and both mean-spirited and vindictive. Ted was virile and good-looking, and in spite of his humble situation in life, he was intelligent and aspiring to better himself. One day, he promised, he would have his own builder's firm. In early 1938, Georgina noticed that she was pregnant with Ted's child. Understandably, Percy flew into a terrible rage when he was informed of this, but he still refused to divorce her. In March the same year, Percy went for one of his 'drying-out' periods in a nursing home, and Ted could come and see his beloved Georgina at No. 35 Lindisfarne Road whenever he wanted to. Her maid Emily Scott kept Ted informed about Percy's movements, and he made sure not to go near Lindisfarne Road on March 22, when Percy was due to return. Instead he had made an appointment to see Georgina in Coombe Lane at 7.30 in the evening. He was met there by Emily Scott, who told him that there had been a terrible scene, and that Mrs Casserley feared for her life. Ted came to see her outside No. 35, and she told him that Percy had threatened to murder her, and that he had access to a loaded pistol.

The strong, muscular Ted armed himself with a cosh and went to confront Percy Casserley. Georgina had kept his identity a secret, so the alcoholic only knew him as the builder who had been working nearby. They shook hands and Percy offered him some whisky. But Ted was not having any of that. He looked his adversary in the eyes and said "I have called to see what the trouble is between you and Mrs Casserley. I have just left her, and she is terribly upset. You know about her condition. I am responsible for it." Percy looked quite dazed and taken aback, before finally growling "So it is you, you swine!" and bounding over to a chest of drawers, from which he pulled out a revolver. Ted rushed forward and seized hold of him before he could fire. Percy's right hand was forced upwards, but with his free hand, he seized hold of Ted's testicles and twisted them hard. Ted grabbed hold of a large torch and struck Percy over the head three times, until he released his painful hold. Percy pleaded for mercy and begged Ted to release him, but once he was free, he cocked the pistol. Ted seized hold of him again, and a gunshot rang out.

Shot in the head, Percy Casserley died on the spot. Ted and Georgina were equally distraught. But the resourceful builder's foreman decided that all was not lost. He put some valuables in a bag to simulate a burglary, threw the torch into the garden, and took the pistol and the cosh away with him. Georgina went out shopping, returning at 9 pm and 'finding' Percy dead in the dining room. Initially, all went well for the guilty pair. Mrs Casserley played her part to perfection, and the police gave credence to the 'burglary gone wrong' theory. But there was no convincing evidence of a forced entry into the house. Percy Casserley's background of alcoholism and ill-health was soon exposed, as was his wife's infidelity. A cartridge case was found in the house, indicating that Percy had been shot by his own gun, presumably by someone he knew and had allowed to enter the house. Ted Chaplin was tracked down to a flat in Epsom. He had a recent cut on his hand, and his coat had marks of blood. It also lacked a button, similar to one found in the murder house. On March 25, he was charged with the murder of Percy Casserley.

After Mrs Casserley had been charged as an accessory after the fact, harbouring and assisting the murderer of her husband, there was much newspaper interest. Many people, women in particular, found this most unfair. On trial at the Old Bailey, Ted Chaplin was ably defended by the celebrated Norman Birkett. The prosecution was unconvinced by Chaplin's own story, as related above; they found it equally likely that he had deliberately knocked Casserley down and then shot him dead with his own pistol. It spoke against him that he had brought a cosh with him into the murder house, indicating intent to injure his rival. Ted Chaplin gave a favourable impression when giving evidence in court, and his story was fully compatible with the known facts about the case, and with the technical evidence. The jury found him guilty only of manslaughter, and Mr Justice Humphries sentenced him to twelve years penal servitude.[30] This far from bonhomous judge then had some choice words for Mrs Casserley. Many foolish people, not a few of them newspaper journalists, had treated her like a heroine, he said, and her case had aroused the most ridiculous nonsense. In reality, she was just a participator in a sordid intrigue, and the less said about the minutiae of the case, the better. This tongue-lashing was her only punishment, however, and she was discharged.

If Ted Chaplin's story contained the full truth and nothing but the truth, his sentence was certainly a harsh one. Throughout the Second World War, when he could have fought for his country in the great conflict, he sat rattling the bars of his prison cell. In the end, Ted served nine years in prison, being released early in 1947. Mrs Casserley was waiting for him, and they were married in the Isle of Wight. According to an internet site, Mrs Georgina Chaplin died in 1974, and her gravestone in Stoke Cemetery, Guildford, mentions that she had a son named Roy. Edward Royal Chaplin lived on until 1986. The murder house at No. 35 Lindisfarne Road still stands, and looks virtually unchanged from the photographs in the police file at the National Archives.

MURDER WITHOUT MOTIVE IN HARTFIELD CRESCENT, 1941

In 1941, the 29-year-old Mrs Doris Eugenia Girl was living at No. 77 Hartfield Crescent, Wimbledon. Her husband was serving with a barrage balloon unit, and their only daughter had been evacuated from London. A homeless young man named Stanley Edward Cole, a 23-year-old wood machinist, was friendly with both Mr and Mrs Girl, and when Mr Girl was away, he slept on a sofa in the kitchen of their house. Just after midnight on August 23 1941, Cole came staggering up to the Wimbledon Police Station, exclaiming "I've killed a woman in Hartfield Crescent! I stabbed her in the back! Why did I do it?" And indeed, the body of Mrs Girl was found at No. 77, with a lethal stab wound in the back. There was no evidence that the pair had been quarrelling or fighting, and Cole seemed to have stabbed her entirely without warning. Although sane, he could not provide a motive for his crime. At the Central Criminal Court, he was convicted of murder, and Mr Justice Hallett sentenced him to death. The verdict was upheld by the Court of Criminal Appeal, and Cole was hanged at Wandsworth Prison on October 31 1941.[31]

MURDER IN ELTON ROAD, 1954

On May 9 1954, the 44-year-old waitress Mrs Nellie Officer was found murdered in her tiny terraced cottage at No. 5 Elton Road, Kingston. The 53-year-old gardener Rupert Geoffrey Wells, of no fixed abode, was also found in the cottage, and taken to Kingston Hospital in a very drunken and intoxicated state. The following day, Wells was discharged from the hospital and taken to the Kingston Police Station, where he was charged with the murder of Nellie Officer.

On trial for murder at the Lewes Assizes on July 28 1954, Wells pleaded Not Guilty. The defence submitted that he had been under the influence of a hypnotic sedative drug, in combination with alcohol, and that he entirely lacked any knowledge what had happened the evening of the murder. The jury found him guilty, however, and he was sentenced to death. An appeal failed, and he was executed at Wandsworth Prison on September 1 1954.[32] The police file on the case is closed until 2030, and newspaper coverage of this obscure murder was quite limited, but the murder house at No. 5 Elton Road still stands.

CHAPTER 5

CROYDON AND SOUTH LONDON SUBURBS

What human creature in the dead of night
Had coursed like hunted hare that cruel distance?
Had sought the door, the window in his flight,
Striving for dear existence?
What shrieking Spirit in that bloody room
Its mortal frame had violently quitted? –
Across the sunbeam, with a sudden gloom,
A ghostly Shadow flitted?

Croydon expanded very rapidly in Victorian times: a humble village south of London became a thriving suburb, home to 140 000 people. Today, it covers an impressive area of land in South London. Since Croydon was extensively 'developed' in late Victorian times, relatively few older buildings remain: thus went No. 35 South End, where John Carver murdered his wife Mary in 1870, and No. 2 Colliers Yard, where Eliza Osborne was murdered in 1877.[1] The majority of Croydon's Victorian and Edwardian murder houses survive in good order, however, with a few notable exceptions. I was particularly sad to find that although much of the Birdhurst Rise conservation area remains intact, the two celebrated murder houses at No. 16 South Park Hill Road and

No. 29 Birdhurst Rise, site of the great Croydon poison mystery of 1929, are no longer standing. It was here that Edmund Duff, Vera Sidney and Violet Sidney were murdered by a mystery poisoner; the main suspect in this classical British mystery was Grace Duff, wife of Edmund and the main financial beneficiary of all three crimes, although she was never tried for the crimes.[2]

Other lost Croydon murder houses include No. 51 Pawson's Road, where Gilbert Wright was murdered by his wife in 1895, the little terraced house at No. 47 Handcroft Road where Mrs Eliza Ray was murdered by burglars in 1934, and No. 113 Gloucester Road, where Elizabeth Bounds was murdered in 1944. The Elgin Court Hotel, where Johanna Hallahan was murdered by the hotel porter Frank Burgess in 1952, no longer frowns on the passer-by. The saddest of Croydon's lost murder houses must surely be No. 14 St Aubyn's Road, where four-year-old Edwina Taylor was murdered by the pervert Derrick Edwardson in 1957. This blot on the landscape no longer stands, although houses on the other side of the road show what it must have looked like. Although there were calls for the death penalty to be brought back for child murder, the creature Edwardson was sentenced to life imprisonment.[3]

Many of Croydon's and South London's historic murder houses still stand today. Admire the grand murder house at Camden Place, shudder at the Tooting Horror, read about the shotgun-wielding maniac of Quadrant Road, marvel at the cunning of the master criminal Richard Brinkley, and ponder the Addiscombe Road Mystery, still unsolved after more than 80 years.

DOUBLE MURDER AT CAMDEN PLACE, 1813

In 1813, stately Camden Place, Chislehurst, was home to the wealthy gentleman Mr Thomson Bonar and his wife Ann. Mr

Bonar was nearly 80 years old, and his wife was around ten years younger, but both remained hale and hearty. The Bonars were generous, charitable people, and very popular locally. On Sunday May 30 1813, the Bonars went for a ride in their elegant carriage, before having dinner and sitting in their drawing-room for a while. Mr Bonar went to bed early, but his wife sat up reading for quite a while, before retiring to their shared bedroom in the wee hours.

The following morning, Mrs Bonar's maid came to rouse her at seven in the morning. The poor girl beheld a most dreadful sight. Her mistress lay dying and insensible on the bed, and the corpse of Mr Bonar was on the floor, his face and head beaten to a pulp, and his hands badly mangled. His nightcap, soaked with blood, lay next to his battered and broken body, with a lock of grey hair still adhering to it. Clearly, the old man, who was still strong and vigorous, had fought for his life against a frenzied and powerful intruder. A bent poker lying on the floor was clearly the murder weapon.

5.1 The murder of the Bonars, from the New Newgate Calendar.

IT WAS IMPOSSIBLE TO IMAGINE A MORE AWFUL SCENE.

5.2 The Bonars are found murdered, from Famous Crimes Past & Present.

The domestics of Camden Place made sure that footmen were dispatched to alert the police, and to fetch a doctor. One of them was the young Irishman Philip Nicholson, who had previously served in the 12th Dragoons as an officer's servant. He rode express to London on one of the best horses in the stable, and called on Mr Astley Cooper, the celebrated surgeon, who drove to Camden Place without delay. His diagnosis was a gloomy one: Mrs Bonar had received very serious head injuries, and would not live long. And indeed, she expired just after eleven o'clock, having remained silent and unconscious apart from once exclaiming 'Oh, dear!'

Leaving Astley Cooper's house, the footman Nicholson visited the Red Lion public house, near Bedlam, where he refreshed himself with three large glasses of rum. He met a man named Dale, a former under-butler in Mr Bonar's household at Camden Place, who had recently been discharged on suspicion of ill conduct. The drunken Nicholson greeted his former colleague with the outcry "The deed is done, and you are suspected; but you are not in it!" He then went on to the Bow Street police office, to give information of the murder; he mentioned his meeting with former butler Dale, implying that this man must be a suspect. One of the Bow Street runners went to the Red Lion to interview Dale; another tried to follow Nicholson, but lost sight of him in Brydges Street.

Examining the crime scene, the Bow Street runners found nothing to suggest that Camden Place had been broken into, or that any object had been stolen by the murderer. Dale was brought to Chislehurst and harshly questioned by the magistrates, but he had an alibi, having been drinking at the Red Lion all night. This led to Nicholson becoming a suspect, since he had tried to implicate his former colleague. The city officer Forrester was dispatched to find Nicholson. After much searching, he spotted the footman at the Three Nuns public house in Whitechapel, in a state of advanced drunkenness. The truculent Nicholson was not at all keen to leave the pub, but Forrester persuaded him with his fists and hauled him to the Giltspur Street Compter, a small

5.3 The gates and gate-house to Camden Place, from an old cabinet card.

debtor's prison situated not far from Newgate. The Lord Mayor personally wanted to question him, but Nicholson was too drunk to say anything coherent.

The next day, Philip Nicholson was brought before the Lord Mayor, at the Mansion House. He said that he had been the only male servant sleeping at Camden Place. He could not explain why he had taken the bloody sheets from Mr and Mrs Bonar's beds, and tucked them underneath his own bed. Nor could he explain his outcry to Dale, or his incessant drinking after he had been sent to London. There was a bloody footprint at Camden Place, on the stairs from the servant's bedrooms up to the main house, but Nicholson said he might have trodden in the blood when gathering the sheets. When he was stripped and examined in a private room, multiple bruises were found, but these were likely to be the result of his scuffle with Forrester. Nicholson was a Roman Catholic, and a firm supporter of the Catholic Bill of 1813, The Act allowed the right to vote to Irish Roman Catholics in England, provided they took the oath of allegiance and a new oath abjuring certain doctrines. Furthermore, they could be elected to all corporations, hold all civil and military offices except the very highest, and to a certain extent keep arms. When this controversial Bill was lost in the House of Commons, Nicholson was furious, more so when he heard Mr Bonar express his high satisfaction at the result.

At the coroner's inquest on Mr and Mrs Bonar, the verdict was wilful murder against Philip Nicholson. At the end of the inquest there was an outcry that Nicholson had cut his throat. He had been confined in the butler's pantry, and had grabbed hold of a razor there, but Astley Cooper the surgeon managed to bandage his wound, which had not affected the windpipe or the major arteries. Some days later, Nicholson made a full confession. He had drunk much beer the evening of the murder, but not enough to become insensible; in fact, he lay awake in bed in the wee hours when he suddenly got the idea to murder his master and mistress. He had sneaked into their bedroom, naked except for his own bed sheet wrapped around his body, and dealt the sleeping Mrs Bonar two mighty blows with the poker. Mr Bonar had leapt out of bed and grappled with him for fifteen minutes, before Nicholson was able to beat him to death. The reason he had been so keen to gather the bedclothes the morning after was that his own sheet had also been lying on the floor.

At the Maidstone Assizes, Philip Nicholson was found guilty of the murder of Mr and Mrs Bonar, and he was sentenced to death. He was hanged at Pennenden Heath on August 23 1813.[4] It has been claimed that he was the last famous murderer to be executed there, but surely that dubious honour must go to Charles Hussey, who was executed for the murder of Mr Bird and his housekeeper at Greenwich in 1818, although doubt has persisted concerning his guilt. The last person to be executed at Pennenden Heath was a certain John Dyke, hanged in 1830 for burning a hayrick, although it later emerged that he was innocent.

Camden Place remained in the possession of Mr Bonar's son, a colonel in the Kent militia, for some time. The wealthy gentleman Nathaniel Strode bought Camden Place in 1860 and made major changes to the building. The most famous residents of Camden Place were the French Imperial family, with whom Strode had close contacts. The Empress Eugenie and the Prince Imperial fled to Britain in 1870 following the capture of her husband Napoleon III after his defeat in the Franco-Prussian War, and were given use of Camden Place by Mr Strode. The Emperor joined her at Camden Place in 1871 after his release, and died there two years later. The Empress remained at the murder house until 1881, when she moved to Farnborough following the death of the Prince Imperial in South Africa. Strode returned to

5.4 Camden Place, from an old postcard.

Camden Place, but the estate was sold after his death in 1890. That very year, it was visited by that indefatigable murder house detective, George R. Sims, who edified his Refereaders about the situation of the blood-bespattered murder room.[5] Some of the land was bought for building by the local developer William Willett, but the house itself and much of the land was sold to Chislehurst Golf Club in 1894, with the house serving as its club house. The large and elegant murder house is still in the possession of this golf club today.

THE PENGE MYSTERY, 1877

In 1875, the 24-year-old auctioneer's clerk Louis Staunton married the eleven years older Harriet Richardson. Mrs Richardson, the bride's mother, knew that her daughter was quite feeble-minded, and suspected that Louis was marrying her to get his hands on the £3000 she had inherited. Since Harriet herself was very keen to get married, she resented her mother's meddling. Although Mrs Richardson applied to the Court of Chancery to have Harriet placed under control as a person of weak intellect, she was unsuccessful to prevent the wedding from taking place as planned.

Louis and Harriet Staunton went to live at No. 8 Loughborough Park Road, Brixton. His brother Patrick lived across the road at No. 9, with his wife Elizabeth. In March 1876, Harriet Staunton gave birth to a son, christened Tommy. But by that time, Louis was already on intimate terms with Patrick's young sister-in-law Alice Rhodes. Harriet was plain and feeble-minded, whereas Alice was young and pretty, and very much in love with the moustachioed, bushy-whiskered Louis. It was probably around this time that the Staunton brothers, two cruel and calculating scoundrels, made plans to dispose of Harriet and little Tommy. Since Harriet was quite half-witted, given to violent temper tantrums, and addicted to the bottle, Louis could no longer stand her. Later in 1876, Patrick and his wife moved to a lonely cottage near Cudham in Kent. Louis decided that Harriet and her child should live with them. Himself, he rented a farmhouse nearby, living there with Alice as Mr and Mrs Staunton.

Harriet did not like Patrick Staunton, and he returned the dislike in full. He struck her more than once, and made sure she was systematically starved. Mrs Richardson suspected foul play, but Louis and Patrick fobbed her off when she demanded to see her daughter. When she went to London and entered the cottage where the Stauntons kept Harriet, Patrick forcibly threw her out. In early April 1877, Louis Staunton took the ailing little Tommy to Guy's Hospital. The wretched child died not long after, from long-standing starvation. Nobody seems to have suspected unnatural death, and Louis went to Guy's under an assumed name

5.5 Harriet Staunton at her wedding and at her miserable death, and portraits of the four Penge miscreants, from the Illustrated Police News, October 6 1877.

to collect the tiny corpse. He drove a hard bargain at the funeral parlour, and Tommy ended up having to share a coffin with another pathetic little London waif.

Later the same month, the brothers Louis and Patrick Staunton, aided and abetted by Elizabeth Staunton and Alice Rhodes, considered themselves close to success. Since they thought Harriet could not live much longer, they removed the feeble, emaciated invalid to No. 34 Forbes [today Mosslea] Road, Penge, where she died the very next day. A careless local doctor, who had only seen the patient in a dying condition, was persuaded to sign a death certificate that Harriet had died of 'apoplexy'.

Would the scoundrelly Stauntons get away with it? They very nearly did. By mere chance, it happened that Harriet's brother-in-law was in a shop in Forbes Road, when a stranger came in to register the death of a lady from Cudham in Kent, at No. 34. The brother-in-law knew that Harriet had been kept in Cudham, and that Mrs Richardson was very keen to trace her current

5.6 The autopsy of Harriet Staunton, and a drawing of the murder house, from the Illustrated Police News, June 2 1877.

whereabouts. He went to see the doctor, and to identify the deceased as his 36-year-old sister-in-law Harriet Staunton. The police were notified, the death certificate withdrawn, and the hastily arranged funeral postponed. An inquest was held, and since a panel of medical experts had assigned Harriet's death to starvation, the Stauntons and Alice Rhodes were committed to stand trial at the Old Bailey for her murder, before Sir Henry Hawkins, who was known for his severity.

Clara Brown, the former housemaid of Patrick Staunton provided some very damning testimony about how he had beaten and mistreated poor Harriet. Mrs Richardson described how Louis had married her daughter for money, and then kept her captive in Cudham. The medical evidence was of a disgusting

5.7 The murder house at No. 34 Forbes Road, Penge

nature. Harriet had been systematically starved, and her weak, emaciated body was dirty and swarming with vermin. Due to the long-standing louse infestation, her skin was thickened to a remarkable degree.

The counsel for the prisoners faced an uphill task. Mr Edward Clarke, representing Patrick Staunton, tried to attack the medical evidence, aided by two doctors who testified that Harriet might have died from meningeal tuberculosis. It is true that the autopsy revealed that she had a small tubercular lesion at the apex of the right lung. The doctors speculated that "some small patches of rough millet-seed like deposit in the meshes of the pia mater" might be a sign of meningeal tuberculosis, but Sir Henry Hawkins pooh-poohed their evidence, remarking that they had themselves not seen the body. In a marathon summing-up, lasting more than ten hours, he effectively closed every loop-hole for the four prisoners; in particular, he reminded the jury that all four were equally culpable.

Due to Sir Henry's oratory, the time was close to 10 pm when the jury finally retired. They sat for ninety minutes before returning a verdict of guilty. Alice Rhodes fainted dead away, and the other three prisoners sat trembling like leaves as Sir Henry Hawkins, who looked even more sinister than normally in the dark, candle-lit court-room, sentenced all four to death for "a crime so black and hideous that I believe in all the records of crime it would be difficult to find its parallel."[6]

5.8 The Stauntons in the dock receiving sentence.

Although there was little sympathy for the Staunton brothers, many people thought Sir Henry Hawkins had gone too far when he sentenced the two women to death. As the medical debate about Harriet's cause of death continued in the *Lancet*, some correspondents still upheld the possibility of meningeal tuberculosis. This led to the Home Secretary reopening the case and respiting the executions. In the end, the three Stauntons were sentenced to life imprisonment, and Alice Rhodes, against whom the evidence had been feeble to say the least, was acquitted. Alice got a job as a barmaid after her narrow escape. One day, she pulled a pint for Sir Henry Hawkins, who remarked that surely, he had seen her somewhere before.

"You have, my Lord. I am Alice Rhodes, and your Lordship once sentenced me to death."

"Good heavens! I hope you are now doing well for yourself?"

"I am, quite well – no thanks to your Lordship!"[7]

5.9 Vignettes from the Penge Murder, from the Illustrated Police News, October 20 1877.

Patrick Staunton died in prison in 1881, and Elizabeth was released three years later. She married an art dealer and led a respectable life until her death, well into her seventies. As for the selfish, cruel Louis Staunton, he became a changed man in prison. A model prisoner and a devout Roman Catholic, he admitted his guilt, and said he deserved his punishment. In 1898, he was released from Dartmoor Prison, having served 22 years behind bars. It is pleasing to recount, in a tale as dark and disturbing as this one, that he was met by his loyal Alice, who had been waiting for him all those years. They were married in Brighton, and had

5.10 The Stauntons in Maidstone Gaol, from the Penny Illustrated Paper, October 20 1877.

offspring. Alice died just before the Great War, but Louis remarried. He was by then a successful estate agent and auctioneer. He died in 1934, aged 83.[8]

Although the Staunton house in Loughborough Park Road has been 'developed' since it was pictured in local historian Dorothy Cox's 1989 book *Brotherly Love; or, the Cudham Quartet*, quite a few of the other houses associated with the Penge Mystery remain. No. 6 Colby Road, Gipsy Hill, where Louis and Harriet lived before she was taken to Cudham, still remains, and Dorothy Cox reproduced recent photographs of both the Cudham farmhouses. Forbes Road was renamed Mosslea Road after the murder, but the houses were not renumbered. A woman growing up there in the 1950s remembers the lurid tales told about No. 34, not far from where her family lived. When it was featured by Dorothy Cox in 1989, No. 34 Mosslea Road was in a rather shabby condition, but when I saw it in 2012, the murder house was looking quite well cared for.

MURDER BY A CROYDON PUBLICAN, 1893

For many years, Mr James Peckham had been landlord of the Oakfield Tavern, situated at the crossing of St James's Road and Oakfield Road, Croydon. In 1886, when he was 47 years old, he married the wealthy widow Sophia Thomson, who was eighteen years his senior, and settled down in a semi-detached house at No. 4 Quadrant Road, Croydon. This was an ill-conceived move, since the marriage seems to have been cursed from the start. Both the Peckhams were fond of drink, James more so than his wife. James was also fond of spending money, whereas his wife was very parsimonious. They were constantly at loggerheads, particularly when drunk. The only respite for poor Sophia came in 1891, when James was admitted to Cane Hill Asylum, where he spent eighteen months suffering from 'melancholy mania'.

But James Peckham emerged from the asylum as angry and mean-spirited as before. In spite of his eighteen months of forced abstinence from alcohol, he drank harder than ever after returning to the family home at No. 4 Quadrant Road, and his temper suffered as a result. The neighbours at No. 6 could hear the Peckhams quarrelling furiously, and James threatening to shoot his wife. This was no idle threat, since the former publican had access to a loaded shotgun, among other firearms.

On January 2 1893, the Peckhams were at loggerheads as usual. Alice Aldous, servant to Mr Veale who lived at No. 6, was fearful that James might injure his wife. She could hear tongs smashing against the kitchen furniture, and moments later, the now 71-year-old Sophia was forcibly thrown out of the house, still holding some formidable-looking tongs. When Alice Aldous went out to comfort her, she saw that apart from a swollen and bloody nose, Sophia seemed unharmed. She asked to be readmitted to No. 4 Quadrant Road, but James twice replied 'If I let you in, I'll murder you!' In spite of this dire threat, the foolhardy old woman, whose instinct of self-preservation was clearly not in good working order, once more went into the house. Moments later, an explosion was heard. Fearful that James Peckham had shot his wife, Alice Aldous ran to fetch a police constable.

But it turned out that Police Constable George Windus had also heard the shot. When he came trudging up to No. 4 Quadrant Road, James Peckham stood outside, dancing a jig. 'I have shot my wife!' he shouted to the police constable. 'Surely not?' he startled constable answered. 'I have, my bonny boy!' shouted James, who appeared very exhilarated. He showed the constable into the kitchen, where Sophia's lifeless body was lying

5.11 James Peckham shoots his wife, from the Illustrated Police News, January 14 1893.

on the floor. A large part of her head had been blown off by the gunshot, and she was quite dead. Indicating the shotgun, James said 'I shot her with the right barrel, and the other barrel is loaded!' There had been two other people in the house at the time of the murder: the lodger Louisa Woodhams, and Sophia Peckham's imbecile sister.

At the coroner's inquest on Sophia Peckham, Louisa Woodhams and Alice Aldous gave evidence about James's drunken ways. He had often been shouting threats to injure or murder her, and kept his arsenal of rifles and shotguns ready for use. It is remarkable, even by the standards of the time, that a person recently committed to a lunatic asylum for eighteen months, was allowed to keep firearms, and a plentiful supply of ammunition. When asked for the motive of murdering his wife, James replied that it had all been an accident: the gun had gone off by mistake. At the Guildford Assizes, several people testified as to James's fierce and angry temper, his fondness for firearms, and his strange and unreasonable behaviour. One man had been held at gunpoint at No. 4 Quadrant Road, and forced to execute an infantry drill until he nearly dropped from fatigue.

It was found that James Peckham had committed the murder in a state of insanity, and he was incarcerated in Broadmoor.[9] He became a very difficult patient, known for his truculence and his foul language. A sturdy, corpulent man, nearly six feet tall and weighing 16 stone, he was a force to be reckoned with when seriously annoyed. Broadmoor records indicate that James Peckham remained a patient for 20 years, before succumbing to diabetes in 1913. The murder house at No. 4 [now 10] Quadrant Road still stands, although another house has been built in its large side garden. James Peckham's old pub, the Oakfield Tavern, was recently pulled down.

THE TOOTING HORROR, 1895

In 1880, the 24-year-old plasterer Frank Taylor married Martha Hocking, the 21-year-old daughter of a well-to-do manufacturer. It was a runaway match, and Martha would receive no further support from her family, since they considered that she had married beneath her station in life. Frank was a steady, industrious man, however. Although he remained a humble labourer, he was able to keep poverty from the door, and put food on the table for their steadily increasing brood of children.

In 1894, the Taylors were living in a small terraced house at No. 12 Fountain Road, Tooting. They had not less than seven children alive, ranging in age from the 14-year-old Frank Jr. to little Georgie aged just twenty months. Later the same year, Frank Taylor lost his job. He tried getting another one, but was struck down with influenza. Due to the severe winter, work was scarce, and once he had recovered, he could not find employment. His family was soon destitute, and they barely had food for the children. In between visiting various shops to look for work, Frank scrambled on the ice for pennies and farthings thrown by well-to-do skaters who made the most of the cold snap. The

5.12 Frank and Martha Taylor, from Lloyd's Weekly Newspaper March 17 1895.

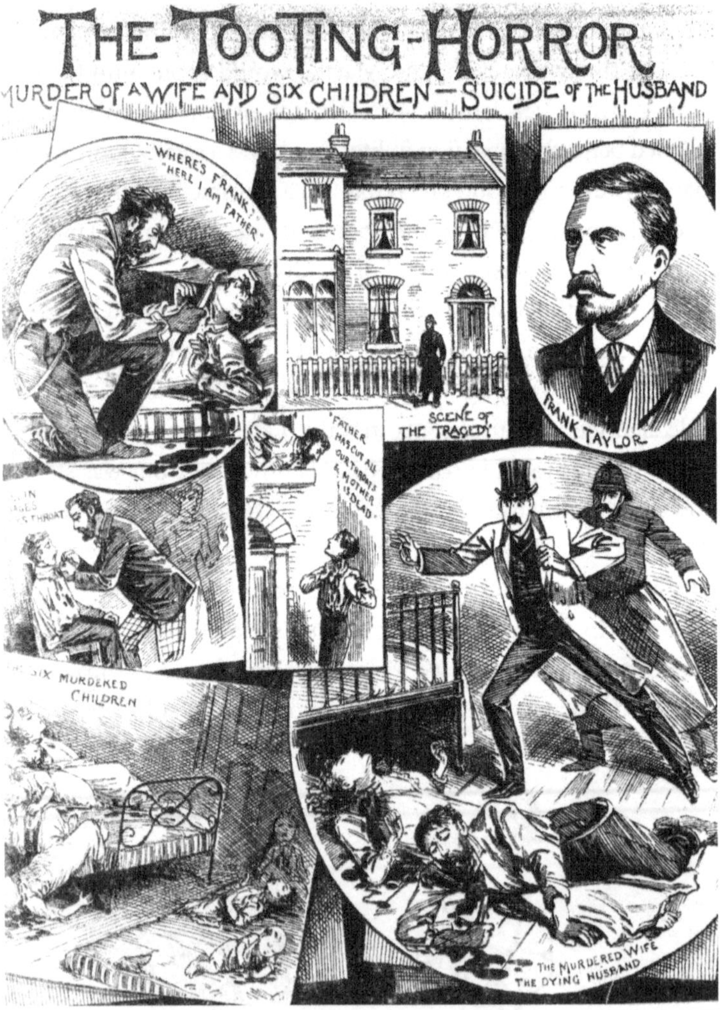

5.13 Sensational Scenes of the Tooting Horror, from the Illustrated Police News March 16 1895.

children were regular visitors to the penny paupers' suppers provided by the Tooting Graveney parish church. Frank Jr. earned a few pennies by carrying fresh water to neighbours whose pipes had frozen, but his father remained unable to find paid employment. For every day that went by, Frank Taylor became increasingly bitter and morose. The family now owed six weeks rent, and in spite of the freezing cold weather, none of the children had boots.

At half past five in the morning of March 7 1895, there was a knock at the door of Mr Richard Henry Hockins, a house-painter living at No. 9 Fountain Road. When he looked out of the window, he could see Frank Jr. standing by the door. Bleeding profusely from the throat, arm and hands, he called out 'Father cut all our throats and mother is dead!' Realizing that something terrible must have happened, Mr Hockins came downstairs, bandaged young Frank's wounds, and made sure the police was called in. The front door to No. 12 Fountain Road was locked and bolted, but the constables broke it down. Inside the cramped little house they met with the grossest scenes. In the back bedroom, they found all six children dead in a bloodbath, with their throats cut. In the front bedroom, they found the body of Martha Hocking with injuries from a terrible struggle; her head was nearly severed from the body. Frank Taylor himself was the only person alive, in spite of a large gash in the throat, but he expired on the way to the Wandsworth & Clapham Infirmary. He had succeeded in exterminating his entire family, apart from Frank Jr.

From his bed at St Thomas's Hospital, Frank Jr. gave his account of the 'Tooting Horror', as the mass murder was called in the newspapers. At about half past five in the morning, his father had come into the tiny bedroom shared by the seven Taylor children, saying 'Frank, where are you?' 'I am here, father', the sleepy lad had replied. His father had then leapt at him like a madman, slashing at him with a large razor. In spite of the deep wounds on his hands and arm, Frank kept fighting back. The other children woke up, and started shrieking and crying. Frank Taylor let go of his severely wounded son, and instead began cutting the throats of all the smaller children, one by one, except the seven-year-old Florrie. He lurched out of the room, sharpened the razor, and dispatched Florrie as well. Frank Jr. heard his father exclaim 'Oh, Lord! Oh, Lord!' and saw him reel out of the room. With considerable presence of mind, the wounded lad took on his mother's jacket, unbolted the front door, and went to seek assistance from Mr Hockins. His father pursued him downstairs, but did not venture out into the road, preferring to bolt the door and cut his own throat as well.

The Tooting Horror was widely reported in the newspapers. Although the irrepressible *Illustrated Police News* exploited the tragedy in some 'thrilling' illustrations, the majority of the press struck a more sombre note. The tragedy caused widespread revulsion throughout Britain. Some people blamed the Tooting authorities for their lack of charity: was it really right that a honest workman should become completely destitute, and driven to desperation, once he had lost his job? The relieving officer for the parish of Tooting retorted that Frank Taylor had been offered work as a stonemason a few weeks before the tragedy, and that he had recently been fined two shillings and sixpence for failing to send his children to school. The local people, who had done very little to help Frank Taylor when he was alive, now sang his praises and those of his family. Frank had been a very honest, upstanding citizen, his wife a hard-working, respectable woman, and the children very well behaved. In particular, golden-haired little Florrie had been a very pretty girl, and quite the pet of the neighbourhood.

The inquest on the murdered Taylors was opened at Tooting Vestry Hall on March 9. The coroner, Mr Braxton Hicks, said that this was one of the most painful and dreadful affairs that had happened in England for many years. Visibly moved, the jury then viewed the bodies. The police constables who had searched the murder house had found a bundle of religious hymns, and also an envelope on which Frank Taylor had written "I love my wife and children too dearly to allow people to jeer. They are all pure." There were also two letters with confused statements about false accusations against Frank Taylor being washed away in the Lord's precious blood. His enemies, who hated him with a cruel hate, had destroyed his life.[10] A writer in the *Pall Mall Gazette* pointed out that the Tooting Horror was the worst family tragedy in Britain since 1834, when the German Johann Nicholas Steinberg had murdered his common-law wife and four children in a bloodbath, at No. 17 Southampton Street [today Calshot Street; the house no longer stands]. Rather flippantly, the journalist commented that the German had fallen short of Taylor's record by two victims.[11]

Amidst loud applause, the Rev. D.H. Morton, Rector of Tooting Graveney, offered to have the murdered Taylors buried free of charge. A gentleman stood up to say that if the Rector had not made his generous offer, he and his friends would have paid for the funeral, so that the Taylor children were spared the indignity of a pauper's grave. There was more applause among the spectators; the Taylors were clearly more popular dead than alive. Commenting that such unseemly and raucous behaviour did not suit this sombre occasion, the coroner went on to read a number of letters from ladies and gentleman all over the country, offering to take care of the boy Frank, who was still recovering in hospital. In a strange ceremony of exorcism, all the furniture, clothes, and other effects of the murdered family was dragged out of the murder house, and burnt to ashes in a field to the rear of the house.

The last we hear of Frank Jr is that having recovered from his wounds, he was taken to the King's College Convalescent Home.

Various charitable individuals had made sure that his future education, and a fair start in life, had been secured for the orphaned lad.[12] In spite of a plaque being sold to commemorate the Tooting Tragedy, with the names of the eight dead members of the Taylor family, it is well-nigh forgotten today, even by the locals. No local history book mentions it, but the Surrey folk singer 'Pop' Maynard has rescued a contemporary song on the subject, which he has performed more than once:[13]

Once in Tooting did reside,
With his children by his side,
Frank Taylor and with him his loving wife.
But from life they are now gone,
Little Frankie left forlorn,
To tell how father robbed them of their life.

O it was just before the dawn,
On that fatal Thursday morn.
It was early there the lad they did behold,
He was crying there with fear:
'O come to mother, dear,
For father's killed them, they are dead and cold.'

'Then, where is my father?' little Frankie cried,
'With your mother and the babies he has died.'
'O here I must remain
and suffer grief and pain,
But we'll all meet up in Heaven side by side!'

So, is Tooting's House of Horrors still standing? This question has been debated on the Tootinglife internet homepage, but without any constructive deductions being made. Interestingly, one of the contributors could remember lodging in a haunted house in Fountain Road, where doors opened and shut on their own accord, and no tenant stayed longer than eight months. Even for an experienced murder house detective, finding the House of Horrors was quite a challenge, particularly since the contemporary accounts gave two different numbers for the house (No. 8 and No. 12). The houses in Fountain Road were renumbered a few years after the Tooting Horror, and the present-day No. 12 (and No. 8) are clearly innocent, since they are of a later style than the murder house.

Two vital clues come from the *Penny Illustrated Paper's* drawing of the House of Horrors: it is situated next to a slightly wider house without a fence, a shop carrying the name J. Lee. Since the Post Office directories put Joseph Lee's grocer's shop at No. 11 Fountain Road, it makes good sense for No. 12 to be next door, and thus it is impossible that the murder house was at No. 8. Secondly, the illustration shows open fields on the opposite side of the road, indicating that the murder house is in the longer

5.14 Three views of the Tooting murder house, from Lloyd's Weekly Newspaper March 17 1895, the Penny Illustrated Paper March 16 1895 and from the Illustrated Police Budget March 16 1895.

terrace of twenty houses seen on the 1894 Ordnance Survey map of Tooting, near the Blackshaw Road end of Fountain Road. The images in the *Penny Illustrated Paper* and *Lloyd's Weekly Newspaper* also show that the murder house is on the western side of Lee's former shop (which can still be seen to be wider than the other houses in the terrace). Importantly, this shop is on a slightly higher level than the houses to the west of it, again agreeing with the original illustrations. The murder house is today's No. 159 Fountain Road, situated just to the west of Lee's former shop at No. 157. It has not changed much since the time of the Tooting Horror.

MURDER IN OAKWOOD ROAD, 1897

George Dawes, a 49-year-old Croydon plasterer, lived at No. 18 Oakwood Road, Thornton Heath. Both he and his wife Sarah had been previously married, and together they had a brood of not less than nine children, all of whom resided at the small terraced house at No. 18.

For many years, George and Sarah had lived happily together, but in 1895 and 1896, he was becoming decidedly odd. Entirely without reason, he became convinced that his wife led a double life as a prostitute. She had been seduced by George Ward, landlord at the 'Bird in Hand' public house, and he had become her pimp, persuading her to receive various men, including sailors and navvies, at the family home when George was away. This disagreeable thought remained with George day and night, but he did not feel brave enough to confront the villainous publican, since he believed that Ward was also a criminal mastermind, who had a number of 'heavies' under his control.

George Dawes' brother Alfred tried to reason with him,

pointing out that Sarah was a respectable, middle-aged woman, and certainly nothing like a typical prostitute. George remained convinced that something very sinister was afoot at No. 18 Oakwood Road, however. When he saw his eldest son, 18-year-old George Jr, sitting in the same sofa as Sarah, he immediately understood that this demonic lad had become one of Ward's henchmen. George confronted his son, saying that he now knew the truth: his own son had been operating a system of light and curtain signals, to let the eager 'customers' waiting outside know that the 'happy hooker' Sarah was ready for their attentions. As a reward for assisting him, Ward had allowed George Jr to enjoy the insatiable Sarah's services himself! George Jr, a decent young man, was so outraged by these wild allegations that he left No. 18 Oakwood Road, never to return.

Unashamed of his outrageous behaviour, George Dawes openly accused Sarah of being a prostitute. When she denied his absurd allegations, he gave her a hard knock in the face. She prosecuted him for assault, and he was ordered to pay two sureties of £10 each to keep the peace for six months. Alfred Dawes and George's other friends put further pressure on him: had he not been making a complete fool of himself with his unbalanced actions? For a while, George tried his best to rein in his abnormal jealousy. He treated his wife with respect, and no longer made any wild threats against the publican Ward. He did not allow his son to return to No. 18 Oakwood Road, however, and sometimes he strip-searched his other children to make sure they were not smuggling in secret messages in their underwear. He also hung differently coloured curtains in the windows of No. 18, to tempt the army of lovers he thought was waiting outside, waiting for them in the hallway, armed with a heavy cudgel.

Late in the evening of Boxing Day 1896, George Dawes went to see his brother Alfred. When Alfred let him into the house,

George said that he had just murdered his wife, through dashing her brains out with a hammer, and cutting her throat. Knowing that George was not always *compos mentis*, Alfred and his wife accompanied him back to No. 18 Oakwood Road, there they found the mangled remains of poor Sarah Dawes in the blood-soaked bed. At Croydon Police Station, George Dawes blamed the publican Ward for what had happened, telling the constables all about how his wife had been seduced by him, and the later disastrous events leading to her death. On trial at the Old Bailey, before Mr Justice Hawkins, he was found guilty but insane, and committed to Broadmoor, where he expired in October 1921.[14] The murder house at No. 18 Oakwood Road still exists, and so does the small 'Bird in Hand' pub at No. 291 Sydenham Road.

THE TALENTED MR BRINKLEY, 1907

5.15 A drawing of Richard Brinkley, from a press cutting in the archives of Mr Stewart P. Evans, reproduced by permission.

In the evening of Saturday April 20 1907, the Fulham carpenter Richard Brinkley visited his friend, the Croydon accountant Reginald Parker. Since Brinkley had recently come into some money, he wanted to buy a large and sturdy bulldog to guard his property. Parker, who had previously helped his friend to draft letters and other documents, had agreed to help him procure one of those animals. When Brinkley came to see the bulldog, at No. 32 Churchill Road, Croydon, he found Parker and his landlord Richard Beck in the living-room, sharing a bottle of ale. Beck, an insurance agent working from home, was joined by his wife and daughter. The jolly Mr Brinkley produced a large bottle of oatmeal stout from his pocket, offering Parker to have a swig or two. This surprised Parker, who knew that his friend was a strict teetotaller, but the Fulham carpenter said that his doctor had recently advised him to take stout regularly, for his constitution. Brinkley poured Parker a glass, before asking for some water for himself. Later, the two friends departed to see the bulldog, which Brinkley purchased for £5 and arranged to have transported back to Fulham.

Later the very same night, Reginald Parker, who had arranged to sleep in the house of a friend, was woken up by the police. They gruffly asked him what he knew about the mysterious deaths of his landlord Richard Beck and his wife Elizabeth, and the serious illness of their daughter Daisy. There was suspicion that these three had all been poisoned. Parker, a somewhat shady character, sobered up very quickly in this dire situation. He explained about the visit by his friend Brinkley, his interest in the bulldog, and the mysterious bottle of stout, from which Parker himself had drunk very little. But what interest would the Fulham carpenter have in murdering the inoffensive Becks, who he did not know at all?

And indeed, the police found traces of prussic acid both in the bottle of stout and in the glasses the Becks had drunk from. A boy told them that Brinkley had purchased a bottle of stout from the shop where he worked, the evening of the murders. Clearly, this strange Mr Brinkley had deliberately brought with him a bottle of poisoned stout to No. 32 Churchill Road. When arrested by the police, the Fulham carpenter exclaimed "Well, I'm sugared! This is very awkward, isn't it!" He reminded them that he was a strict teetotaller, and a hard-working man of good character, and asked permission to send word to his Masonic lodge.

But the police made good headway in solving the Churchill Road mystery. Although Brinkley denied being near that part of Croydon the evening of the murders, an acquaintance had seen him at the railway station. And then there was the pharmacist, from whom Brinkley had purchased prussic acid to poison a dog, returning a few days later for a second dose since he had spilt the first one. But the most spicy revelations regarded the will of a 76-year-old Fulham widow of German ancestry, named Johanna Maria Blume. She had owned a house at No. 4 Maxwell Road, just south of where the Chelsea football club is today, and lived there with her granddaughter Augusta. Mrs Blume had a daughter named Caroline, but they were on bad terms since Caroline was living in sin with a man, with whom she had several children. The cunning Richard Brinkley had insinuated himself into the gullible old woman's affections, calling her 'granny' and giving her a hand with various daily chores. In late 1906, Mrs Blume made a will in favour of Brinkley, leaving him her entire estate, valued at £725 in total. Strangely enough, Caroline Blume told the police, her mother had died just two days after this will had been drawn up!

The police tracked down old Mrs Blume's will, which looked fully legitimate. It was duly signed by the old lady, although the granddaughter said that the old lady had only signed a paper regarding some Masonic outing. Augusta the granddaughter also remembered that Brinkley had seemed much affected by Mrs Blume's death, asking the doctor to make sure the dear old lady was not 'cut up' to determine the cause of her death. A benevolent doctor had made out a diagnosis of 'apoplexy' for her death certificate, but Mr Ingleby Oddie, the Coroner for London, insisted on an autopsy. No obvious cause of death was forthcoming, but the pathologist suspected a cerebral haemorrhage and death through natural causes. The talented

5.16 Mrs Blume is exhumed, from the Illustrated Police News, May 11 1907.

Brinkley was very pleased to receive this good news, and he went out partying with the pretty, 21-year-old Augusta Blume, who worked as a pantomime actress. When he told young 'Gussie' that he had been 'granny's' wish that they should get married, she wanted nothing of that, however.

One of the witnesses to Mrs Blume's bogus will turned out to be none other than Reginald Parker. But when questioned, this individual denied all knowledge of this will, or of old Mrs Blume of No. 4 Maxwell Road, although he could remember signing what was purportedly a document concerning some Masonic outing! After Brinkley had claimed all old Mrs Blume's property, Caroline had stated her intention to challenge the will. At first, the Fulham carpenter had tried to appease her by offering her his hand in marriage, saying that this had been old Mrs Blume's wish, but she wanted nothing of that. Clearly, this audacious Mr

5.17 Brinkley in the dock, and Mrs Blume being resurrected, from the Illustrated Police Budget, May 11 and May 18, 1907.

Brinkley had then decided to 'eliminate' Parker who had been tricked into signing the bogus will. And this plan might well have succeeded, had not the thirsty Becks come in the way, and drunk the poisoned stout themselves. There was considerable newspaper interest in the sensational 'Croydon Poisoning Case': the *Illustrated Police News* published a drawing of the exhumation of Mrs Blume, and its fellow sensation newspaper the *Illustrated Police Budget* also too a great interest in this extraordinary murder mystery, publishing drawings of Brinkley in the dock, Mrs Blume being exhumed, and Reginald Parker lounging in a chair with the sturdy bulldog sitting on his lap. In the end, the exhumation of Mrs Blume's remains yielding nothing interesting, but she had been dead a long time, and traces of certain volatile poisons may well have disappeared.

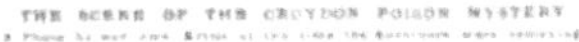

5.18 The murder house at No. 32 Churchill Road, Croydon, and Reginald Parker holding the large and sturdy bulldog that was intended to guard Brinkley's ill-gotten gains, from the Illustrated Police Budget, May 11 and June 1, 1907.

The police strongly suspected that the talented Mr Brinkley had been up to further mischief in the past. He had been born in 1855, probably in Eye, Lincolnshire. In 1875, he married Miss Clara Emily Sorrell in Chelsea. The 1881 Census found him at No. 6 Tullet Place, Kensington [it no longer stands], living with his wife and three children: Richard Langtry Brinkley born in 1875, Annie Louisa Brinkley born in 1877 and Clara Maria Brinkley born in 1878. He described himself as a cabinet maker, and two lodgers, a French polisher and a young plumber, lived in his house. Mrs Clara Emily Brinkley died in 1883, aged just 28. Her death certificate gives the cause of death as complications to deep venous thrombosis, a less than common ailment in one so young, then as well as now. The mention in the 1881 Census is the last we hear of the two little girls.

In 1893, a 17-year-old young woman named Laura Jane Glenn had died mysteriously at No. 21 Marlborough Square, Chelsea. She was a penniless prostitute, and had more than once been evicted from her lodgings, due to her immoral life. It was suspected that she had committed suicide from drinking arsenic tincture from a medicine chest belonging to her much older boyfriend William Ridgeley. Although a carpenter by trade, he took an interest in veterinary medicine and practiced as a 'dog doctor', dosing the hapless Chelsea canines with various chemicals from his large medicine chest. When inspected by the police, this chest was full of dangerous poisons of every description. As cool as a cucumber, Mr Ridgeley told the constables that as a dog-fancier, he needed some medicines to make use of when his valuable animals were taken ill. The police suspected that after Ridgeley had tired of the young floozie Laura Jane Glenn, he had given her some poison to drink, and forged a suicide note. There was a good deal of newspaper publicity about the 'Chelsea Mystery', as the case was called, and the proceedings from the coroner's court were reported in full.

At the coroner's inquest on Laura Jane Glenn, William Ridgeley's son, the 17-year-old Richard William Ridgeley, gave evidence in his father's behalf. Importantly, he admitted that although Ridgeley was his proper name, he sometimes used the name Brinkley! His father's intentions towards the deceased had been fully honourable, and he had in fact employed her to keep house for him. When the elder 'Ridgeley' faced a hostile questioning about what use he made of this great quantity of dangerous poisons, he told them about his sympathy for ailing canines, and also about some chemical and electrical experiments he was making. He had been very fond of the deceased, and his intentions had been fully honourable. 'Ridgeley' described himself as a friend and helper of London's downtrodden young 'unfortunates', but the coroner did not believe a word of what he was saying. Mrs Childs, the landlady at No. 21 Marlborough Square, described her experiences with the sinister 'Mr Ridgeley' and with the silly young Laura Jane Glenn, who was fond of telling 'porkies' about her father being an army captain, her mother a Maid of Honour to the Queen, and the opera singer Adelina Patti one of her best friends! In reality, she had been kicked out by her family after stealing £10, and she had been living with an army soldier before moving in with 'Ridgeley'. After deliberating for half an hour, the coroner's jury returned a verdict of suicide, adding that Ridgeley deserved severe censure for having such a quantity of poison in his possession. The police ought to find out "how he came possessed of them, and for what purpose".[15]

But although the police detectives still suspected that 'Ridgeley' had murdered Laura Jane Glenn, they were unable to find any further conclusive evidence against him. Interestingly, they found another 'unfortunate' young woman, who called herself Emily George, who had once cohabited with the talented Richard Brinkley, who sometimes used the name William Rigby. She had three illegitimate children with him, one of whom had died mysteriously at an early age. The 'dog doctor' Brinkley had often dosed her and the children with various powders and tinctures from his medicine chest, and she had sometimes felt very ill after taking her medicine. In 1890, Brinkley had been sentenced to nine months of hard labour for stealing a quantity of bicycles and skates from a store. Detective Inspector George Jeffrey, who led the retrospective police investigation into Brinkley's past misdeeds, could report that the volatile Emily George had once attracted notice in Salisbury, where she had moved, by declaring that if she liked to open her mouth, she could get Brinkley sent to penal servitude. Inspector Jeffrey also retrieved the death certificate of 'George Brinkley', age just three hours, dead from 'congenital debilitude' in late 1889. Then there was the matter of another young London floozie, the 20-year-old Jane Kemp, who had lived with Brinkley for a while in 1888 and 1889. She gave birth to a male child named 'Charles Richard Kemp', who died in July 1889. The mother followed him into the grave four months later, from what was believed to be 'consumption'. Dead people do not talk, but the various close friends of the talented Mr Brinkley certainly had a very short life expectancy!

In *The Secret History of Great Crimes*, a small book published in the 1920s, the Brighton journalist and cinematograph owner Walter Harold Speer quoted a Scotland Yard detective involved in the Laura Jane Glenn case as saying that the 'Chelsea Mystery' had been a very black case, and that 'Ridgeley' was fortunate not to have been charged with murder. W. Harold Speer added that there was no doubt in his own mind that 'Ridgeley' "had poisoned the girl, and, in fact, public opinion became so hot against the man that he thought it advisable to leave the neighbourhood." Speer went to Brinkley's former lodgings in Brixton, where the landlady gave him an arsenic pill, which this miscreant had left behind after experimenting on her chickens. He also learnt that Brinkley's young wife had died unexpectedly after a very unhappy life. W. Harold Speer decided to keep an eye on this slippery customer, and he could report that after his narrow escape in the Laura Jane Glenn case, Brinkley had made himself scarce.[16] He was active as a street agitator, preaching socialism to crowds of labouring men at the street corners of Hammersmith. In 1900, he successfully took his employer to court for wrongfully detaining his tools, after he had been dismissed from his job as a foreman carpenter.

When he was on trial for murder at the Surrey Assizes in Guildford, things were not looking good for the mysterious Mr Brinkley. Reliable witnesses made it clear that he had brought the bottle of poisoned stout to No. 32 Churchill Road. The problem was that he had clearly not intended the Becks to be his victims, but the judge informed the jury that if the prisoner had taken poison into the house with the intent to murder some person, it did not matter who, then he was guilty. Found guilty of murder and sentenced to death, Richard Brinkley was hanged at Wandsworth Prison on August 13 1907.[17] The most remarkable aspect of the Brinkley case is how such an unremarkable man, a hard-working teetotaller and Freemason, could concoct such a deliberate murder plot. And how many people had this mystery man done to death? His wife, his mistress Laura Jane Glenn, several other floozies he has associated with, and more than one of his illegitimate children, had all died under suspicious circumstances. It would seem very likely that old Mrs Blume had also received a dose of poison, after Brinkley had forged her will, although this could never be proven at the time. It was unwise of Brinkley to try to murder Parker instead of swearing him into the plot, and clumsy of him to leave the bottle behind with the Becks. But the greatest question still remains to be answered: what had the talented Mr Brinkley, who took such an interest in London's prostitutes, been up to in 1888, the year of Jack the Ripper?

MURDER AND SUICIDE IN CHATFIELD ROAD, 1908

In 1908, the little semi-detached house at No. 27 Chatfield Road, Croydon, was home to the widow Mrs Mary Jane Manser, her son Francis and her daughter Mary. Her married daughter Eva also lived in the house, with her husband Walter Jennings. Francis Manser, a gloomy and solitary young man, is listed in the 1901 Census as apprentice to a civil engineer, and he later worked at Mr Cow's india-rubber factory at Streatham Common. In early 1908, he lost his job, and went unemployed for several months. Francis Manser was an expert revolver shot, and often went practicing at the local shooting range.

Leading a vegetating existence at No. 27 Chatfield Road did not agree with the 25-year-old Francis Manser. After suffering badly from the influenza, he became severely depressed. None of the other inhabitants of the house seems to have suggested that perhaps he should see a specialist doctor, or at least to have made sure that he did not have access to loaded firearms. On July 7, Walter and Eva Jennings went out, but Francis Manser remained at No. 27 Chatfield Road with his mother and sister. It was his habit to sleep all day and be awake all night, something that did not benefit his prospects of finding paid employment. But this particular day, the demented young Manser went out of bed, grabbed his revolver, and shot his mother and sister dead as they lay sleeping in bed. He then killed the two family dogs. Standing in front of a mirror, he finally shot himself straight through the head. Since there was a thunderstorm outside, none of the neighbours reacted to the gunfire. It was not until Mr and Mrs

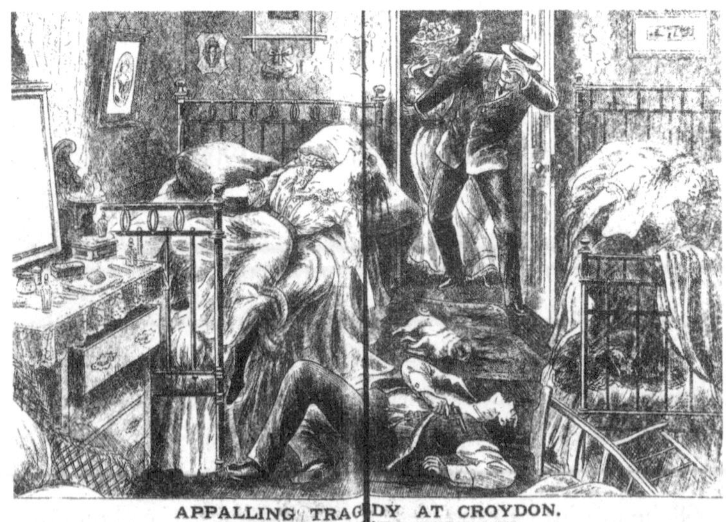

5.19 The carnage left behind by Francis Manser is discovered, from the Illustrated Police News, July 18 1908.

Jennings returned home at five in the afternoon that the carnage was discovered. Francis Manser, who was still alive, was at once conveyed to the Croydon General Hospital, where he expired just after nine o'clock. He had left a letter saying 'Bury us all at Southsea with Father.'

At the inquest on Francis, Mary Jane and Mary Manser, the family GP gave evidence as to attending Francis in April for a severe bout of influenza. Two years earlier, he had fallen off a machine at work and landed on his head. Mrs Manser had told the doctor that Francis had been feeling depressed and anxious about his work, but this had not prompted the medical man to refer him to a mental specialist. Mrs Jennings had not noticed anything untoward when leaving the house, nor had her husband.

5.20 The murderous Francis Manser, and the house at No. 29 Chatfield Road, from the Illustrated Police Budget, July 18 1908.

There had been no quarrel, nor had Francis given any indication of going over the edge. Walter Jennings said that although he knew that his brother-in-law "had been rather disappointed in life", he had not appeared capable of causing mass carnage in the household. The coroner's jury returned a verdict of wilful murder against Francis Manser, who had afterwards committed suicide while mentally deranged.[18]

CARNAGE IN ALEXANDRA ROAD, 1909

In early 1909, Mr Ernest Harvey Blundell, an insurance agent living at No. 27 Alexandra Road, Croydon, was very ill with what was diagnosed as influenza and 'neuritis'. His eyes were chronically inflamed, and it was feared that he might lose his eyesight. Not at all unreasonably, Blundell became depressed and despondent, and worried that he would no longer be able to work and support his wife and children. There was already a lodger in the little terraced Croydon house: an elderly lady named Miss May Hope Jay, who occupied two rooms on the first floor. Mrs Blundell confided in her that since her husband could no longer work due to his headaches, the family had to economize.

On February 11 1909, after the Blundells' 13-year-old daughter had gone off to school, Miss Jay was alarmed to hear gunfire and screams from the Blundells' bedroom. She went up to the door and said 'What is the matter, Mrs Blundell? Can I do anything?' Since there was no response, Miss Jay boldly opened the door. She saw the nine-year-old boy Graham Blundell lying dead on the floor, blood pouring from a gunshot wound in his chest. His father was lying not far away, bleeding profusely from the head. When the terrified Miss Jay asked what had happened, he just said 'My poor wife! I wish I were dead!'

5.21 Miss Jay enters the Alexandra Road chamber of horrors, from the Illustrated Police News, February 20 1909.

Miss Jay ran out of the room, looking for Mrs Blundell, who was nowhere to be found. Had some armed robber broken into No. 27 Alexandra Road, intent on gunning down the entire Blundell family? The terrified old lady ran out of the house, screaming 'Murder! Murder!' all the way to the surgery of Dr J.H. Thompson, the local practitioner. She

5.22 The police find Mrs Blundell in the coal cellar, from the Illustrated Police News, February 20 1909.

managed to describe the bloodbath she had witnessed, and the doctor sent a boy for the police and accompanied her back to the murder house. He found young Graham Blundell in a small bedroom, dead from a revolver shot to the chest. Ernest Harvey Blundell had one bullet wound to the forehead, and one to each temple, but remarkably, he was still alive. A small-calibre revolver was lying on the floor next to him. He explained that he had murdered his wife and son, and then shot himself in the head three times. Surprised and dismayed that he was still alive after this determined attempt at self-destruction, he had tried to cut his throat and wrists with a blunt old pen-knife, but with as little success. He urged the doctor to "give him two or three more shots to finish him off" but Dr Thompson's respect for the Hippocratic oath did not allow for such rash actions.

In the meantime, Miss Jay and a police constable went in search of Mrs Blundell. The heard groans emanating from the coal cellar, and in there, they found Mrs Blundell, still alive but bleeding profusely from a bullet wound just below the ear. Both the Blundells were taken to Croydon General Hospital, where they lay in a serious condition. Poor Miss Jay, who had witnessed such horrors, had to be put to bed in a state of nervous exhaustion.

At the time of the coroner's inquest on Graham Blundell, both his parents were too ill to take part. Ernest Harvey Blundell had always been a sober, industrious man, and very religious, but he had suffered badly from the influenza, and also from inflammation of the eyes that might end in blindness. He had left various confused notes behind in the murder house, and witnesses testified that Mrs Blundell had feared that her husband was losing his mind. The coroner's inquest returned a verdict of wilful murder against Ernest Harvey Blundell.

In early March 1909, the newspapers announced that Mrs Blundell was now out of danger, although the bullet was still lodged in her skull. Amazingly, Ernest Harvey Blundell himself also made it out of the hospital alive. The plan was to bring him before the Croydon magistrates, but Blundell was found insane and unfit to plead, and was incarcerated in Broadmoor, where he lived on until 1940.[19]

MURDER AND SUICIDE IN CRANBROOK ROAD, 1927

John O'Leary, a young Croydon railwayman, joined the army in 1914 and served in the trenches throughout the Great War. On leave back home in 1915, he married his sweetheart Rose Coomber. Serving in the Royal Engineers, John was twice gassed and survived many dangers, but in 1919, he returned home to Croydon and settled down in a small terraced house at No. 25 Cranbrook Road.

In 1927, John O'Leary was working as a goods clerk at Waddon Station. A steady, industrious man, he had two little daughters, to whom he was devoted. The neighbours found him and Rose friendly and likeable, albeit very reserved. But on May 5 1927, when his daughter Rona returned home, she found her mother's dead body in the front room. She had been beaten to death with a large black shillelagh, which was lying nearby. The little girl alerted a neighbour, and a police constable was soon at the scene. In a small scullery by the coal cellar, he found John O'Leary dead, his throat cut from ear to ear.

Initially, it was believed that an intruder had entered the house and murdered both the O'Learys, but there was no sign of a forced entry, nor had anything been stolen from the house. The absence of signs of a struggle led the police to suspect that John O'Leary had beaten his wife to death, before going into the scullery and cutting his throat with a razor that was found on the floor not far away.

At the inquest on John and Rose O'Leary, no clue was forthcoming as to why John had decided to murder his wife and then take his own life. The neighbours had found them a devoted couple, and both John's father and his father-in-law denied that the quiet Croydon railwayman had ever showed signs of violence or insanity. His experiences in the Great War had taken their toll on his health, both bodily and mentally, and he had been suffering from headaches, sleeplessness and depression. The very day he had murdered the wife, he had an appointment to see a doctor about these problems. The coroner's verdict returned a verdict that John O'Leary had murdered his wife, afterwards committing suicide, adding that he had not been in his right mind when he committed these acts.[20]

SYPHILOPHOBIA IN FRANCHE COURT ROAD, 1930

Robert Frederick Montague was a young South London labouring man. In the 1920s, he contracted syphilis, and attended St Thomas's Hospital for treatment, with a good effect. He regularly attended the hospital for check-ups, to make sure the disease did not recur. In December 1929, he married his wife Jessie, and they settled down in the upstairs flat at No. 9 Franche Court Road, Tooting.

In August 1930, Robert Frederick Montague developed some kind of skin disease. He had a healthy fear of syphilis, and was fearful the disease had recurred. The doctors at St Thomas's Hospital pooh-poohed his concerns, and told him that these small spots on the skin certainly had nothing whatsoever to do with syphilis, but Montague remained convinced that his syphilis was not cured, and that he had infected his wife and unborn child with this loathsome disease.

In the early morning of September 2 1930, Robert Frederick Montague came into Earlsfield police station, to give himself up for murdering his wife. And indeed, Jessie Montague was found dead in the bedroom at No. 9 Franche Court Road. In his deranged condition, Robert Frederick Montague had thought it best to kill his wife and unborn child. A psychiatrist found him depressed and morose, and a severe case of syphilophobia, but he was fit to plead and stand trial for his crime, which he did at the Central Criminal Court on October 14 1930. The 30-year-old Robert Frederick Montague was found guilty but insane, and was sent to Broadmoor.[21]

THE NORTHWAY ROAD MATRICIDE, 1931

In the early 1920s, No. 10 Northway Road, Croydon, was home to the builder Mr James Alfred Hurley, his wife Annie Elizabeth, and their four children. After Mr Hurley had died prematurely in 1923, his widow lived on in the house. Her eldest son James became a civil servant and moved to a flat of his own, but in 1931, the invalid son Henry, the daughter Beatrice and the 14-year-old schoolboy Thomas were still living in the parental home. Henry had a partially paralysed right arm, and some kind of muscle disease as well. His bowels were not in good working order, something the doctors blamed on a 'nervous stomach condition'. He was no longer able to work as a stocktaker, and in 1930, he had been in a mental hospital for six weeks, and very much resented his mother for having committed him there. He was angry and spiteful towards her, and the family life became increasingly stressful, particularly after Annie Elizabeth herself had been diagnosed by a serious bowel complaint.

On May 5 1931, Annie Elizabeth Hurley was found lying on the first floor landing, strangled to death. Henry was nowhere to be found, but before the police started searching for him, the invalid came into the South Norwood police station, stating that he had strangled his mother to death, since she had been nagging

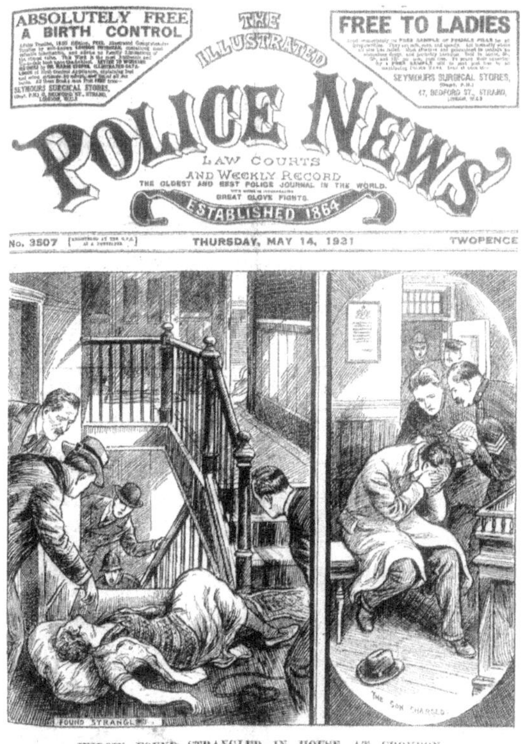

ABSOLUTELY FREE
A BIRTH CONTROL

SEYMOURS SURGICAL STORES

THE ILLUSTRATED

POLICE NEWS

LAW COURTS
AND WEEKLY RECORD
THE OLDEST AND BEST POLICE JOURNAL IN THE WORLD.
GREAT GLOVE FIGHTS.
ESTABLISHED 1864

FREE TO LADIES

SEYMOURS SURGICAL STORES,
47, BEDFORD ST., STRAND,

No. 3507 THURSDAY, MAY 14, 1931 TWOPENCE

FOUND STRANGLED.

THE SON CHARGED

WIDOW FOUND STRANGLED IN HOUSE AT CROYDON

5.23 James Alfred Hurley strangles his mother to death, from the Illustrated Police News, May 14 1931.

him. When examined by the prison doctor, he showed no sign of emotion when his crime was discussed; in fact, he expressed relief that his mother was no longer able to annoy him. Abnormally morose and taciturn, this strange Henry Hurley had a general resentment for every person he encountered, the doctor wrote. But although far from sane, he was found fit to plead and stand trial. On trial at the Central Criminal Court for matricide, Henry William Hurley was found guilty but insane, and he was incarcerated in Broadmoor.[22]

THE ADDISCOMBE ROAD MYSTERY, 1932

Mr Ellis Dagnall, a 72-year-old actor and theatrical producer, lived in the semi-detached house at No. 61 Addiscombe Road, Croydon, with his 56-year-old housekeeper Susan Emberton. When Mr Dagnall returned home on March 18 1932, he found the house in great disorder, and a large suitcase packed full of silver stood in the hall. Mr Dagnall immediately ran out and called the police. They arrived three minutes later, but the burglar or burglars had fled. Miss Emberton was found lying on her bed with serious head injuries. Dr Dorothy Day, who practiced at No. 59 Addiscombe Road next door, was called in, and she predicted that although the housekeeper had received some serious knocks to the head, she would eventually recover. All Miss Emberton could say was 'Oh, my poor head! My head hurts, who did it?'

In spite of the lady doctor's optimistic prognosis, Susan Emberton died on March 20 without saying anything further, and

5.24 A postcard showing Addiscombe Road, Croydon.

5.25 Susan Emberton is found murdered, from the Illustrated Police News, March 24 1932.

the case was now one of murder. A fair amount of money and jewelry had been stolen from the ransacked murder house, but the unexpected arrival of Mr Dagnall had meant that the burglars had not been able to take with them the suitcase they had loaded full of silver. An old police truncheon marked '1848' was found on the premises; it was stained with blood, and presumed to be the murder weapon. The house at No. 61 Addiscombe Road was for sale, and Miss Emberton, who had been housekeeper to Mr Dagnall for eight years, was entrusted to show the premises to prospective buyers. The detectives were interested to find that there were some promising witness observations of the comings and goings at the murder house. At 11.50, a good-looking young woman had been seen to exit the premises; at 12.45, Miss Emberton received a crate of beer from a delivery driver; at 3.45 a telephone inspector called but nobody answered the door. At 5.20, a young man was admitted into the house by a woman wearing a white apron, and at 5.55, two men were admitted by a woman, leaving a blue saloon car outside. Strangely enough, another witness had seen Miss Emberton walking towards Croydon with a large empty shopping basket at 6 pm, something that was in disagreement both with the middle-aged housekeeper's daily routine, and with the other witness statements quoted above.

The detectives presumed that Miss Emberton had admitted two burglars into the house, quite possibly after they had posed as prospective house buyers. One of them had knocked her down, and they had then proceeded to ransack the house. A police informant soon named the Croydon burglars turned murderers as Alfred 'Bottles' Philpot and another man nicknamed 'Musha'. 'Bottles' had been the man who had knocked the Addiscombe Road housekeeper down. It turned out that Philpot the burglar was already serving time in Brixton Prison, for two 'jobs' at Kensington and Finchley. He was a tough character, and the other inmates treated him with respect. When questioned by the police, Philpot claimed to have an alibi for the 'Croydon job', having transported a bedstead to his sister at the time of the murder. The police were convinced that he had made this alibi up in advance, and persuaded his parents and sister to lie for him. They tried their best to find the elusive 'Musha', and succeeded in tracking down a suspected burglar named Louis Bura who sometime was addressed by this nickname, but there was nothing to tie him to the Croydon murder. Many known criminals were questioned by the police, in the hope that they could be persuaded into giving evidence against Philpot, but they had respect for this tough London burglar, and were unwilling to 'squeal' on him.[23]

Mr Dagnall finally managed to sell the murder house at No. 61 Addiscombe Road in August 1933; he moved into a flat at Shaftesbury Avenue. The police file on the murder of Susan

Emberton was closed in August 1934, and it remains unsolved to this day. Alfred Philpot remained the only serious suspect, but the case against him wholly depended on the reliability of the police informant who 'fingered' him. The murder house looks more or less unchanged since the 1930s; curiously, the house next door is still a doctor's surgery.

MURDER IN PRESTON ROAD, 1959

In 1959, the 58-year-old James Joseph Tyrrell was employed at a telephone operator at the Croydon Interchange. He lived in an end-of-terrace house at No. 55 Preston Road, Upper Norwood, with his 88-year-old father and namesake. On March 12, he was visited by his former colleague William John Storie, who had been promoted to be temporary night supervisor at the Wallington exchange office, after 25 years of service in Croydon. Tyrrell was the collector for the Mutual Aid Insurance, and Storie wanted his funds transferred to Wallington. Storie thought Tyrrell rather muddled with regard to his book-keeping ability, but they parted good friends.

Early the following morning, Tyrrell heard a noise from downstairs. He bravely went down to confront the burglar, but a fist shot out and hit him hard on the nose. When the intruder grabbed Tyrrell by the throat, the telephone operator bit his hand hard. But his opponent, who was much the stronger, flung him on a bed, jumped on him, and struck him six hard blows on the head. When Tyrrell screamed for help, his elderly father came lurching into the room, but only to receive another brutal beating. Since Tyrrell was still groaning loudly with pain, the intruder gruffly said 'Stop shouting!' The battered telephone operator recognized his voice as that of William John Storie.

The police soon arrived at No. 55 Preston Road. William John Storie, who was still on the premises, was taken into custody, and the two battered Tyrrells were driven off to hospital. Storie could not explain why he had gone on a rampage, and beaten up his colleague and his elderly father so very badly; in fact, he seemed genuinely appalled at what he had just done. He could remember boarding the bus on his way home from work, but then he had completely blacked out. Since old Tyrrell died a few days later, the case became one of murder. It turned out that Storie's personal life had been very sad: his wife had been bombed out, and her sister killed in a V1 attack during the war. Her nerves shattered, she had nagged him ceaselessly, but he had remained with her for the sake of their daughter. An experienced psychiatrist suspected that Storie had suffered from an epileptic fugue and automatism when he had attacked his harmless colleague and the old man, and found reason to argue diminished responsibility on psychiatric grounds. On trial at the Central Criminal Court on June 17 1959, Storie was found guilty of manslaughter and was sentenced to four years in prison.[24]

THE TRITTON ROAD DOUBLE MURDER, 1960

Alfred Rubython Hickman was born in 1905, and left school at the age of fourteen, working as a messenger boy for a while, before joining a telephone manufacturing company in 1921. He married his wife Winifred, and they had a daughter named Jean. Alf Hickman's mental health was far from good: he suffered from recurrent bouts of depression, and was an inpatient at the Bethlem Royal Hospital in 1949. Still, he kept beavering away at the telephone company, as a veteran employee with 39 years of service.

In early 1960, the now 55-year-old Alf Hickman lived in the

upstairs flat at No. 8 Tritton Road, West Norwood, with his 50-year-old wife Winifred and the 18-year-old daughter Jean, who worked as a shop assistant. When a young family moved into the ground floor flat, which had long stood empty, there was immediate trouble, since the Hickmans were the proverbial Neighbours from Hell. There were angry quarrels about the decoration of the shared areas, and particularly about the shared bathroom and WC, which the Hickmans regarded as their own property since they were accessed from the stairs on the first floor. Winifred kept watch nearly around the clock, and if the neighbours attempted to sneak upstairs to make use of the facilities, she would yell 'They're snooping their noses round our flat, Alf!', and the short-tempered paterfamilias would come running downstairs, swearing angrily and waving his fists about. After Alf had beaten his ground floor neighbour up on three occasions, he was summoned for assault, and likely to face a hefty fine.

But Alf Hickman had troubles closer to home. His wife Winifred was an angry, nagging woman, who urged him to take drastic action in the feud against the neighbours. Poor Alf's mental state kept deteriorating, and in early March 1960, he went to see the family GP, saying that he felt strong urges to destroy himself and his entire family. The GP immediately sent him to the Maudesley Hospital, where a foolish young doctor referred him for outpatient treatment and sent him home.

The gloomy Alf took the bus back to No. 8 Tritton Road. At night, he got a strong impulse to murder his wife and daughter. He went out of bed, grabbed a large hammer, and bashed both women's brains out in a veritable bloodbath, before making himself a cup of tea in the kitchen. He then tried cutting his arms and wrists, but without much determination. At 8.15 the following morning, the long-suffering downstairs neighbour received yet another shock when Alf came calling at his doorstep, wearing only his underpants and covered with blood from head to foot. Alf politely asked for the police to be called, since he had just murdered his wife and daughter.

Due to its extreme brutality, the Tritton Road double murder caused widespread revulsion. The doctors at the Maudesley Hospital received some well-deserved newspaper chastisement for allowing a homicidal maniac to walk free, after his family GP had done the right thing and referred him as an urgent case. In the end, Alf Hickman, who had wiped out his entire family, was found insane and unfit to plead, and incarcerated in Broadmoor.[25] He appears to have emerged from its walls, since there is reason to believe that he died in Canterbury in 1971.

WIFE MURDER IN PURLEY ROAD, 1963

In 1963, the terraced house at No. 33 Purley Road, Croydon, was home to the telephone engineer Idris Pierce, his wife Una, and their two daughters. A native of Wales, Idris had been born in 1929. Una had a part-time job at the Little Topper café in Mead Place, something that her husband did not approve of. He suspected that she was up to no good with one of the regular customers, a married man named Godfrey Arthur Hone. Since Hone was richer and more attractive than Idris himself, he was becoming fearful that his wife was about to leave him.

It must be said that Idris Pierce was a nasty piece of work: a cruel wife-beater who regularly disciplined his wife with his fists. But Una went to see the family GP Dr Moffat, to show him her various injuries. The angry doctor treated Idris to a severe tongue-lashing, threatening to report him to the authorities if he beat his wife again, and the coward agreed to improve himself.

But Idris Pierce continued his wicked ways, and Una

eventually had enough of his violence. She moved out of the family home, into lodgings of her own in Harold Road, Upper Norwood. Unwisely, she left her two young daughters at No. 33 Purley Road, probably because she thought it would be too traumatic for them to be removed from their home. Dr Moffat tried to bring about a reconciliation, but Una refused to return to her violent cad of a husband. The jealous Idris suspected that she was seeing the man Hone on the side, and he might well have been right.

On November 2 1963, the desperate Idris Pierce sent one of his daughters to Una's lodgings, to try to persuade her to return home. This she refused to do, although she became worried about her children's welfare and wanted to check on them at No. 33 Purley Road. But Idris was waiting for her there, in a furious temper. He attacked her with a large carving knife, stabbing her repeatedly until she was dead.

Aghast at what he had done, Idris Pierce called the police and an ambulance, and made a full confession to his crime. When he was on trial for murder at the Old Bailey, his barrister pointed out his previous unblemished record, and stressed that he had given himself up and confessed to the police. Idris was convicted of manslaughter on the grounds of diminished responsibility, and was sentenced to eight years in prison.[26] According to an internet source, he served his sentence, returned to Wales, and lived on until 1998. There is no record of him remarrying, or ever committing any other serious crime, and the police files on the case are still closed.

MURDER AT COLLEGE ROAD, 1969

In September 1969, the 35-year-old homosexual chauffeur Colin George Saunders picked up the 19-year-old drifter Stanley Wrenn,

5.26 A postcard showing College Road, Bromley.

in the concourse of the Piccadilly Circus underground station. Saunders, who had previous convictions for importuning and gross indecency, took Wrenn to his ground floor front bedsit in the Victorian terraced house at No. 13 College Road, Bromley, where they shared the double bed. Wrenn was later to say that for the coming weeks Saunders had sex with him every night. But after three weeks, Wrenn found that he had been infected with rectal gonorrhoea, and this infuriated him so much that he decided to kill his host. He bought a fisherman's knife, took a gas-ring from another room in the house, and concealed them until he was ready to strike. Once the cowardly youngster was satisfied that Saunders was asleep, he struck him on the head with the gas-ring and stabbed him repeatedly.

Stealing some of Saunders' possessions, Stanley Wrenn left in the chauffeur's elegant grey Humber Imperial which was parked in the drive behind the house. But since he had never driven a car with an automatic gearbox before, he put it in reverse by mistake and cannoned backwards into another car. The careless murderer had to exchange names and addresses with its angry driver, who said that he would phone the police. Wrenn said he would himself do this from his home in nearby College Road, went back there, and then returned to the scene saying he had made the call. He abandoned the Humber and took a train into London. Meanwhile police investigated the car accident and went to Saunders' room at No. 13 College Road, where they found his body. After spending the night sleeping rough in the West End, Wrenn bought a newspaper in the morning. When he saw his name linked with Saunders' death, he went to the nearest police station to give himself up. Charged with murder, he pleaded guilty at his trial at the Old Bailey and was jailed for life. He was released ten years later, and disappeared back into obscurity.[27] The murder house still stands, not far from the crossing with Hammelton Road. It has not changed much since the time of the murder, as judged from the police photographs kept in the Wrenn police file in the National Archives.

CHAPTER 6

DISCUSSION

The BLOODY HAND significant of crime,
That glaring on the old heraldic banner,
Had kept its crimson unimpaired by time,
In such a wondrous manner!
O'er all there hung the shadow of a fear,
A sense of mystery the spirit daunted,
And said, as plain as whisper in the ear,
The place is Haunted!

How ancient is the concept of a 'murder house'? The feeling of some degree of reluctance to move into a house, inside which the previous occupant has been brutally murdered, is likely to be quite deep-rooted, among superstitious people at least. Yet I have looked into a number of celebrated eighteenth-century London murders, without finding any evidence to suggest that the houses involved were given any particular attention by the rather primitive newspaper press of the time. In the early 1700s, Jonathan Wild's house achieved a fair deal of notoriety, but no person was murdered inside the abode of this well-known thief-taker and kingpin of the criminal underworld. The house of Mary Blandy, who was executed for murdering her father in 1752, still stands today in Henley-on-Thames. In 1929, when this venerable murder house was admired by the crime writer A. Salusbury

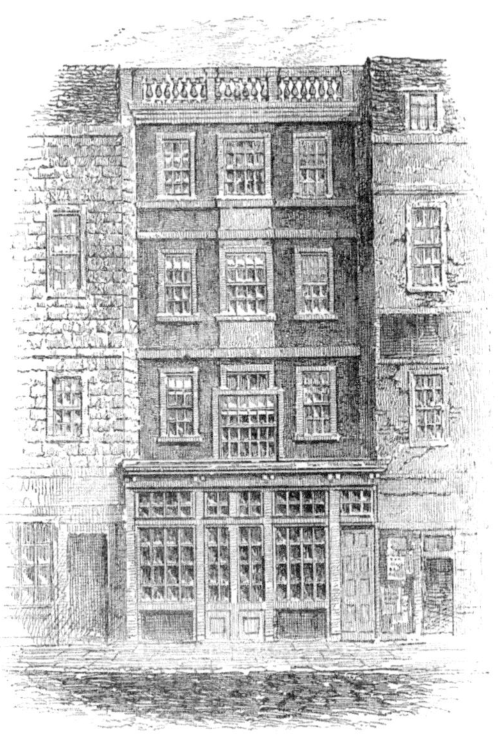

6.1 Jonathan Wild's house at 'The second door south of Shop Court, Old Bailey', from Walter Thornbury's Old and New London.

McNalty, it was occupied by a doctor, but today it is the Blandy House dental surgery. It has a reputation for being haunted, but this yarn is of relatively modern origins, and dubious veracity.[1]

The concept of a murder house would change in late Georgian and early Victorian times, however. Firstly, the growth of literacy, and the rapid development of the popular newspaper press, meant that news about the recent murders would reach the Londoners with rapidity. Secondly, some London houses were numbered already in the 1760s, and this practice became widespread in late Georgian times; the house-numbers were of course an essential

6.2 Mary Blandy, from Horace Bleackley's Some Distinguished Victims of the Scaffold.

tool for the throng of mainly lower-class people who wanted to gawp at the murder house.[2] The London murder house mania was at its height from the 1830s until the 1890s. Some of its finest flowers were, in chronological order, Eliza Grimwood's house at No. 12 Wellington Terrace, Waterloo Road [1838]; the gloomy abode of the Mannings at No. 3 Miniver Place, Bermondsey [1849]; Youngman's house at No. 16 Manor Place, Walworth [1860]; the murder houses left behind by Jack the Ripper [1888]; Mrs Pearcey's house at No. 2 Priory Street [1890]; and the celebrated 'murder shop' at No. 22 Wyndham Road, Camberwell, where Edgar Edwards wiped out the entire Darby family [1903].

In 1863, the London murder house enthusiasts acquired a valuable ally upon the foundation of the *Illustrated Police News*. This somewhat disreputable weekly newspaper specialized in depicting murder and mayhem, with London as its epicentre of reportage, and seldom failed to publish drawings of the most recent murder houses, along with information concerning their numbers and locations. The *Illustrated Police News* prided itself on the accuracy and quality of its illustrations; rightly so, in my estimation, since its drawings of various historic London murder houses have been instrumental in solving several long-standing mysteries. The role of the *Illustrated Police News* in fanning the flames of the London murder house mania cannot be overestimated. Albeit frowned upon by respectable people, this newspaper became something of a Victorian institution, reaching a very considerable circulation between the 1870s and 1890s.[3] For a while, it even had a downmarket competitor, the *Illustrated Police Budget*, with tacky and often inaccurate illustrations.[4] In the 1880s and 1890s, even the mainstream weeklies, like the *Penny Illustrated Paper*, *Reynolds' Newspaper*, and *Lloyd's Weekly Newspaper*, regularly published drawings of murder houses, and details where to find them.

Throughout Victorian and Edwardian times, the vast majority of newspapers, metropolitan and provincial alike, saw it as a public service to publish the full addresses of the current murder houses. After the Great War, the newspaper attitude to murder houses would change, however. It was no longer considered obvious that their full addresses should be published, and from the 1920s onwards, this happened much less frequently. Although the *Illustrated Police News* remained the murder house detective's best friend, this newspaper was no longer fashionable, and its quality during its declining years in the 1920s and 1930s leaves much to be desired. Today, the full address of a murder house is never openly divulged in the newspapers, although photographs of the crime scene can occasionally be revealing.

★★★

How often did it happen that London murder houses got a reputation for being haunted? Quite often, in Victorian times. Indeed, a remarkable 1902 newspaper article stated that "it is a fact that over one thousand houses in London are tenantless because they are supposed to be haunted. Seventy-one of these have been the scenes of murder… "[5] In particular, the Bloomsbury 'Murder Neighbourhood' was notorious for its wealth of haunted murder

6.3 Three of London's haunted murder houses, from Lincoln Springfield's article about 'London's Undiscovered Murders' in Harmsworth's Magazine for December 1898. From left to right: No. 12 Great Coram Street, No. 4 Burton Crescent and No. 4 Euston Square.

houses. No. 12 Great Coram Street, where the prostitute Harriet Buswell was murdered by an unknown assailant on Christmas Eve 1872, was reported to be haunted: all the tenants moved out, and the house was put up for sale. A lady evangelist bought it for a knockdown price and reopened it as Miss Stride's Home for Destitute Girls and Fallen Women. The haunting continued for several decades: the second floor back room, where the murder had been committed, was always kept locked, due to the eerie, unworldly sounds emanating from it at night.[6]

Burton Crescent, situated just at the epicentre of the Murder Neighbourhood, is today known as Cartwright Gardens. The reason the street name was changed in 1908 were the unsolved murders of two women: old Mrs Samuels at No. 4 in 1878 and the prostitute Annie Yates at No. 12 in 1884. Both murder houses were reputed to be haunted, although the ghosts lacked the persistence of the spectre of Harriet Buswell.[7] Another notorious murder house in these parts was not far away: No. 4 Euston Square, where the elderly spinster Matilda Hacker was found murdered in the coal cellar in 1879. Although the servant girl Hannah Dobbs stood trial for the murder, she was acquitted, and Miss Hacker's murder remains unavenged. The murder house acquired a very sinister reputation: it was reported to be haunted, and strange groans and screams were heard in Miss Hacker's old room. The bloodstain on the floorboards in the murder room could not be removed by any amount of scrubbing, and no dog would pass this room of horrors without snarling and whining, and giving indications of intense terror.[8] Still, the haunted house stood for several decades, before becoming a victim of the reconstruction of Euston Station in the 1960s. Some old houses in the southern part of Euston Square, which was renamed Endsleigh Gardens as a result of the murder, still stand.

THE NEW

NEWGATE CALENDAR,

CONTAINING THE

REMARKABLE LIVES AND TRIALS OF NOTORIOUS CRIMINALS, PAST AND PRESENT.

No. 61.—Vol. II.] SATURDAY, DECEMBER 24, 1864. [One Penny.

THE MURDER OF ELIZA GRIMWOOD.

6.4 Eliza Grimwood is murdered, from the New Newgate Calendar.

One of London's most celebrated early murder houses was No. 12 Wellington Terrace, where Eliza Grimwood was murdered in 1838. The house was besieged by a throng of murder-mongers, and got a very bad reputation indeed. Rumours soon spread that the empty house was haunted by Eliza's restless spirit. When that intrepid ghost-hunter, Mr Elliott O'Donnell, made some inquiries about local ghosts in the 1890s, he found a street hawker named Jonathan who had been a boy at the time when Eliza Grimwood was murdered. Jonathan's mother, who had known Eliza, used to say that she was "as tidy a looking girl as was to be found in the 'ole neighbourhood." A certain Mrs Glover had twice seen Eliza's ghost, dressed just as she had been in her lifetime, making the bed in the murder room. People in Wellington Terrace saw the ghost looking out through the ground floor window so often that they got used to it, and were not alarmed.[9] As we have seen, the Staunton, Bravo and Pearcey murder houses also became quite notorious, and the latter two are reputed to have been subjected to exorcism rituals in modern times, to get rid of the persistent ghosts.

One of the most notorious haunted murder houses of modern London was the grocer's shop at No. 36 Leinster Terrace, just at the crossing with Craven Hill Gardens, where the manager Mr Edward Creed was murdered by an unknown intruder in 1926. The motive was thought to be robbery, but excessive violence had been used against the hapless shopkeeper. Elliott O'Donnell declared the shop to be haunted by Creed's ghost, after staying there overnight and experiencing many unexplained and uncanny phenomena.[10] More steady and balanced people than this jittery ghost-hunter also felt the ghost's presence, and as a result, the shop became quite notorious locally. It is said to have stood until the 1960s, although becoming increasingly derelict. In the end, the murder shop was demolished, along with No. 35, and a

6.5 The haunted murder shop at No. 36 Leinster Terrace, and other images from the murder of Mr Creed, from the Illustrated Police News, August 5 1926.

small restaurant, hopefully without any resident ghost, was constructed on the site.

The majority of the haunted houses of London appear to fit nicely into four categories. Firstly, there are the houses presumed to be haunted by some famous personage [Oliver Cromwell, Lord Nelson, Charles Dickens &c] who had once lived there. Secondly, there is the poltergeist type of haunting, which tends to be geographically limited, but independent of the misdeeds committed by former inhabitants of the house; sceptics believe that mischievous adolescents are responsible for many of the historical instances of poltergeist activity. Thirdly, it was not uncommon that houses of a very dilapidated and neglected appearance became notorious in the neighbourhood. They might fit into a 'Miss Havisham' or 'Dirty Dick' legend, and be considered the abode of some tragic recluse who had once been crossed in love, or an alternative legend that they were once the site of a gruesome murder, and shunned ever since because of the subsequent haunting. Examples of the former topos are Nathaniel Bentley's old house in Leadenhall Street, which no longer stands; Dirty Dick's Tavern in Bishopsgate purchased some of Bentley's paraphernalia, but has nothing to do with the original legend.[11] There was a similar story about No. 19 Queen's Gate, Kensington, around the turn of the century, due to the house's neglected and begrimed appearance.[12] Richard Whittington-Egan investigated a Liverpool legend involving a neglected old house at No. 1 Mulgrave Street, said by many people to have been the home of a 'Miss Havisham' character, but the truth turned out to be that it had been deserted for many years after its owner died in 1906, since his maiden sister thought it harboured too many painful memories.[13] A good example of the pseudo-murder house variant was the 'haunted house' at No. 43 Stamford Street, Blackfriars, wrongly said to have been the site of a terrible murder, and

THE HISTORY OF THE

Mysterious House

And alarming Appearances

AT THE CORNER OF STAMFORD ST., BLACKFRIARS ROAD,

Well known to have been unoccupied for many Years, and called

The Skeleton's Corner!

ALSO THE PARTICULARS OF THE

FEMALE SPECTRE

Which appeared at the Window;

And an account of who are the

VICTIMS OF SEDUCTION AND MURDER.

The wonder and excitement caused by the appearance of the house, and also by the curious and

Extraordinary Disappearance of the Inmates.

Alarming noises and strange shadows; the curiosity exited on passing the house, and an account of what has been reported to have been seen of the

Skeleton and Apparitions.

THE REPORT OF THE BUTCHER, BAKER, AND THE PIEMAN,

And other interesting particulars. Spectre visit of that strange Female in Black, and

FATE OF THE YOUNG LADY

Supposed to be a tenant many years ago; also an account of an old haunted Mansion in the country, and the courage displayed by a young Officer.

LONDON: PUBLISHED BY W. JENKINSON, 91, LEATHER LANE, HOLBORN,
And Sold by all Booksellers.

6.6 The title-page of a 1850 pamphlet about the [bogus] haunted murder house in Stamford Street.

haunted ever since. The truth was that in the 1850s, the house belonged to an eccentric old lady, Miss Angelina Reid, who deliberately allowed it to go to ruin, in order to spite her nephew and heir. At night, she and her elderly servant sometimes surveyed the dusty, decaying rooms by the light of an old lantern, thus giving rise to the haunting legend.[14] Fourthly, there are the genuine murder houses, which often developed a reputation for being haunted, particularly if the house was close to central London, and if the murder was high-profile and/or unsolved, with 'blood crying out for vengeance'. In many cases, these reputed hauntings were mere rumours, indicative only of the house's bad reputation, and the sensitive nerves of resident servant maids. In a few instances, the haunting lasted for decades, like in the tales of No. 12 Great Coram Street, No. 4 Euston Square, and No. 36 Leinster Terrace. None of these three houses stands today, and hopefully their restless ghosts have found peace.

★★★

The pioneer of London murder house detection was the author, poet and playwright George R. Sims (1847-1922).[15] He was exceedingly popular in his own lifetime, and people likened him to Charles Dickens for his social conscience, and his obvious sympathy for London's poor. When Sims joined the *Referee* newspaper in 1877, he assumed the pen-name 'Dagonet' and

6.7 An autographed postcard sent by George R. Sims to one of his admiring Refereaders.

wrote a weekly 'Mustard and Cress' column. This column, which would continue for 45 years until Sims died in harness, became enormously popular and did much to keep his name in the public eye. His punning and laborious wit, and frequent 'lapses into poetry', appealed to the literary taste of his contemporaries. Sims also became known for his overblown and ultra-sentimental ballads like 'Christmas Eve in the Workhouse' and 'Billy's Rose', which were fashionable recital pieces in Victorian times. His plays, *The Lights of London* in particular, were equally popular, and provided Sims with a generous income, most of which he spent on gambling and high living. When liver trouble forced the hard-drinking Sims to take to the lemonade bottle, his output of ballads ceased completely, and the remainder of his output also became less sprightly.

George R. Sims sometimes edified his 'Refereaders' about London's history of crime, an area where he was quite well informed. He was always on the prowl for new items to add to his private crime museum. Sims had the knocker from Thurtell's house in Elstree, and a kitchen chair from Mrs Pearcey's murder house, among other items of criminal memorabilia. He also managed to buy the hanging beam of old Newgate, a 'Jack the Ripper' letter, and various relics of the murderers Percy Lefroy Mapleton, Henry Wainwright, Herbert Bennett and James Canham Read.[16] Sims took an interest in tracking down famous murder houses in London and its vicinity, exclaiming "Whenever there is a fine, bright day I say to myself, 'Hurrah! Let's have a drive to a place where a murder was committed.'" After visiting Camden Place in Chislehurst in 1890, to see the room where Mr and Mrs Bonar had been beaten to death, he promised that "I have several magnificent murders up my sleeve, and directly we get a few decent days which will allow me to drive down and take notes on the spot, Refereaders will have the benefit of my investigation.

Some of the murders I have unearthed in the country around London are simply enthralling."[17] In his 1906 book *Mysteries of Modern London*, Sims devoted an entire chapter to notorious murder houses, including the two Huelin houses at No. 15 Paulton's Square and No. 24 Wellington Square, Chelsea, Madame Riel's house at No. 13 Park Lane and the murder shop at No. 22 Wyndham Road, Camberwell.[18]

George R. Sims was not the most reliable of murder house detectives, and when writing some reminiscences in 1911, he could well remember an 'unpleasant journalistic adventure' back in 1890. When describing Mrs Pearcey's murder house at No. 2 Priory Street, he got the number of the house right but the name of the street wrong. The owner of the wrongly accused house was not at all pleased with these shenanigans, and Sims had to resort to bribery and "apply golden ointment to his wounded feelings", as he expressed it. When visiting the Phyllis Dimmock murder house at No. 29 St Paul's Road [today Agar Grove], the poetic Sims commented that "In the window of the murdered girl's room, a canary was singing gaily."[19]

The second trailblazer in the annals of London murder house detection was the journalist and author Guy Logan (1869-1947), whose interest in criminal history started already when he was a schoolboy. He often made expeditions to celebrated murder houses, and later wrote on the subject in a crime periodical:

The writer has actually stayed – for one night only – at No. 16, Manor Place, Walworth Road, where, in the 'sixties,' that unexampled young villain, Youngman, killed his mother, sweetheart, and two brothers in order to procure the pitiful sum of £100. My rest was not disturbed by the memories of these ill-deeds, nor was it when I passed a night some five years ago at the Leicester Hotel, in Upper Grenville Street, Liverpool, though the tavern alluded to was the house at which Gleeson Wilson

6.8 An autographed photograph of Guy Logan, another pioneer murder house detective.

murdered the Henrichson family in 1849. I have been over the house – in Priory Street, Kentish Town, at which the somewhat mysterious Mrs Pearcey slew her rival, Mrs Hogg, and the little house in Church Villas, Richmond, where Kate Webster killed and mutilated Mrs Thomas, is sufficiently familiar to me. Houses in Montagu Street, Bedford Place, in Harley Street, in Euston Square, in Burton Crescent, all of which still stand, have the stain of unavenged blood upon them, as has Great Coram Street, not so very far away from those mentioned. The warehouse in the Whitechapel Road, in which Henry Wainwright killed and buried his paramour, Harriett Lane, has not been done away with, and the dwelling in which the ruffian Seaman killed Mr Levi and his housekeeper – hard by the Commercial Road East – still frowns upon the passer-by.[20]

Guy Logan, whose knowledge of criminal history was well-nigh encyclopaedic, later went on to write seven books about true crime, but his plans to produce a full-length book on the Murder Houses of London came to nought after he had been at the receiving end of a libel suit instigated by a vengeful Baroness.[21]

* * *

How do you become a murder house detective? Thirty years ago, you needed an encyclopaedic knowledge of the capital's criminal history, an equally impressive grasp of the topography of the streets of the great metropolis, and a pair of good walking shoes to visit all the possible murder houses on foot. Nowadays, the Internet and the growth of online databases of every description has changed the prospects of the enterprising murder house detective beyond recognition. Newspaper databases provide an invaluable source of long-forgotten murders, with details of their location, and sometimes a drawing of the murder house itself.[22] The Old Bailey proceedings is an independent and reliable source of trials from 1674 until 1913. Other online databases include TrueCrimeLibrary and BritishExecutions, and although the valuable Casebook and JtRForums online repositories mostly deal with Jack the Ripper, they do contain material about other crimes. Another important source are the Metropolitan Police murder ledgers, giving details of murders in London from 1891 until 1966, often including the number of the murder house.[23] In the relatively few instances when they do not, ordering a copy of the murder victim's death certificate from the General Register Office can sometimes be informative.

Making a huge trawl from the Internet newspaper databases,

the Old Bailey proceedings, the Metropolitan Police murder ledgers, and various reference books, it is possible to accumulate a huge number of London murders. After eliminating those that have little interest [botched illegal abortions, child murders by insane mothers, wife murders by drunken husbands], Google Maps can be consulted to see whether the more promising murder houses still stand. These maps are easy to use, and valuable when it comes to eliminating that a murder house exists today. Sometimes, this does not even require a house number: if the crime in question took place in 1890 and the street does not contain a single older building, the work is done and the house can be eliminated. To identify a murder house with certainty, it is required to visit it on foot, looking out for other nearby landmarks connected with the crime in question. It is useful to be able to 'tell' the age of houses from their architectural style, and this is something that comes with experience: it hardly takes a PhD in architecture to tell if a house is Georgian, early Victorian, late Victorian, Edwardian, 1920s/1930s, or Modern.

For most London murder houses, their detection has been fairly straightforward. For example, it hardly taxed the intellect to find Lord Lucan's house in No. 46 Lower Belgrave Street: it is very well known, and easily accessible, as is the Plumber's Arms public house nearby, into which the injured Lady Lucan took refuge from her attacker, calling out for help. On the other hand, the thinking cap had to be applied to pin-point the remains of Henry Wainwright's murder house in Whitechapel Road, since the houses had been renumbered, and since the relevant section of the road had been 'developed'. The British Library's large-scale Ordnance Survey maps were instrumental in establishing where the house had been. Although only the 1938 edition of these maps provides house numbers, the earlier editions from the 1880s and 1890s are also valuable, providing admirable topographical exactitude. The useful book 'Names of Streets and Places in the Administrative County of London' and various Internet registers can be made use of in cases where there is suspicion that street names have been changed, or houses renumbered; the Post Office directories remain another valuable resource in this respect.[24] The Stamford 1863 London maps are another valuable resource for the murder house detective, as are the commercially available replica Ordnance Survey maps and the various editions of Bartholomew's Reference Atlas of Greater London.

But even when you have ascertained that a murder house is likely to be still standing, it is sometimes not entirely straightforward to find it. Many London streets have been renamed, and house numbers have changed. Moreover, in Victorian times, a 'Terrace' was a row of terraced houses in a certain road, similar in build and structure. These Terraces had different names, meaning that the houses in one road could have twenty different names, and as many numbering systems. Sometimes, the Terrace [sometimes called Villas, Place or Row] was named after the builder, sometimes after the road itself, and at other times from patriotic motives. The profusion of 'George Terraces', 'Queen's Terraces' and 'King's Terraces' in every street confounded the Victorian postmen, since provincial letter-writers often did not include the name of the road on which the Terrace stood. Furthermore, the naming of roads also had serious deficiencies at the time, since there was a 'George Street', a 'King Street' and a 'Victoria Street' in every district and suburb.[25] To decipher an address like 'Grove House, Frederick Villas, George Street, King's Avenue, Ball's Pond', the postman needed to know his district very well, and to appreciate that the letter writer had provided the name of the house itself and that of the Terrace, the road in which it stood, the closest main road, and the name of the district. If some clueless out-of-towner left either of these vital pieces of evidence out, the letter was at risk of never reaching its proper destination. In the 1880s and 1890s, when the London street nomenclature and house numbering had become insufferably confused, there was a determined move to abolish all these 'Terraces', 'Places' and 'Rows', to rename the streets in a more imaginative manner, and to renumber the houses going from the centre to the periphery. This makes it a challenge to find some of the older murder houses, since it is often difficult to pinpoint the location of the erstwhile 'Terrace', which may or may not still be in existence, with the houses renumbered, in a busy modern road.

The trouble with these 'Terraces' is not confined to murder house detection, but has been recognized by genealogists and historians alike. The National Archives has some useful street indexes from the 1861 and 1871 Censuses, but although these occasionally give the name of the road in which the Terrace once stood, they provide no clues about the numbering of the houses in the Terrace, or about the renumbering of the houses when the Terrace ceased to exist. The London Post Office directories, of which a good collection is kept on the open shelves at the National Archives, are a more useful source. Using these directories, the 'Names of Streets and Places in the Administrative County of London', and various online repositories, it can be ascertained what year the Terrace ceased to exist and the street was renumbered. Since people did not move particularly often in Victorian times, analysis of the names of the residents in the Post Office directories dating immediately before, and immediately after, the renumbering of the houses, should provide useful hints about the numbers of the houses in the former Terrace. Then it is time to open Google Maps, to see if these numbers refer to a row of similar-looking houses at the predicted site of the former Terrace, with [even slightly] different houses around it; if this is the case, we know the present-day location, and number, of the murder house.

In the first volume of this work, these methods helped to solve the mystery of No. 10 Rylston Terrace, Rylston Road, Fulham, which is today No. 44 Rylston Road. The case of No. 19 Canonbury Terrace was more difficult, but this was a high-profile murder, with several helpful drawings of the murder house, eventually it was possible to track it down to No. 1 Alwyne Villas, Islington. In the second and third volumes, it was not difficult to demonstrate that the murder houses at No. 1 Florence Terrace and No. 10 Alma Villas were still standing, using the relevant Post Office directories. The case of No. 3 Herbert Villas, of Acton Atrocity infamy, was more difficult, but again a contemporary drawing of the house helped to solve the case. In the present volume, Tooting's house of horrors in Fountain Road was the most difficult murder house to 'detect', and it took two years of pondering the available evidence to identify it, through an accumulation of local knowledge, and careful analysis of the available illustrations of the murder house.

The methods described here can be applied to identify not just a murder house, but *any* house. A literary historian trying to find the house where Charles Dickens once ate a beefsteak can make use of them, as can a genealogist hoping to identify the house where his great-grandfather lived. Nor are these methods geographically restricted: I have made use of them in Paris, where a surprising amount of important murder houses are still standing, and in Edinburgh, which is also home to a quantity of historic murder houses.

BIBLIOGRAPHY OF SOME KEY WORKS

M. Baggoley, *Surrey Executions* (Stroud 2011)

F. Barker & D. Silvester-Carr, *Crime & Scandal: The Black Plaque Guide to London* (London 1991)

I. Butler, *Murderers' London* (London 1973)

D. Cargill & J. Holland, *Scenes of Murder* (London 1964)

P. de Loriol, *South London Murders* (Stroud 2007)

R.A. Downie, *Murder in London* (London 1973)

M. Fido, *Murder Guide to London* (London 1986)

G. Howse, *A-Z of London Murders* (Barnsley 2007)

B. Lane, *The Murder Club Guide to London* (London 1988)

C. Maxton, *Foul Deeds and Suspicious Deaths in Croydon* (Barnsley 2006)

J. Oates, *Unsolved Murders in Victorian and Edwardian London* (Barnsley 2007)
Foul Deeds and Suspicious Deaths in Lewisham and Deptford (Barnsley 2007)
Unsolved London Murders of the 1920s and 1930s (Barnsley 2009)
Unsolved London Murders of the 1940s and 1950s (Barnsley 2009)
Foul Deeds and Suspicious Deaths in Richmond and Kingston (Barnsley 2010)

E.S. Shaw, *A Companion to Murder* (London 1960)
A Second Companion to Murder (London 1961)

L. Stratmann, *Middlesex Murders* (Stroud 2010)
Greater London Murders (Stroud 2010)

MAJOR NEWSPAPERS CONSULTED

DE	Daily Express
DM	Daily Mirror
DMa	Daily Mail
DN	Daily News
DT	Daily Telegraph
ET	Evening Telegraph
Ind	Independent
IPB	Illustrated Police Budget
IPN	Illustrated Police News
LWN	Lloyd's Weekly Newspaper
MC	Morning Chronicle
MP	Morning Post
NYT	New York Times
PIP	Penny Illustrated Paper
RN	Reynolds' Newspaper
Sta	Standard

NOTES

INTRODUCTION

1. The first is J. Bondeson, *Murder Houses of London* (Stroud 2014).
2. The five major modern sources on London's topography of capital crime are Cargill & Holland, *Scenes of Murder*, Butler, *Murderers' London*, Downie, *Murder in London*, Fido, *Murder Guide to London* and Barker & Silvester-Carr, *Black Plaque Guide to London*. On celebrated suburban murders, these book receive support from the 'Foul Deeds' series, particularly the useful books by Dr Jonathan Oates.

1. SOUTHWARK, CAMBERWELL AND LAMBETH

1. G. Logan in *Famous Crimes Past & Present* 10(125) [1905], 174.
2. Oates, *Unsolved Murders in Victorian and Edwardian London*, 13-19.
3. G. Logan, *Verdict and Sentence* (London 1935), 17-60.
4. M. Alpert, *London 1849, A Victorian Murder Story* (London 2004), 94.
5. G. Logan in *Famous Crimes Past & Present* 7(82), [1904], 56.
6. *Times* Aug 31 1860 9g.
7. Downie, *Murder in London*, 147, de Loriol, *South London Murders*, 33-5.
8. *MP* Dec 25 1886, *LWN* Dec 26 1886; *Times* May 4 1918 4b, *IPN* March 28 1918.
9. On Robert Ward, see Howse, *A-Z of London Murders*, 165-7.
10. G. Logan, *Guilty or Not Guilty* (London 1930), 245-6.
11. G.R. Sims, *Mysteries of Modern London* (London 1906), 68.
12. G. Logan, *Verdict and Sentence* (London 1935), 165-80; G. Howse, *Foul Deeds and Suspicious Deaths in London's East End* (Barnsley 2005), 138-67.
13. *Sta* Nov 9 1863, *LWN* Nov 15 1863, *Glasgow Herald* Nov 14 1863, *Examiner* Nov 21 1863.
14. On the little-known Coppen case, see Baggoley, *Surrey Executions*, 96; OldBaileyOnline, TrueCrimeLibrary and www.robshistory.co.uk; *Times* Aug 28 9c, Aug 31 9d, Sept 19 5b, 1874, *Sta* Aug 28 and Sept 4 1874, *LWN* Aug 30 1874, *MP* Sept 29 1874, *York Herald* Sept 24 1874, *Bradford Observer* Nov 14 1874.

15. On the Soper case, see NA MEPO 3/122 and a useful 'Summary of the Murder of Jane Soper' available on Ancestry; *Times* Oct 29 1875 8f and Feb 15 1876 12a, *Sta* Oct 9 1875, *LWN* Oct 24 1875 and Feb 13 1876, *RN* Oct 24 1875 and Feb 20 1876, *DN* Feb 8 1876, *Leeds Mercury* Jan 25 1876.
16. On the little-known case of James Banbury, see Baggoley, *Surrey Executions*, 120-2, OldBaileyOnline and TrueCrimeLibrary; *RN* July 10 1892, *PIP* July 9 and 16 1892, *IPN* July 9 and 16 1892.
17. H.L. Adam (Ed.), *Trial of George Chapman* (Notable British Trials, London 1930), Butler, *Murderers' London*, 174-7, R.M. Gordon, *The Poison Murders of Jack the Ripper* (Jefferson NC 2008), 89-92, 194-8; Casebook and PubsHistory.
18. H. Wojtczak, *Jack the Ripper at Last* (Hastings 2013).
19. On the sad story of the Maces, see *Times* Jan 2 1932 7b and Jan 6 1932 7e, *DM* Jan 2 1932, *DMa* Jan 5 1932, *IPN* Jan 7 1932 and *Western Daily Press* Jan 6 1932.
20. On the Vent case, see NA MEPO 3/1697; *British Journal of Psychiatry* 81 [1935], 439-40; *DM* Feb 16, March 5, 6 and 14 1935.
21. NA MEPO 3/2291, M. Lefebure, *Evidence for the Crown* (London 1955), 185-92, *Brixton Free Press* March 23 1945.
22. NA MEPO 20/10; *Times* Nov 30 1965 5c, Jan 13 6e, Jan 14 6e, Jan 15 12c, Jan 18 7b, 1966, *DMa* Jan 18 1966.
23. *Times* Nov 9 1967 1f, Feb 15 1968 3b, Feb 16 1968 2d, March 12 1968 3b, *DE* Nov 21 1967 and April 30 1968, *DM* Nov 9, 18, 20 and 21, Dec 1 and 20, 1967 and Feb 15 1968, *DMa* Nov 9, 14 and 21 1967 and Feb 15 and April 30 1968.
24. TrueCrimeLibrary, W. Clarkson, *Moody* (Edinburgh 2003); *DMa* Aug 5 1991, June 3 1993, Oct 4 2001, *Ind* June 3 1993.

2. WANDSWORTH

1. G. Logan in *Famous Crimes Past & Present* 10(125) [1905], 174. An original drawing of the stables at Granard Lodge show that they are in no way identical to the buildings still standing there.
2. On the Watson case, see de Loriol, *South London Murders*, 44-7.
3. Fido, *Murder Guide to London*, 170.
4. Butler, *Murderers' London*, 164, Cargill & Holland, *Scenes of Murder*, 171, Fido, *Murder Guide to London*, 165-6; *Times* Nov 26 1981 6a, Jan 16 1982 2d and Jan 5 1983 1g, *Daily Record* May 17 2008 and Nov 19 2012.
5. The Bravo police file in NA MEPO 3/123 is not very capacious. Books

on the case include, in chronological order, F.J.P. Veale, *Verdict in Dispute: The Bravo Case* (London 1950), Y. Bridges, *How Charles Bravo Died* (London 1956) [Improved second edition in 1972], J. Williams, *Suddenly at the Priory* (London 1957), E. Jenkins, *Dr Gully* (London 1972), B. Taylor & K. Clarke, *Murder at the Priory* (London 1988) and J. Ruddick, *Death at the Priory* (London 2001); see also *Journal of Psychological Medicine* NS 2 [1876], 341-56, W. Roughead, *Malice Domestic* (Edinburgh 1928), 3-39, W.E. Swinton (*Canadian Medical Association Journal* 123 [1980], 1262-4), R. Whittington-Egan, *Speaking Volumes* (Malvern 2004), 10-13, Fido, *Murder Guide to London*, 170-3, de Loriol, *South London Murders*, 51-6.

6. J. Clark, *Haunted Wandsworth* (Stroud 2009), 9-20.
7. J. Ruddick, *Death at the Priory* (London 2001), 105-6.
8. On the Relton case, see *Famous Crimes Past & Present* 7(73) [1904], 165-6; *Times* March 22 1884 12d and April 24 1884 12a, *RN* March 23 1884, *Sta* May 7 1884, *DN* March 19 and 20 1884 and *Western Mail* April 25 1884.
9. *Times* Jan 16 1894 5b, *DN* Jan 16 1894, *PMG* Jan 12 1894.
10. *MP* May 7 1888, *Western Daily Press* May 7 1888.
11. NA CRIM 1/45/2; *Sta* April 11 and 14 1896, *PIP* April 18 1896, *MP* April 14, May 4 and June 11 1896, *LWN* April 12 and June 14 1896.
12. 10. *MP* June 6 1896, *RN* June 7 1896, *LWN* June 7 1896, *Sta* June 3 and 6 1896.
13. On Brown of Linom Road, see NA CRIM 1/46/6; Baggoley, *Surrey Executions*, 124-5; OldBaileyOnline; *Sta* Nov 10 1896, *MP* Dec 10 1896, *LWN* Nov 11 and Dec 6 and 20 1896, *IPN* Dec 12 and 19 1896, *PMG* Jan 5 1897.
14. On the mysterious murder of Mary Kate Waknell, see *Sta* May 14 and 15 1900, *LWN* May 13 1900, *IPN* May 19 1900, *IPB* May 19 1900, *Auckland Star* June 30 1900 and a text entitled 'Murder in Brixton 1900' on the Brixton Guide website.
15. On the obscure Franklin case, see *DM* July 10 1906 and *IPB* July 14 1906.
16. On the equally obscure Warren case, see NA CRIM 1/103/9; also OldBaileyOnline and *Times* Aug 29 1906 8e and Sept 1 1906 4f.
17. M. Macnaghten, *Days of my Years* (London 1914), 229-37; E. Villers, *Riddles of Crime* (London 1928), 153-69; H.L. Adam, *Murder by Persons Unknown* (London 1931), 67-74; A. Lambton, *Echoes of Causes Celebres* (London n.d.), 207-16; E. Jepson in M. Pemberton (Ed.), *Great Stories of Real Life* (London n.d.), Vol. II, 231-40; A. Armstrong in *Great Unsolved Crimes* (London n.d.), 146-52; J. Goodman, *Acts of Murder* (London

1986), 92-103; B. Taylor in *Perfect Murder* (London 1987), 163-205; Oates, *Unsolved Murders in Victorian and Edwardian London*, 163-71. *Times* July 25 1910 4b and Sept 19 1910 3a, *NYT* Aug 22 1910, *Grey River Argus* Sept 27 1910, *DMa* Feb 23 2007.

18. On Thomas Frederick Anderson, see the article by N. Atkinson in *Dictionary of New Zealand Biography*, Vol. 4, 1998.
19. Mr Whittington-Egan has intimate knowledge of the Atherstone case, about which he is working on a monograph.
20. On the case of Ada Annie Williams, see NA CRIM 1/143/3, HO 144/19785 and PCOM 8/337; *DM* Nov 10 and 13 1913, *ET* Nov 21 1913.
21. *DM* Dec 13 and 20 1913, *NYT* Dec 12 1913, *Evening Post* Jan 1 1914.
22. On her later adventures, see NA PCOM 8/337.
23. NA MEPO 3/1578; *Times* July 15 5b and Sept 8 7c, 1922, *DM* July 13, 15, 17 and 22, Sept 8 1922, *IPN* July 20 1922.
24. NA MEPO 3/1703; RootsChat; *Times* Dec 5 1935 9c and Dec 7 1935 14a, *DM* Dec 4 1935, *DMa* Dec 19 1935.
25. I. Oddie, *Inquest* (London 1941), 195-201, J. Symons, *A Reasonable Doubt* (London 1960), 172-81, Cargill & Holland, *Scenes of Murder*, 167, Oates, *Unsolved London Murders of the 1920s and 1930s*, 102-14, Howse, *A-Z of London Murders*, 52-3
26. NA MEPO 3/1704; *Times* April 6 9a, April 18 9f, April 20 7d, April 27 11d, May 2 16e, May 9 11b, May 14 11d, June 16 5e, 1936, *DM* April 20 1936, *DE* May 2 1936.
27. Shaw, *Companion to Murder*, 265-6; *Times* March 19 14c, April 29 18e, May 14 14c, 1938, *DM* March 5, April 29 and May 14 1938.
28. NA MEPO 3/2279. There was no major newspaper coverage of this obscure case.
29. NA CRIM 1/2349; *Times* Aug 17 3c, Aug 18 3c, Sept 16 4g, Nov 4 3g, Dec 2 7e, 1953, *DM* Aug 26, Sept 9 and 16 1953, *DMa* Aug 17 and Nov 4 1953.
30. On the Ross case, see NA CRIM 1/2676 and DPP 2/2483; Cargill & Holland, *Scenes of Murder*, 168; *Times* Nov 10 6e, Nov 11 4f, Dec 14 6d, 1955 and Jan 31 5e, Feb 1 4e, Feb 2 15f and March 5 3b 1956, *DM* Nov 9 1955, *DE* Nov 9 1955 and *DMa* Nov 9 1955.
31. Cargill & Holland, *Scenes of Murder*, 175; *Times* June 22 1962 6e, *DM* June 6 and 22 1962, *DE* June 6 1962, *DMa* June 22 1962.
32. *DE* Aug 29 1962.
33. *Times* Aug 14 3c, Sept 14 5g, Sept 15 12a, Sept 18 6d, 1962.
34. M.J. Freeman, *I, Pornographer* (ten volumes); *Times* Dec 9 3a, Dec 11 4e, Dec 12 4f, Dec 13 3a, Dec 18 2e, 1969, *DM* May 29 1970.

3. LEWISHAM, DEPTFORD AND GREENWICH

1. Anon., *The Trial of Charles Hussey, for Murdering Mr Bird* (London 1818); *MC* Feb 16, March 17 and 19, April 10 1818, *MP* Feb 18, April 4, Aug 3 and 4, 1818.
2. On these five cases, see respectively, Oates, *Foul Deeds and Suspicious Deaths in Lewisham and Deptford*, 94-104; *RN* June 13 1897, *DN* June 17 1897, *IPN* June 12 1897, *LWN* June 20 1897; OldBaileyOnline and *Times* July 16 1901 11e; Oates, *Foul Deeds and Suspicious Deaths in Lewisham and Deptford*, 110-4, and *Times* Sept 5 1902 8f; *Times* Feb 4 1905 4f and Feb 11 1905 4b.
3. On these four cases, see respectively, *Times* April 7 1928 9c; Oates, *Foul Deeds and Suspicious Deaths in Lewisham and Deptford*, 173-7; NA MEPO 16/21 and *Times* Nov 26 1969 18c and Feb 19 1970 4f; *DM* March 11 and Nov 11 and 13, 1975, *DMa* Nov 13 1975.
4. Knapp & Baldwin's *Newgate Calendar* (London 1828), vol. 4, 341-2, *New Newgate Calendar* (London 1864), Vol. 1, 225-6, *MC* Dec 21 and 25 1822.
5. NA MEPO 3/86; Oates, *Foul Deeds and Suspicious Deaths in Lewisham and Deptford*, 78-81; *Times* June 30 1870 9f, *MP* Aug 29 1868, *LWN* Sept 6 1868, *Sta* June 30 1870.
6. On the case of Mrs Tyler, see Oates, *Unsolved Murders in Victorian and Edwardian London*, 132-7; *MP* Aug 16, Sept 15 and Oct 13 1898, *DN* Oct 13 1898, *RN* Oct 16 1898, *Sta* Aug 16 1898, *IPN* Aug 20 and Sept 24 1898, *Bristol Mercury* Aug 18 1898, *Trewman's Exeter Flying Post* Aug 20 1898.
7. OldBaileyOnline; *IPN* May 25 1901 and *West Australian Sunday Times* June 30 1901.
8. M. McNaghten, *Days of my Years* (London 1914), 149-56, Fido, *Murder Guide to London*, 175-6, Oates, *Foul Deeds and Suspicious Deaths in Lewisham and Deptford*, 115-24, de Loriol, *South London Murders*, 85-95, Stratmann, *Greater London Murders*, 189-65, Lane, *Murder Club Guide to London*, 82-4; *Times* March 28 11f, April 6b, May 6 19a, May 8 4d, 1905, *DM* March 29 and 30, April 19 and 26, May 3, 6 and 8, 1905.
9. *Yarmouth Independent* Feb 25 1911.
10. On the Thompson case, see NA CRIM 1/97/3; OldBaileyOnline; *Times* Feb 9 1905 10f, *PIP* Feb 18 1905, *Auckland Star* May 6 1905.
11. NA CRIM 1/111/3; OldBaileyOnline; Oates, *Foul Deeds and Suspicious Deaths in Lewisham and Deptford*, 131-5; *Times* Nov 21 1908 12e, *DM* Nov 21 and Dec 23 1908.
12. NA CRIM 1/179/6; Oates, *Foul Deeds and Suspicious Deaths in Lewisham and Deptford*, 136-40.

13. NA MEPO 3/895; Oates, *Foul Deeds and Suspicious Deaths in Lewisham and Deptford*, 165-72, *Times* July 16 14e, Aug 25 7d, Oct 4 9b, 1934, *DM* July 12 1934.
14. Cargill & Holland, *Scenes of Murder*, 203-4; *Times* July 21 2b, July 24 2g, Sept 15 2d, Oct 7 2c, 1942, *DM* July 17, 21, 22, 23 and 24, Sept 15 1942.
15. E. Roberts, *Fifty Years a Medium* (London 1975), 78-80.
16. NA MEPO 3/2224; *ET* July 6 1942, *Derby Evening Telegraph* July 6 1942, *DMa* July 6 1942.
17. On the Frith case, see NA CRIM 1/2854 and DPP 2/2723; *Times* Aug 28 8g and Sept 13 5g, 1957, *DM* Aug 28 and Sept 4 1957, *DMa* Sept 4 and 25, Oct 30 1957.
18. L. Price & J. Caplan, *The Confait Confessions* (London 1977), Fido, *Murder Guide to London*, 177, de Loriol, *South London Murders*, 117-20, Lane, *Murder Club Guide to London*, 76-81; *Times* Oct 18 1975 1a and 3e, *DM* Nov 25 1972, Nov 8 1974, Oct 10 and 18, Dec 19 1975.
19. D. McBarnet (*Modern Law Review* 41 [1978], 455-63), *DM* Oct 1 1976.
20. *DM* Jan 28 and Aug 5 1980, June 19 1981.
21. *Times* April 25 1980 4a and June 17 1983 3g, *DM* May 7 1981.
22. *DMa* Oct 26 1985.

4. WIMBLEDON, RICHMOND AND KINGSTON

1. H.L. Adam (Ed.), *Trial of George Henry Lamson* (Notable British Trials, London 1951).
2. NA MEPO 20/1.
3. On the Smethurst case, see OldBaileyOnline; A. Newton, *The Case of Thomas Smethurst MD* (London 1859), L.A. Perry (Ed.), *Trial of Dr Smethurst* (Notable British Trials, London 1931), E.A. Perry, *The Drama of the Law* (London 1924), 269-76, C. Kingston, *Enemies of Society* (London 1927), 9-13, L.R. Gribble in *Great Unsolved Crimes* (London n.d.), 57-64, Butler, *Murderers' London*, 214-5, Oates, *Foul Deeds and Suspicious Deaths in Richmond and Kingston*, 24-36; *PIP* Aug 12 1876, *IPN* Sept 23 1882.
4. Mr Serjeant Ballantyne, *Some Experiences of a Barrister's Life* (London 1898), 212-22,, L.A. Perry, *Some Famous Medical Trials* (New York 1928), 193-207, and *Trial of Dr Smethurst* (Notable British Trials, London 1931). The most recent book on the case is P. Maggs, *Smethurst's Luck* (London 2013).
5. E. O'Donnell, *Trial of Kate Webster* (Notable British Trials, London 1925), C. Kingston, *A Gallery of Rogues* (London 1924), 186-200, R. & M.

Whittington-Egan, *The Bedside Book of Murder* (Newton Abbot 1988), 27-38; Butler, *Murderers' London*, 211-4, Barker & Silvester-Carr, *Crime & Scandal*, 287-9, Oates, *Foul Deeds and Suspicious Deaths in Richmond and Kingston*, 53-67, Stratmann, *Greater London Murders,* 221-30.

6. G. Logan, *Wilful Murder* (London 1935), 99.
7. J. Clark, *Haunted Wandsworth* (Stroud 2009), 80-2.
8. G. Logan, *Monsters of Crime* (Dublin 1938), 86-7.
9. G. Logan, *Wilful Murder* (London 1935), 80-1.
10. *DMa* July 6 2011 and *Ripperologist* 121 [2011], 107. A dissenting voice has objected that no conclusive tests were performed on the skull, and that the authorities at New Scotland Yard were not prepared to spend large amounts of money on the matter. And why would Kate Webster take the risk of disposing of the skull in such close proximity (50 yards) to the murder house, in a busy pub stable yard? Also, she stated she had thrown the skull, in a bag, into the Thames along with other body parts, and at that stage had no reason to lie.
11. TrueCrimeLibrary and OldBaileyOnline; *Times* March 12 1902 12d.
12. *Times* Aug 1 1905 11c, *DM* June 22 and July 17 1905.
13. *Times* Sept 11 1906 5c, *DM* Sept 11 1906, *DE* Sept 11 1906, *IPN* Sept 15 1906.
14. On the Partridge case, see NA CRIM 1/116/5; OldBaileyOnline; *Times* May 16 1910 13f and May 25 1910 14f, *DM* May 17 1910.
15. On the Churchman case, see OldBaileyOnline; *Times* Feb 28 1912 13g and March 4 1912 4c, *DM* Feb 29 and March 21 1912.
16. On Captain Tighe, see *The Handstand* Dec 2003 and *Wimbledon Society Newsletter* Sept 2010, p. 5.
17. NA CRIM 1/170/4 and HO 144/1475/332065; *Times* Nov 19 1917 5e, Dec 13 1917 5f, Jan 29 1918 4e, Feb 13 1918 5f, *DM* Nov 15, 19 and 23, Dec 13, 14 and 31, 1917, *IPN* Nov 27 1917 and Nov 25 1937.
18. J. Doughty, *The Rochdale Hangman* (Oldham 1998), 306-10.
19. On the Wilkinson case, see NA MEPO 3/1693; *Times* May 31 16a, June 1 4g, June 2 16d, June 15 13f, 1934, *DM* May 31 1934, *IPN* June 7 1934.
20. NA MEPO 3/1712; Oates, *Foul Deeds and Suspicious Deaths in Richmond and Kingston*, 119-26, Stratmann, *Middlesex Murders*, 108-24, TrueCrimeLibrary; *Times* July 11 9c, July 22 18e, July 23 7d, Aug 13 7c, Sept 7 9e 1936, *DM* July 10, 11,14, 22, 23, 25 and 26, Sept 26 1936, *DE* July 17 and 23, Sept 24, 1936, *DMa* Aug 6 and Sept 25 and 26 1936, *ET* July 13, 22 and 29, Aug 5 1936.
21. *DM* Sept 26 1936.
22. *DMa* Oct 28 1936, *Gloucester Citizen* Oct 28 1936.
23. *Hampshire Advertiser* June 24 1889.

24. *Daily Herald* March 24 1917.
25. NA MEPO 3/1724; Oates, *Foul Deeds and Suspicious Deaths in Richmond and Kingston*, 127-38; *DM* Nov 24 and 27 1937, *DE* Nov 24 and 27 1937, *IPN* Dec 2 1937.
26. NA MEPO 3/1737; Oates, *Foul Deeds and Suspicious Deaths in Richmond and Kingston*, 139-47; *Times* Dec 27 5f, Dec 30 12e, Dec 31 9d, 1938 and Jan 18 9c and Jan 19 9f, 1939, *DM* Dec 27 and 28 1938.
27. *Times* Feb 16 11c and Feb 17 16e, 1939.
28. *Times* March 14 5d, March 30 11g, March 28 11g, 1939, *DE* March 30 1939.
29. *DE* May 22 and 25, 1939.
30. On the Casserley case, see NA MEPO 3/877; D.G. Browne & E.V. Tullett, *Bernard Spilsbury, His Life and Cases* (London 1961), 362-4, Fido, *Murder Guide to London*, 184; *Times* March 24 14f, March 25 11f, March 26 9c, March 28 11a, April 1 13e, April 27 11c, April 28 7e, 1938, *DM* March 24 1938.
31. *Times* Sept 9 1940 9g, Oct 16 1940 9g, Nov 1 1940 2f, *DM* Aug 31, Sept 13, Oct 16 1940, *DE* Aug 24 and Nov 1 1940.
32. *Times* May 10 4d, May 11 5a, July 29 4c and Aug 31 2e, 1954, *DMa* May 10, July 29 and Aug 18, 1955.

5. CROYDON AND SOUTH LONDON SUBURBS

1. Maxton, *Foul Deeds and Suspicious Deaths in Croydon*, 12-20, 116-21.
2. R. Whittington-Egan, *The Riddle of Birdhurst Rise* (London 1988).
3. Maxton, *Foul Deeds and Suspicious Deaths in Croydon*, 44-9.
4. Knapp & Baldwin's *Newgate Calendar* (London 1828), Vol. 4, 102-10, *New Newgate Calendar* (London 1864), Vol. 1, 693-6, *Famous Crimes Past & Present* 7(84) [1904], 92-4, G. Logan, *Masters of Crime* (London 1928), 219-25; *Times* June 1 3d, June 2 3c and Aug 25 3c, 1813, *MC* June 2 and 7 1813, *MP* June 2 and 9, Aug 21 1813.
5. *Referee* Nov 16 1890.
6. Butler, *Murderers' London*, 193, Fido, *Murder Guide to London*, 177-9, Lane, *Murder Club Guide to London*, 95-100, Barker & Silvester-Carr, *Crime & Scandal*, 273-4, de Loriol, *South London Murders*, 57-61.
7. C. Kingston, *A Gallery of Rogues* (London 1924), 78-82.
8. D. Cox, *Brotherly Love* (Buckingham 1989).
9. On the Peckham case, see Maxton, *Foul Deeds and Suspicious Deaths in Croydon*, 145-9; *Times* Jan 4 1893 3f, *RN* Jan 8 1893, *IPN* Jan 14 and 21

1893, *North-Eastern Daily Gazette* March 4 1893, *Leicester Chronicle* Jan 19 1895.

10. On the Tooting Horror, see *LWN* March 17 1895, *IPN* March 16 1895, *IPB* March 16 1895, *PIP* March 15 1895, *Sta* March 8, 9 and 11 1895, *MP* March 8 and 9 1895, *Hampshire Telegraph* March 9 1895; also N. Freeman, *1895, Drama, Disaster and Disgrace in Late Victorian Britain* (Edinburgh 2011), 83-4.
11. On the parallel to the Steinberg case, see *PMG* March 9 1895; also G. Howse, *North London Murders* (Stroud 2005), 9-12.
12. *Taunton Courier* April 3 1895.
13. *DMa* Dec 24 2008. See also the internet article 'The Ballad of Willie Cummins' by Mike Yates, and the TootingLife web page.
14. On the Dawes case, see OldBaileyOnline and Maxton, *Foul Deeds and Suspicious Deaths in Croydon*, 38-43; *Times* Jan 14 1897, *IPN* Jan 2 1897, *Hampshire Telegraph* Jan 2 1897.
15. NA MEPO 3/177; *Sta* Feb 23 1893, *LWN* Feb 26 1893, *IPN* March 4 1893. Richard Langtry Brinkley, only surviving son of the murderer, lived on for many years and had three sons of his own, two of whom lived into the 1970s and 1980s.
16. W.H. Speer, *The Secret History of Great Crimes* (London n.d.), 7-17. Speer is far from a credible source, but there are such obvious similarities with the contents of NA MEPO 3/177 that he must have been truthful about his contacts with the police. See also R. Whittington-Egan, *Murder Files* (London 2006), 200-3.
17. NA MEPO 3/177; I. Oddie, *Inquest* (London 1941), 118-27, J. Janeway, *Surrey Murders* (Newbury 1988), 67-74; Maxton, *Foul Deeds and Suspicious Deaths in Croydon*, 122-8; *Times* April 30 7f, May 7 12d, May 13 5f, July 24 10e and July 26 11d, 1907, *DM* April 23, July 24 and Aug 14 1907.
18. On the Manser case, see *Times* July 8 1908 16b and July 10 1908 9d, *Auckland Star* Aug 22 1908, *Marlborough Express* Aug 26 1908.
19. On Blundell, see *Times* Feb 12 1909 2c, Feb 15 1909 14f, March 8 1909 8c, *DM* Feb 12 1909, *PIP* Feb 20 1909.
20. Maxton, *Foul Deeds and Suspicious Deaths in Croydon*, 93-6; *ET* May 9 1927, *Gloucester Citizen* May 9 1927.
21. NA CRIM 1/522; *ET* Sept 9 1930.
22. On the Hurley case, see NA CRIM 1/557; *DM* May 6 1931, *IPN* May 14 1931, *Western Daily Press* May 7 1931 and *ET* May 13 1931.
23. NA MEPO 3/887; Oates, *Unsolved London Murders of the 1920s and 1930s*, 144-50; *DM* March 21 and 22, Oct 8 1932, *DE* March 21, 23 and 24, and April 13 1932, and Sept 5 1933, *DMa* March 21 and 22 1932, *IPN* March 24 1932.

24. NA CRIM 1/3178 and DPP 2/2916; Maxton, *Foul Deeds and Suspicious Deaths in Croydon*, 33-7; *Times* March 31 4d, April 16 7f, April 21 7a and June 18 14e, 1959.
25. On the Hickman case, see NA CRIM 1/3379 and DPP 2/3075; Cargill & Holland, *Scenes of Murder*, 189; *Times* March 14 1960 6a and March 15 1960 16g, *DM* March 14 and 31 1960.
26. BritishMurders; Maxton, *Foul Deeds and Suspicious Deaths in Croydon*, 81-6.
27. NA CRIM 1/5290/1-2; TrueCrimeLibrary; G. Honeycombe, *Murders of the Black Museum* (London 1992), 552-5.

6. DISCUSSION

1. It is at No. 29 Hart Street, Henley-on-Thames; see W. Roughead (Ed.), *Trial of Mary Blandy* (Notable British Trials, London 1914) and I. Butler, *Murderers' England* (London 1973), 124-6.
2. Prior to that time, houses and shops were identified by their names and signs, and their proximity to certain taverns, but addresses like 'Mr. Smith, near the Ball and Acorn, Queen-street, Cheapside' quickly became outdated as London grew in Georgian times; see A. Heal (*Notes and Queries* 183 [1942], 100-1), D. Garrioch (*Urban History* 21 [1994], 20-48) and A. Tantner (*Histoire & Mesure* 24(2) [2009], 7-30).
3. S. Jones, *The Illustrated Police News* (Nottingham 2002), L. Stratmann, *Cruel Deeds and Dreadful Calamities* (London 2011) and J. Bondeson (*Fortean Times* 274 [2011], 50-3).
4. S. Wyndham (Ed.), *Dreadful 'Twas* (Old Greenwich, Conn. 1958), J. Bondeson, Introduction to G. Logan, *The True History of Jack the Ripper* (Stroud 2013), 17-21.
5. *Edinburgh Evening News* Sept 8 1902, quoted from the *Echo* newspaper.
6. E. O'Donnell, *Ghosts of London* (London 1933), 47.
7. E. O'Donnell, *Ghosts of London* (London 1933), 45-6.
8. *LWN* Feb 6 and 13 1898; G. Logan, *Dramas of the Dock* (London 1930), 19-39, E. O'Donnell, *Rooms of Mystery* (London 1931), 84-5.
9. E. O'Donnell, *Confessions of a Ghost-Hunter* (London 1928), 216.
10. E. O'Donnell, *Rooms of Mystery* (London 1931), 270-82.
11. H. Sculthorp (*Notes & Queries* 6s. 5 [1882], 269-70), R. Fraser (*Nineteenth-Century Fiction* 9 [1955], 301-7).
12. *IPB* Sept 7 1907. The house today looks spotlessly clean.
13. R. Whittington-Egan, *Liverpool Ghosts and Ghouls* (Liverpool 1986), 54-6.

14. *Leeds Mercury* Dec 16 1871, *Star* Dec 19 1871; H. Price, *Poltergeist over England* (London 1945), 155-63.
15. On Sims, see A. Calder-Marshall [Ed.], *Prepare to Shed Them Now: The Ballads of George R. Sims* (London 1968), 1-48 and W.J. Fishman, *Into the Abyss* (London 2008).
16. George R. Sims' serial 'My Criminal Museum' appeared in *Lloyd's Weekly News* from July 21 until October 6 1907. See also *Sunday Post* Oct 15 1922 and *Havera & Normanby Star* Jan 11 1923.
17. *Referee* Nov 16 1890.
18. G.R. Sims, *Mysteries of Modern London* (London 1906), 64-71.
19. *Yarmouth Independent* Feb 25 1911.
20. *Famous Crimes Past & Present* 10(125) [1905], 174.
21. On Guy Logan, see J. Bondeson, Introduction to *The True History of Jack the Ripper* (Stroud 2013).
22. These would be: British Library 19th Century Newspapers, British Newspaper Archive, Times Digital Archive, UKPressOnline [has Daily Express and Daily Mirror, 1905-], Daily Mail Historical Archive [1896-2004], ProQuest [has old issues of Guardian and Observer], PapersPast [has many New Zealand newspapers, which syndicated articles from the London press] and Trove [from the National Library of Australia]. In addition, there are many useful American newspaper databases, which are of less relevance when searching for London material.
23. These are MEPO 20/1 (1891-1917, minus 1911-1912), MEPO 20/2 (1919-1932, early entries lack house numbers), MEPO 20/3 (1933-1944), MEPO 20/4 (1945-1953), MEPO 20/5 (1954-1958), MEPO 20/6 (1959-1960), MEPO 20/7 (1961), MEPO 20/8 (1962), MEPO 20/9 (1963), MEPO 20/10 (1964-1965) and MEPO 20/11 (1966).
24. 'Names of Streets and Places in the Administrative County of London' was published by the London County Council in 1901, 1912, 1929 and 1955; the latter edition is of course the most useful. There was a short supplement for 1955-1966.
25. In 1842, there were 15 George Streets, 12 William Streets and 17 Queen Streets in London; in 1876, the numbers had risen to 23, 17 and 22, respectively. After the street renaming had taken effect, the 1888 Post Office directories lists 10 George Streets, 13 William Streets and 14 Queen Streets. Today, there are 8 George Streets, 5 William Streets and 7 Queen Streets. The George Street in Marylebone, the William Street in Knightsbridge, and the Queen Street in Mayfair are the only ones in central London.